CARIBBEAN
THE LESSER ANTILLES

Authors:
Eva Ambros, Steven Cohen, Janet Groene,
Laurie Werner, Ute Vladimir, Deborah Williams,
Claire Walter

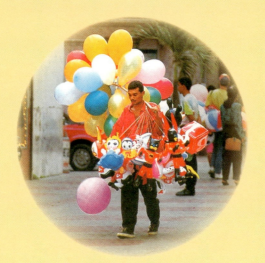

An Up-to-date travel guide with 156 color photos and 20 maps

Second Revised Edition
1998

IMPRINT / LEGEND

Dear Reader,

Being up-to-date is the main goal of the Nelles series. To achieve it, we have a network of far-flung correspondents who keep us abreast of the latest developments in the travel scene, and our cartographers always make sure that maps and texts are adjusted to each other.

Each travel chapter ends with its own list of useful tips, accommodations, restaurants, tourist offices, sights. At the end of the book you will find practical information from A to Z. But the travel world is fast moving, and we cannot guarantee that all the contents are always valid. Should you come across a discrepancy, please write us at: Nelles Verlag GmbH, Schleissheimer Str. 371 b, D-80935 München, Germany, Tel: (089) 3571940, Fax: (089) 35719430.

LEGEND

CARIBBEAN
The Lesser Antilles
© Nelles Verlag GmbH, 80935 Munich
All rights reserved

Second Revised Edition 1998
ISBN 3-88618-112-X
Printed in Slovenia

Publisher:	Günter Nelles	**Cartography:**	Nelles Verlag GmbH
Chief Editor:	Berthold Schwarz	**Color**	
Project Editor:	Steve Cohen	**Separation:**	Priegnitz, München
Editors: Dr. B. Peyer, Marton Radkai		**Printed by:**	Gorenjski Tisk

No part of this book, not even excerpts, may be reproduced without prior permission of Nelles Verlag
- X05 -

TABLE OF CONTENTS

Imprint / Legend 2
List of Maps 7

HISTORY AND CULTURE

History of the Lesser Antilles 15

Culture 35

TRAVELING IN THE LESSER ANTILLES

TURQUOISE SAILING GROUNDS 55
U. S. Virgin Islands 60
British Virgin Islands 72
GUIDEPOST: Hotels, Restaurants, Sights 76

SEASIDE IDYLLS AND CRUISES 81
Anguilla 81
St. Martin / Sint Maarten 83
GUIDEPOST: Hotels, Restaurants, Sights 90

BEACHES AND DIVING DELUXE 95
St. Barts / St. Barthélémy 95
Saba 98
St. Eustatius 101
GUIDEPOST: Hotels, Restaurants, Sights 103

CARIBBEAN CHARMS OF YORE 106
St. Kitts 106
Nevis 110
Montserrat 113
GUIDEPOST: Hotels, Restaurants, Sights 116

A BEACH FOR EVERY DAY 121
Antigua 121
Barbuda 127
GUIDEPOST: Hotels, Restaurants, Sights 129

BEACHES, FORESTS AND VOLCANOES 131
Guadeloupe 131
Dominica 137
GUIDEPOST: Hotels, Restaurants, Sights 141

TABLE OF CONTENTS

THE BEAUTIFUL TRIO 145
Martinique 145
Barbados 148
St. Lucia 152
GUIDEPOST: Hotels, Restaurants, Sights 158

NUTMEG AND VANILLA 163
St. Vincent 163
Grenada 167
The Grenadines 172
GUIDEPOST: Hotels, Restaurants, Sights 176

CARNIVAL, CALYPSO AND WHITE SAND 181
Trinidad 181
Tobago 189
Isla de Margarita 190
GUIDEPOST: Hotels, Restaurants, Sights 191

THE DUTCH ABC 195
Aruba 195
Bonaire 198
Curaçao 202
GUIDEPOST: Hotels, Restaurants, Sights 206

FEATURES

Sailing 210
Diving, Hiking and Camping 216
The Tourism Quandary 220
Caribbean Cuisine 222
Gambling 225
Reggae, Rastafari and Steelbands 227
Hurricanes 232
Shopping 234

TABLE OF CONTENTS

GUIDELINES

Preparation 236
   Climate 236
   Arriving in the Caribbean 238
   Departure 239
   Currency and Exchange 239
   Customs 240

Traveling in the Lesser Antilles 240
   Airlines 240
   Cruise Directory 241

Practical Tips 243
   Accomodation 243
   Accomodating the Handicapped 244
   Accomodation Information 244
   Business Hours 245
   Clothing 246
   Crime 246
   Driving 246
   Electricity 246
   Emergencies 246
   Etiquette 247
   Festivals and Holidays 247
   Guides 247
   Photography 248
   Postal Services 248
   Telephone Service 248
   Time 248
   Tipping 248
   Tourist Information 248

Authors 248

Photographers 249

Index 250

LIST OF MAPS

LIST OF MAPS

The Lesser Antilles 6-7

Virgin Islands 58-59

Anguilla / St. Martin / Sint Maarten 80

St. Barts / Saba / St. Eustatius 98

St. Kitts / Nevis 107

Montserrat 114

Antigua 122

Barbuda 127

Guadeloupe 132-133

Dominica 139

Martinique 144

Barbados 149

St. Lucia 153

St. Vincent / The Grenadines 165

Grenada 169

Trinidad / Tobago 182-183

Isla Margarita 190

Aruba 196

Bonaire / Curaçao 200-201

Airports / Cruise Ports 240-241

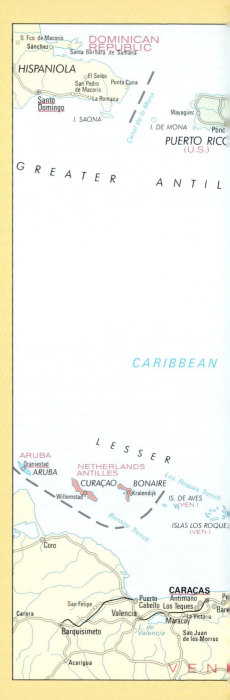

THE LESSER ANTILLES

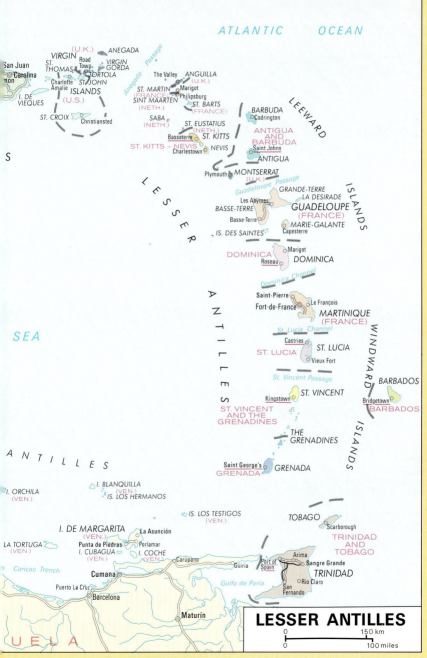

HISTORY

HISTORY OF THE LESSER ANTILLES

Before Time Began

Many millions of years ago the crust of a restless earth heaved and cracked, producing a violent hissing sound as hot lava hit cold ocean, then groaned as it splintered like a split emerald into a million multi-faceted green jewels. Countless islands emerged from the Caribbean Sea, yet scientists today like to call the Antilles "geologically unfinished" because their development is still going on. Those who have either seen the bubbling sulphur springs and smoking volcanoes that exist on St. Lucia or Montserrat, or the unique pitch pits on Trinidad, agree that there are quite a number of indications suggesting that some dramatic geological events may yet take place.

The West Indies are thought to have been a chain of mountains on a huge continent that a long time ago connected Europe and the Americas. The mountains then proceeded to sink into the sea as the continent broke in two and only their tops remained, leaving a scattered sprinkling of islands on a sparkling sea surface.

It is standard human hubris to assume that geological change is a thing of the distant past to be studied in the shaded groves of academia. The geological turmoil goes on and on, as a few volcanoes continue to spit fire and tireless oceans scrub at coastlines. Limestone becomes pitted and sculpted by rains, lakes boil and hurricanes rearrange lives and landscapes.

Fossils found in the Caribbean today show that the marine fauna of the Miocene was similar to that of the eastern Pacific. It is assumed that the formation of the isthmus of Panama during the Pleistocene Period closed off the channel between the two bodies of water and organisms evolved separately in each ocean from then on.

The islands differ markedly in their physical geography. Antigua, for instance, is made up of both volcanic rock and coraline limestone. St. Lucia is dominated by volcanic mountains, while Barbuda is a flat coral island that seems to float on the sea like a silk veil. Most islands are rimmed with wide white beaches that appear to have been lifted straight out of an ad for tourism. Others have volcanic beaches with sand as black as a tuxedo. Barbuda's sands, like those of Eleuthera in the Bahamas, are pink as a baby's cheek. Saba perches on cliffs that tower high over the ocean and has no beaches at all. Skyscraper-size rocks, like those found on Virgin Gorda and Aruba, seem to have been flung there by furious giants, while other islands are spread with rolling pastures and fertile fields.

Further differences among the islands are caused by weather, which can vary even though all these islands lie in the same, torrid zone between ten and twenty degrees latitude. In the higher islands, rain forests grow in moist mountain regions while lowlands turn to swamp or desert.

In low islands and along shallow beaches, salt-tolerant mangroves weave elaborate root systems that catch any driftwood, seaweed, or else coconuts that float by. Coon oysters fasten onto the matted mangrove roots, forming an even tighter net that captures ever smaller bits of flotsam. Gradually, inch by inch, a new cay is formed.

Fortunate is the traveler who has the opportunity to sail from island to island, along the entire archipelago. This is the ideal way to discover the many natural

Preceding pages: Enchanting Martinique. Market day in Castries, St. Lucia. Still life, real life? Left: Petroglyphs on St. Vincent.

HISTORY

facets of the Caribbean while at the same time enjoying a relaxing vacation.

Christopher Columbus Arrives

In his search for a sea route to the East Indies, Christopher Columbus blundered ashore in the Bahamas (although there are many claimants, San Salvador seems the most likely candidate) in 1492. After that, further events seemed to succeed at an amazing speed.

Landing on Hispaniola and building a few shelters from the timbers of his wrecked ship, the *Santa Maria*, Columbus left a colony of 38 men to keep a modest foothold in the new land. They were never heard of again, but when Columbus returned in 1494 with a flock of 1000 settlers, including "professionals" such as priests, doctors, blacksmiths and farmers, a permanent colony was founded, and the first mass was said in the New World.

In all, Columbus made four voyages from Europe to the Americas and there is hardly an island in the West Indies where you will not be shown a specific place, identified by a plaque and probably surrounded by numerous vendors peddling souvenirs and other wares, where Columbus made a landfall.

By 1502, when another wave of 2000 immigrants arrived, a firm Spanish presence truly took root in the New World. It is their leader, Nicolás de Ovando, who is credited with founding a new Spanish empire, while the Columbus clan returned to Spain in disgrace.

Yet, while Spain's foothold in the Greater Antilles was secure, and Spanish is today the language of Puerto Rico, Cuba and the Dominican Republic, the smaller islands of the Windwards and Leewards (except for Trinidad, which they held until 1797) were of little interest to Spains' colonial predacity. Only the names remain in the original Spanish,

Above: Columbus, the man who discovered and named most of the Caribbean islands.
Right: European tools of dissuasion.

HISTORY

and then usually in an abbreviated or anglicized version if it.

Santa Cruz became St. Croix, Santa María la Antigua changed to Antigua, Santa María de Guadalupe was reduced to Guadeloupe, San Cristóbal and San Bartolomé were irreverently renamed St. Kitts and St. Barts, and San Eustacio was cropped down to Statia. Columbus' Concepción metamorphosed to Grenada and his La Trinidad, named for the Trinity when he spotted three hills from the sea, was robbed of its definite article.

It is a strange quirk of history that the Caribbean was named after cannibals, that the Americas owe their name to Amerigo Vespucci, whose role in the discovery of the New World was a minor one, that Columbus' name merely designates two cities in Ohio and Georgia. The great discoverer died in 1506, forsaken by his queen and bitterly disappointed that he had failed to find a route to India.

Barbados, which is one of the few islands not visited by Columbus, is also one of the few that was not named for a saint (because discovery was made on that saint's day). Nobody quite agrees whether the name Barbados had something to do with beards – whether it refers to the beards on the Indians or the beard-like Spanish moss on the trees – but Bajans love to discuss their theories on the subject. Columbus did, however, name Tortola for turtles, Anguilla for eels, and equally Aruba *(Oro Uba)* for the traces of gold found there.

It was from its foothold at Santo Domingo that Spanish power spread throughout the Americas. Worked on by Indian slaves brought here from other parts of the West Indies, plantations flourished and galleons stocked up on provisions here for their lengthy raids on North and South America. Then, laden with gold looted on the mainland, ships stopped once again at Santo Domingo on their way back to Seville. For years Hispaniola was the traffic hub of the Antilles.

The golden era lasted until 1521, when Cortez' unexpected discovery of Aztec gold turned Spanish attention to Mexico.

HISTORY

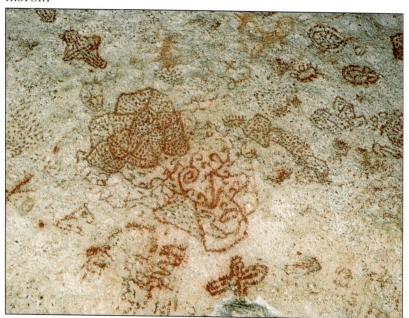

Queen Isabella's interests shifted away from Hispaniola to the mainland of Central and South America, and therefore a slow but certain decline in Spanish power occurred in the West Indies.

Ironically, in their thirst for the easy gold stolen on the mainland, the Spanish ignored one of the few mother lodes in the islands. They certainly knew it was there, having named the island Oro Uba, but it was not until 1825 that mining actually began on the island we know today as Aruba. The precious metal made its jolly way to Dutch coffers well into the 20th century. Remains of smelters and former mining towns can still be seen on the island.

Gold was a fever that shaped lives, built and broke governments, and populated a continent with a new race while destroying the old. The aborigines, who had been torn from their native islands by the Spanish and then cast into slavery or slaughtered (or both), disappeared almost without a trace – and all that for gold.

Indians of the Lesser Antilles

Today, housewives of Aruba keep the area around their homes immaculately swept clean of debris, grass and even flowers. Any decorative plants are put in containers, not in the soil. Even most modern-day Arubans probably do not realize that the custom is a carryover from the ancient Indians, who kept the ground bare so they could immediately spot intruding snakes or dangerous insects.

Aruba's first known inhabitants were the Caiquetios, a branch of the peaceful, agrarian Arawaks who grew yams, tobacco and maize for uncounted centuries before the Conquistadores arrived to the Antilles. Students of the matter assume that they made their way there from the Paraguaná peninsula of Venezuela, only 17 miles from Aruba, in large dugout canoes. They spread throughout the Dutch

Above: The artistry of the original inhabitants of the islands consisted of petroglyphs.

West Indies – probably maintaining stronger ties with the mainland than with each other because of inter-island currents that kept Aruba isolated for a great length of time.

Other Amerindians doubtlessly drifted down the chain of islands from the north, having crossed to the Bahamas from Florida and worked their way south over the centuries. Scholars have a long way to go in learning where the original settlers came from, and how they reached each island group.

Evidence has been found of Indian settlements at Curaçao as early as 2540 B.C. Aruba, which was probably settled at about the same time by different clans of the same tribe, is unique because its indigenous inhabitants survived well into the 19th century. On most other islands, Arawaks disappeared by the thousands, within merely a few generations. It is thought that as many as two million natives perished in less than a hundred years after contact with Europeans.

The Spanish stopped at Aruba in 1513 to round up the populace for transport to Santo Domingo, but Indians continued to stream to the island from the mainland. Then, in 1527, the Spanish brought some of the Indian laborers back from Santo Domingo to work the cattle and horse ranches they were establishing on Aruba. As a result, Aruba remained one of the few islands where aborigines survived well into modern times. The last full-blood Amerindian on the island is said to have died in the early 1860's.

Before the Spanish came to the Antilles, settlement was shaped mainly by ocean currents, the search for food and *Lebensraum*, and the age-old warring between the Arawaks and the ferocious Caribs. With the Europeans, however, came slavery and death. Those Indians who were not slaughtered or enslaved died of European diseases, against which they had no immunities.

There were a few holdouts, however. In 1639, Caribs massacred every one of the British who had settled St. Lucia, and they were able to hold on to the island for several decades. The spot on St. Kitts where English and French soldiers, with a rare sense of cooperation, battled the Caribs in 1629 is still known as Bloody Point. Caribs on Dominica and St. Vincent held out so long, putting up such a ferocious and consistent defense, that the English and French finally were forced to give up both islands in 1784. As a result, the handful of Caribs who have survived on the islands still live here, primarily on the island of Dominica.

Caribs and a growing population of shipwrecked black slaves mingled in St. Vincent, forming a mixed race that fought fiercely against the Europeans for decades. Some Caribs remain on St. Vincent today, representing a mere fraction of those who survived the final, successful attack by the English and then were shipped to Honduras.

Eventually, however, most of the Indians died (many of European disease against which they had no immunity) or were absorbed into the new population. The last Indian survivors of Grenada committed suicide by jumping off a cliff still known today as *Carib's Leap* rather than surrender to the brutality of the Europeans. Many took their own lives by eating raw cassava which had also been their staple food. But unless properly prepared, the root is highly poisonous.

Petroglyphs from Indian times can still be seen along the main road near Romney Manor on St. Kitts, on cave wall in Aruba and at The Fountains in Anguilla. Some sacrificial Carib altars and petroglyphs have remained in St. Vincent. On display in the Archaeology Museum in Oranjestad, Aruba, are rare Caiquetio artifacts as well as the remains of people who had been buried in urns.

One of the most significant archaeological finds made in the Antilles is an Amerindian bat effigy carved from stone

HISTORY

and dating to about A.D. 700. It was unearthed near what is today the airport on St. Vincent and is exhibited in a small archaeological museum at Kingstown. Another good Amerindian collection is on display in the Museum of Antigua and Barbuda at St. John's. Not very long ago, in 1972, some Arawak teeth, bones and beads dating back to at least five centuries before the Spanish arrived, were unearthed in Martinique.

Occasional finds continue to be made, but in fact a great deal remains to be learned about those peoples who lived in this island paradise before Columbus came. Probably most of their secrets will never be known, but fragments of their spirit survive in place names throughout the archipelago, in Arawak words such as *hurricane* and *hammock* that became part of the English language, and in rhythms

Above: The last of the true Caribs can be found on the island of Dominica. Right: Horatio Nelson was one of Britains most successful navy men.

beyond compare that have been incorporated into West Indian folk dances.

Europe Comes to the Caribbean

As European adventurers and soldiers of fortune swashbuckled through the Caribbean, they brought with them their European wars. In fact, some European governments rose and fell according to their gains and losses in the Caribbean. The stakes were cocoa, spices, coffee and the all-precious sugar, which at one time commanded so high a price it was kept in locked cupboards and brought out only on very special occasions.

Molasses, a by-product of the sugar-making process, yielded yet another bonanza in the form of rum. The boom came to an abrupt end after Europeans developed the process by which they could make sugar from their own sugar beets, but not until hundreds of fortunes had been won and lost, and thousands of heads had quite literally rolled.

The Dutch, at war with the Spanish in

HISTORY

the 17th century, muscled into Curaçao to wrest it from Spain. During a turbulent 13-year period, when the Dutch roamed the Antilles with a flotilla of some 800 warships, they captured 30 million pounds worth of booty from Spanish and Portuguese ships.

Holland became a powerhouse in the Antilles, fortifying its islands to the teeth, and placing the canny Peter Stuyvesant at the helm. Peg-legged Stuyvesant went on to become governor of an up-and-coming place called New Amsterdam, in our days better known to the public as New York. There is still some dispute among certain people over whether his amputated leg was buried in Curaçao or Sint Maarten. Horatio Nelson, battling the French off the coast of Barbados, was credited by the planters there for saving their sugar profits. They even designed and established a Trafalgar Square in Bridgetown in his honor, many years before the one in London was built. Even today, Bridgetown policemen wear uniforms fashioned after those worn by Nelson's seamen. A letter, written by Nelson himself with his left hand after he lost his right one, can be seen in a museum in Nevis.

Antigua, settled by English families who had migrated from St. Kitts, was occupied briefly by the French, until it was ceded to the British in the Treaty of Breda in 1667. Irish residents of British St. Kitts drifted to Montserrat in the 1630's as a result of the usual religious and political conflicts between Protestants and Catholics. Still, the island's telephone book features many McSomeones and O'Somebodies, as well as a volcano named Galway Soufrière. They fly the Union Jack, but a piece of their heart belongs to the Shamrock, which is the official seal.

In 1644 the French took Montserrat, lost it in 1668, regained it in 1782, then had to return it to the English in 1783. It is still a British Crown Colony, with St. Patrick's Day as a national holiday.

The French won St. Barts from the Knights of Malta, then exchanged it with Sweden in 1784 for the right to enter the port of Gothenburg. Although the island still remains French today, its capital is Gustavia, named after the King of Sweden, and very many of its residents have the blond hair and the blue eyes of their Scandinavian forebears.

During America's Revolutionary War, the West Indies, with its English bastions, and French and Dutch islands generally sympathetic to the American rebels, were both a bane and a blessing to the rebellious colonists. St. Eustatius became a storage area for supplies on their way from North America's European friends to George Washington's militia. The ruins of warehouses where gunpowder and muskets were stored still stand today as historic landmarks of this period.

Washington had visited the West Indies already as a young man, accompanying his brother, who had gone to Barbados to relieve his tuberculosis. While there, Washington caught smallpox,

HISTORY

which left him pockmarked for life. Some say that the immunity he got from this rather mild case of the pox caught here later, during the American War of Indepenence, protected him from the epidemic of smallpox that ravaged his army.

Almost every island, especially those where Americans are popular visitors, claims to have fired the first salute, raised the first flag, or somehow been among the first to recognize the United States after its declaration of independence in 1776. A more official claim is made by St. Eustatius, where a plaque at Fort Oranje commemorates the "first salute to the flag of the United States". The British lost their stiff upper lip and showed their true colors: In 1781, an English fleet surrounded the neutral island and proceeded to devastate Oranjestad.

Generally, the European powers acted like scrappy terriers who yanked little is-

Above: The unmistakable Dutch touch in the Caribbean. Right: Plantation days revived in the Musée de la Canne, Martinique.

lands back and forth like little pieces of tasty gristle. Trinidad was alternately raided by the Dutch, French and English until 1783, when a royal proclamation in Spain offered free land in Trinidad to any Roman Catholic. Catholics from around the Caribbean swarmed in, only to find themselves under British rule after the Treaty of Amiens in 1802.

So many battles were fought between France and England for control of Dominica that the Caribs named it *Waitookoobooli*, or Place of Many Battles. France finally sold the island to the British for 12,000 Pounds Sterling, but only after burning the capital, Roseau, in a final fit of pique.

The island of St. Lucia passed back and forth between the British and the French no less than 14 times. Sint Maarten changed hands all of 16 times before becoming a permanent Dutch holding. And St. Eustatius changed ownership 22 times! Practically the only exception to this trend is Barbados, lying so far to the east that it was not discovered by Columbus, but only later on by the Portuguese. It was settled by the British in 1625, and British it remained after independence.

Fires that were sparked in Europe were stoked by local slave uprisings, scandals and wars of independence. The result was a spicy stew of intrigue and freebootery that continues to this day in some cases. To student of European history these are mere sidelights on the stage of wars and treaties, of congresses and secret meetings, but to the tourist it means an unending variety among islanders' language, dress, food and attitudes. One can vacation in the Antilles forever and still find each island group different and delightful in an individual way. The more one learns about their legends and loyalties, customs and idiosyncracies, the richer the travel experience becomes. And then there is that other historic factor that inspired the likes of Errol Flynn to no end.

Piracy Rules the Seas

In a period of lawlessness that makes Dodge City look like a kindergarten, the Antilles were for centuries braved and brutalized by a myriad of small fleets under the command of free-lance rascals variously called buccaneers, pirates, freebooters or privateers.

There is a difference. Strictly speaking, a pirate, freebooter or buccaneer is nothing else but a stateless, lawless plunderer. A privateer, on the other hand, was commissioned by his government to raid merchant ships of enemy nations. In short, one man's privateer was another man's pirate. For the most part, a national hero in one nation was a fiend in another. John Hawkins, Thomas Cavendish and Francis Drake were even knighted by Queen Elizabeth I for their extended piratic activities that so miserably hindered the Spanish merchant ships.

Later, American businessmen got involved in the profitable system of legalized highway robbery as well, commissioning pirate ships or buying and selling loot seized by the freebooters. The Dutch entry in the privateering racket was heralded by the notorious Piet Heyn, whose stockholders reaped a hefty 50 percent dividend on their investments.

At one time France had as many as forty commissioned corsairs in service, all of them preying on Spanish ships. The French role in piracy diminished after they made peace at home with Spain, but English pirates stayed in the fray to the bitter end. Distinctions blurred between national hero and international outlaw, and most pirates were probably a bit of both, which led to their being romanticized later. They had a sort of honor code, dividing booty scrupulously among their men. Most of the loot, of course, was promptly redistributed into the pockets of waterfront prostitutes, rum merchants and gamblers.

Once, while partitioning a particularly large haul with his crew, Francis Drake dipped into his captured treasure chests and gave each of his men sixteen bowls

HISTORY

full of silver and gold. He made his most formidable catch in Panama, when he hijacked an entire 200-mule caravan that was unloading its gold and emeralds for the Spanish fleet. Drake was known to his men as a fair divider of the spoils, and some of them retired rich. It was a tempting occupation for men who had left Europe in the first place because they had nothing in their pocket and little future to look forward to.

The defeat of the Spanish Armada in 1588 is known to every schoolboy on both sides of the Atlantic, but it is less well known that the first Armada was assembled not to cross the English Channel but to put an end to Sir Francis Drake's seemingly unbreakable string of naval successes in the West Indies and Central America. Drake got wind of the build-up, swiftly headed for Spain and torched the entire fleet while it lay at Cadiz with such speed and cunning that the Spanish admiral died of shock. In this manner, Sir Francis effectively neutralized the Spanish navy for the next three years.

Captain Kidd even gave his men an elaborate contract, and other pirates also issued written articles, usually based loosely on the formal letters of marque drawn up between sponsors and their privateers. Even the meanest and most illiterate crews were, for example, entitled to a hundred pieces of gold, or eight or six slaves if they lost an arm or leg in combat. They were also entitled to the most agonizing punishments for disobedience, cowardice, desertion or mutiny. Punishment by *walking the plank* is more popular in fiction than it used to be in practice – only one pirate is said to have used it – but floggings were frequent, severe and very often fatal.

The code of honor rarely extended to the fairer sex, but one true story reads like a Hollywood cliché. Captain Henry Jackson, after a bitter battle, captured the *John and Jane* off Swan Island. When he

Above: Agricultural methods have hardly changed since the colonial days. Right: These cabins used to house slaves.

HISTORY

noticed one of his men trying to rape a female passenger, he pulled and cocked his pistol and gallantly came to her rescue. The woman and her belongings were set free, and she eventually returned to Jamaica and told her tale for posterity.

Henry Morgan, thought by some to be the most vicious of pirates and by others to be a mere victim of social ills, so infuriated the Spanish by using nuns and priests as a shield when he attacked Portobello that a formal protest was made to Queen Elizabeth. She ordered him to London, went through a few perfunctory attempts at discipline by stowing him in the Tower for a small while, and then made him Sir Henry Morgan and sent him back to Jamaica as lieutenant governor. It seems his luck held up to the very end. He died in his own bed four years before an earthquake and a tidal wave obliterated Port Royal and swept its human dwellers into the sea.

No apocalypse became involved in the life and legend of Sam Lord either, who made a fortune as a landlocked pirate by setting out false lights along the treacherous coast of Barbados. Passing ships saw the lights, trustingly used them as beacons, and sailed right up on the jagged reefs. Lord then dispatched any seamen who had not had the foresight to go down with their ships, and salvaged enough cargo to fund a lavish retirement in what is still known as Sam Lord's Castle. It is nowadays part of a plush resort.

One of the legendary pirates of the era was Blackbeard (not to be confused with Bluebeard) who wore his beard in spiky braids. Legend has it that, to give himself a more frightening appearance, he plaited fuses in his beard and lit them (something for our late-20th-century rave scene).

In the end, it was a pirate who ended piracy. Woodes Rogers, a British hero who had sacked Guayaquil and captured treasures worth hundreds of thousands of pounds, was commissioned by the British to clear the seas once and for all.

With Nassau as the new pirate's stronghold after the destruction of Port Royal, Rogers was sent to New Providence with orders to clean up thoroughly. He was so feared and so admired, that many of the pirates even joined him in his ventures. The Bahamas Latin motto is still *Expel Pirates, Restore Commerce*.

Three Centuries of Slavery

Slavery. The word itself has a wealth of ugly connotations, the concept is unthinkable in modern times. But in the 16th century, slavery was not new either to the New World or the old. Long before Columbus claimed the Indies, Caribs had been preying on the more peace-loving, agrarian Arawaks, killing their men in battle and making slaves of their women. Indians of the Americas often enslaved their conquered foes, and those made slaves could even consider themselves the lucky ones. The less fortunate were sometimes brutally tortured before they were finally put to death.

HISTORY

From the moment Spanish conquerors came ashore, slavery became the key to an economy based on cheap labor. Arawaks and Caribs were the first to be enslaved, and they were transported by the thousands to Santo Domingo, where the first Antillean plantations flourished, and to other agricultural islands.

Within only a few decades, the increasing demand for slaves so outstripped the supply of Indians that a lucrative trade in Africans developed. Thousands of blacks – as many as 75,000 a year at slavery's peak – were shipped from the Gold Coast of Africa by Dutch and English slave traders. Some had been hunted down and captured, others were simply purchased from African warlords who had, in time-honored tradition, enslaved those tribes they bested in battle. At its zenith, slavery was a $7 million-a-year enterprise, a considerable amount for that period.

Above and right: Their ancestors not so long ago arrived under inhuman conditions in slave ships from Africa.

Many other slaves came from England where, during the Cromwell era, Catholics were sold into West Indian servitude along with political prisoners who had chosen the wrong side in the Civil War. Still others were innocent travelers taken by pirates, who sold them for whatever price or ransom they would fetch.

The island of Barbuda was settled, it is said, by a man whose business was the breeding of slaves – scrutinizing their bloodlines as carefully as one would to breed dogs or horses – for the hard work of clearing fields and cutting cane. His name was Cordington, the name of Barbuda's capital and of most of the people living on the island.

Even the cold, calculated breeding of humans was not new to the islands. Long before white men arrived and colonized the islands, the Caribs had purposefully selected the best breeders from captured Arawak women, to bear them the next generation of warriors.

It will never be known just how many slaves died during the crossing from Af-

HISTORY

rica, from diseases, or simply disappeared into the great maw of human turmoil. It is said that some islands were originally settled by blacks who were pitilessly thrown overboard from ships when cholera or another epidemics broke out. Those who made their way ashore survived in the wild and stayed free.

On a few islands, slaves who arrived as cargo of a ship that had been seized in war, were often given their freedom. So passionate was anti-slavery sentiment among the British by the 1830's, that they liberated their own slaves, then sent out ships to capture slavers and set the human cargo free. Unfortunately, an equally brisk trade was going with ships called "blackbird hunters". They rounded up the poorly defended freed slaves, and spirited them off to other islands where slavery was still legal.

These were centuries of unspeakable cruelty and opportunism, tempered occasionally by acts of kindness and justice. On Barbados, where races have long lived in harmony, planters wrote affectionately of "Negroes whom we ought to have a special care of, by the labour of whose hands our profit is brought in."

One of the more tragic, true stories is that of Thomas Inkle, who was shipwrecked sometime in 1647. He and other survivors made their way ashore, only to be attacked by Indians. All were killed except Inkle, who was hidden in a cave and nursed back to health by an Indian maiden. They soon fell in love, and Inkle pledged his lady a European life of silks and satins. Later they were able to set sail for Barbados, where Inkle had an abrupt change of heart. The Indian woman who had looked so good to him in the wild was not quite so attractive when compared to rosy-cheeked lasses of British Barbados. So he sold her.

Another true story, one that rocked the West Indies and shocked Europe, involved Arthur William Hodge of Tortola. Infuriated when a slave failed to take proper care of a mango tree, Hodge killed him. Hodge was well born and highly connected. Still, he was brought to trial,

HISTORY

convicted and promptly hanged. His defense, the common one of the times, was that a slave was personal property to be used as one wished. The prosecution, taking a cue from the liberal winds that were already blowing in from England, charged that, while a slave was property, he was first a man, one who should be accorded protection under English laws against cruelty.

Slave Uprisings

During much of the slave era, an uneasy peace prevailed between servant and master, but just the whisper of a slave uprising was enough to send chills through the planter community. In 1801, after a slave rebellion in Tobago, 39 of the rebels were captured. The governor terrorized the island's blacks when he hanged the prisoners one by one. It was

Above: A broken chain, the symbol of the end of an inhuman era. Right: A face to tell many tales.

not until later that the subdued slaves learned that it had been a merciful charade. They had seen 39 hangings, but only the ringleader had actually been executed. His body, swaddled in rags and chains, had been repeatedly carried up to the gallows and hanged.

In 1733, slaves in St. John attacked the massively outnumbered whites with machetes, killing some 50 of them, and took complete control of the island for six months. One of the bloodiest uprisings took place in St. Vincent. It was here, in the late 17th century, that a slaver was shipwrecked with its human cargo. The survivors were adopted by the Caribs and a new race, Black Caribs, was born. In time they allied with the French against the English and went about the business of wholesale slaughter until British reinforcements arrived and restored order. More than 5000 Black Caribs eventually were rounded up and shipped to Honduras, slaves once again.

Emancipation was declared at various times throughout the islands. Slaves were

HISTORY

indeed freed in 1793 in Haiti, but only temporarily. The French governor of Guadeloupe freed the slaves there in l794 in the wake of the French Revolution – which had generously passed a number of emancipatory laws – and therefore also executed many slave holders. Slavery returned with a new governor in l802, but was abolished again in l848.

In l834 emancipation also came to the British islands; St. Vincent liberated its slaves in 1838 along with the island of Jamaica, where the trade in slaves had already ended by 1907. The Virgin Islands, still in the hands of the Danes, followed suit in 1848 and the Dutch West Indies did the same in 1863.

When a white man injured a black in Tortola in l853, two decades after the official emancipation, there was another insurrection in which villages and greathouses were looted and leveled, and cane fields burned. By l893 there were only two white inhabitants left on the island.

The freeing of the slaves did not, however, completely dampen the thirst for cheap labor. The Lesser Antilles saw waves of immigration from the Orient and Middle East. As late as l9l4, landowners in Trinidad were importing indentured servants from India and the Middle East.

Into the 20th Century

By the beginning of the 20th century, however, the balance of power had considerably changed in the entire Caribbean region. Spanish hegemony was dwindling. In 1865, it relinquished Santo Domingo, and in 1898 it lost Cuba to American intervention brought about by the mysterious sinking of the *USS Maine*. The U. S.A., which was beginning to feel its oats in the region, also gained Puerto Rico in the bargain. In 1917, it used more direct means to acquire the Virgin Islands from the Danes, namely 25 million US dollars. Naturally, the Monroe Doctrine

of the early 19th century, the self-proclaimed right of intervention into any situation perceived by the US as threatening to its interest, was followed to the letter.

The European wars, which used to have some repercussions in the Caribbean, did so again, but indirectly. World War I bled England and France, and with Spain out of the picture, the US strode into the seat of regional power broker.

Two further circumstances changed or helped the Caribbean during this period: The opening of the Panama canal in 1917 connected the islands with the Pacific. And Prohibition in the USA opened up a huge smuggler's market in rum.

The years of World War II found the Lesser Antilles suspended in a timeless sea, but hardly immune from the turmoil that racked the world at large. The island waters were a battleground for ships and, in l942, two large vessels were torpedoed in St. Lucia's Castries Harbor. When a German submarine was surrounded by a number of Dutch marines at Aruba, the

HISTORY

captain scuttled his vessel rather than surrender. Furthermore, German prisoners of war were interned at Bonaire.

Airstrips were built on every island that could provide enough level space. Harbors were dredged to accommodate naval ships. Refineries at Aruba and Trinidad worked at full capacity to fuel the Allied cause. Rich bauxite reserves in Jamaica flowed into Canada, providing aluminum for the war effort, and planters everywhere worked overtime to produce everything from sisal to bananas.

Islanders signed up to fight for their mother countries, primarily for Britain. French Guadeloupe and Martinique sided at first with the Vichy regime and were blockaded by the Allies, but before the end of the war they switched their allegiance to the Free French.

World War II brought hardship to some islands and undreamed prosperity

Above: Such sugar trains used to chug their way across Guadeloupe. Right: Political campaigning in the post-colonial era.

to others, not just to the local economy but also in the form of multi-million-dollar harbors and airports that are the foundation of today's tourism industry.

Some islands, forced to create their own industries because imports were not available from the mother country during the war, remain self-sufficient today in the production of shoes, canned milk or textiles. St. Kitts is one of the few islands that still has a sugar industry. The war also brought thousands of new faces to the Antilles, faces from the four corners of the world. Many of them fell in love with the islands and returned later, as tourists, investors or immigrants.

Contemporary History

Though tourism had already begun on the islands as early as the 19th century, the real boom set off in the post-World-War II decades. New prosperity in the USA, now fully recovered from the Depression and prosperous as no country in the world, spurned droves to come and

seek the tame exotism of the Caribbean and spend their money.

The Cold War had its effect on the political life, particularly in the US hovering over the area like a mother hen, worrying about its "interests." The situation was aggravated by the victory of Castro and his rebels in Cuba. Even though Castro had appealed to America's alleged sense of justice as he ousted the monstrous Batista, he was unable to find support from the State Department. Ultimately he found an ally in America's great Cold War enemy, the Soviet Union. Since it came to the region, the US has kept a nervous finger on the trigger. When Grenada threatened to slip into the hands of "anti-American" elements, President Ronald Reagan sent in an enormous contingent of marines and rangers to oust not only the local government, but also a handful of Cuban construction workers who were building a landing strip. Still, in spite of – or perhaps because of, here the opinions diverge – Washington's long shadow, the Carribean nations have been by and large progressing well. Most earned their independence from Britain in the 1960s, while remaining in the Commonwealth.

Although Haiti and Trinidad continue to face severe social problems, and there are spasms of racial, political or labor unrest on other islands from time to time, a golden era of amity, plenty and hope has settled over most of the Lesser Antilles.

Even Cuba is coming out from behind the sugar-cane curtain and will again become a major factor in the world-wide tourism business Independence has, of course, been the battle cry of the century – never mind that many of the little islands cannot even feed, let alone defend, themselves. At first, it was independence from European powers. Then several economic and political associations were formed, notably in 1968 the CARIFTA (Caribbean Free Trade Area), later the CARICOM (Caribbean Community). In 1975 came the Caribbean Development and Cooperation Committee (CDCC) and, finally, in 1981 the Organization of

HISTORY

Eastern Caribbean States (OECS). And now islands are breaking away from other islands. Anguilla declared its independence from a federation with Nevis and St. Kitts. The "ABC" islands broke from Holland, then Aruba parted with Bonaire and Curaçao. They draw their economic strength partly from refining Venezuelan oil. Antigua and Barbuda are one federation within the Commonwealth. Dominica is an independent state within the Commonwealth, as are St. Lucia, St. Vincent, the Grenadines, and Barbados, which has the oldest parliament in the western hemisphere.

Trinidad and Tobago are in the unique position in the West Indies of not having to rely on tourism. The islands are rich in oil, still have viable sugar and asphalt industries, and are the home of world-famous *Angostura Bitters*. Both countries form an independent republic together.

Above: Small businesses mean a livelihood for many Antilleans. Right: Hurricanes are the West Indian Sword of Damocles.

Montserrat is a British Crown Colony. One of the Indies' most amazing successes is the tiny island of Sint Maarten/St. Martin, which remains part Dutch, part French. Spend francs, guilders or dollars – nobody cares which, as long as the money is spent.

France still remains a vibrant presence in the West Indies, in islands that are not colonies but actual departments of the mother country. St. Barts is a dependency of Guadeloupe, which had been a dependency of Martinique until recently.

A Heritage of Hurricanes

What is by no means varied in the Caribbean is nature's occasional fury. Travelers in the Antilles soon sense that hurricanes are more than just a meteorological phenomena. They are plaited inseparably into every phase of island life and lore. On some remote islands, where people have little sense of time, they even date important events such as a child's birth, a mother's death, or the building of a new home. "It was two years after the Great Storm," they might say about the purchase of a new house.

Of great storms there were many, but since storms tend to skip and skirt the islands, massive damage can occur in one island while its neighbor is spared. Few hurricanes have affected the entire Antilles, so each island has its own hurricane memoirs. In recent years, the hurricanes have had names – giving them an even more exalted role in history and myth.

In the 1930's, a hurricane swept across low-lying, defenseless Cayman Brac and carried away every tree, building and landmark on the island. When stunned survivors straggled out of the caves and back to where their homes should have been, they could not identify even enough to know where their property lines were. Most left the Brac, and the island did not recover for years.

HISTORY

The fledgling cotton industry in the British Virgin Islands was in no time flattened in the hurricane of 1916; another severe hurricane in 1924 dashed any modest hopes for economic progress before the Great Depression struck in 1929.

In this century, major storms have included *Betsy* in 1956, *Ines* in 1966, *David* in 1979. Then came *Frederick, Gilbert, Hugo* and so on. The irony is that some islands go for generations without seeing a major storm. Memories fade. Building codes soften or are ignored. Defenses, both physical and psychological, weaken. Then the island is hit by a hurricane like *Janet,* which flattened Grenada in 1955, or *Hugo,* which brought 200-mph winds and wholesale destruction to Montserrat and the Virgin Islands in 1989. And a new legend is born in terror, grief and a profound sense of loss that lasts for generations.

Equally dramatic, but less frequent on the calendar of calamities in the Lesser Antilles, are both earthquakes and volcanic eruptions. In 1902, when Soufrière exploded on St. Vincent, 2000 people were killed. What would have been a major news story even in today's press was almost forgotten because, within a couple of days, Mt. Pelée on Martinique also erupted, killing some 29,000 people within two minutes and eradicating the entire city of St. Pierre. Monserrat's volcano was the latest to erupt: August 1997.

One of the most popular West Indies legend tells of that disaster's sole survivor, a lucky man who was found safely encapsuled in the city's lone jail cell. He was set free at once, and thereafter lived out a happy life touring as a sideshow attraction with a circus.

In 1692, an earthquake hit Port Royal, a pirate stronghold of Jamaica, and shook most of it into the sea. In what some saw as a kind of biblical retribution for the port's wicked ways, thousands of homes and about 2,000 people – not to mention millions upon millions of dollars in pirate treasure – sank in the murky deep harbor. Jamestown, the first capitol of Nevis, was completely destroyed in an earthquake and tidal wave in 1680.

CULTURE

CULTURE

About 700 miles separate Anguilla from Trinidad, and much of that space is taken up by water, yet the myriad of little nations making up the Lesser Antilles, while sharing a common colonial past, boasts a colorful and diverse cultural life. Several different languages are spoken here, a range of festivals of varying ethnic, national or religious origin are celebrated on the islands; some prefer cricket, the British national sport, while others tend more toward the American baseball. Cock fighting, a predominantly Hispanic game of chance, if you will, is accepted in some places, but definitely frowned upon elsewhere in favor of less violent casino gambling. Currencies are of course different and even electrical power has two versions: 110 volts in the north and 220 volts in the south.

To the curious visitor preferring to get a sense of local cultures rather than sink into a sun-stroked stupor, this gentle bracelet of islands represents an endless reservoir. All traditional art forms from dance to literature have found representation, be it in calypso rhymes or in such powerful works as the *Rue des Cases Nègres* by the Martinique-born author Joseph Zobel, or *Exile* by the Nobel Prize winner (1960) Saint-John Perse (1887-1975) from Guadeloupe. Other famous authors from the Lesser Antilles are: Vidiadhar Naipaul from Trinidad, whose articles and stories regularly appear in print in the USA and Europe; George Lamming from Barbados, author of the autobiographical *In the Castle of my Skin*; Jean Rhys from Dominica is the author of *The Wide Sargasso Sea*. Even a small film industry has started growing, spawning among other works a fine version of the aforementioned *La Rue des Cases Nègres*, which unfortunately and undeservedly failed to find interest amongst movie-goers in the western hemisphere.

France, Spain, England, Holland and even Sweden and Denmark all partook in the colonial feast, which certainly accounts in part for the cultural diversity of the Lesser Antilles. They also virtually entirely eradicated the existing Indian culture. Relics of the Carib and Arawak cultures are therefore extremely rare. Later came the slaves from Africa with their own artistic expression, one that was inevitably linked to suffering and resistance to their brutal drivers. To a certain degree these countries still act as surrogate mothers to the artistic strivings on the islands inasmuch as they frequently provide training and education to insular talents, especially in the field of literature. Africa has a special place in the inspirational world of Antillan artists, in particular with regards to music.

Left and right: The multicultural side of the Caribbean is most apparent during the festivities of the carnival season.

CULTURE

Carnival and Festivals

Exactly which of the many European nations that colonized the Caribbean brought this celebration with it to the Caribbean is unclear to this date, though the French are the suspects number one. Suffice it to say that the wild day or days ushering in Lent are among the great attractions for visitors. It is a time for dancing and music making, for revelry of all sorts and for basically "letting it all hang out". The actual celebrations include an array of events from colorful parades with dazzling masks, to calypso and steel band competitions.

There are of course differences from island (Aruba, Bonaire, Curaçao), to island. In the Catholic islands and on the ABC islands with their Dutch heritage, frenzied *Carnaval*, called *Vaval* in the French islands and spelled *Carnival* on others, is held just before Lent. In Martinique, it is celebrated every weekend from New Year's to Ash Wednesday. In Guadeloupe, it is the *Fête Annuelle* along the waterfront at Saint-François, in October. In Trinidad, carnivals go on almost around the calendar, thanks to the island's across-the-board ethnic mix. Just before Lent, a Mardi Gras-type of carnival takes place here with feasting and tippling.

Trinidad's seemingly year-round carnival is further enhanced by the religious feasts of two of the island's minorities, both taking place in the fall. Muslims celebrate the *Hosein* festival, and *Divali,* the Hindu Festival of Lights takes place not very long before the Spanish *Parang,* the Christmas festival.

In Tobago, the same events are held along with the additional thrill of a raucous goat and crab race festival on the tuesday after Easter.

On British islands, an equally flamboyant carnival takes place at different times of year and it may, or may not,

Above and right: Mardi Gras on Martinique gives everyone a chance to step out of the closet and really live it up.

CULTURE

have religious undertones. In Anguilla, for example, carnival commemorates Emancipation Day, in August. In St. Vincent, a week-long carnival wing-ding occurs in July. Saba's, Barbuda's and Antigua's carnivals also takes place in July.

The carnival in St. Kitts, which has a Christmas theme, is held in late December. Carnival dates in the Grenadines and St. Vincent have been moved up to the end of June and early July, an appropriate time for prospective visitors as hotels offer cheaper summer rates.

In Bonaire the famous harvest festival of *Simadan* is celebrated in February. Carnival, however, is a springtime affair in the U.S. Virgin Islands. Its star performer is *Mocko Jumbi*, who teeters on seventeen-foot stilts, and brings the spirit of this gay festival to other joyous events throughout the year.

Other nations' holidays are also celebrated by islanders, who are always game for a party, a jump-up (spontaneous parade), or just an excuse for a good time. Favorites include Guy Fawkes Day in the English islands (recalling the man who tried unsuccessfully to blow up the British Parliament), Bastille Day (14th of July) in the French islands, and 4th of July in the Dutch islands.

Although they are more informal than the elaborately costumed carnivals, the traditional Friday night street events at Gros Islet, in St. Lucia, are becoming increasingly popular with tourists and islanders alike.

Music and Dance

When the Spanish arrived, they found music and dance already a part of Indian culture. Arawaks had no stringed instruments, but they enlivened their festivities and ceremonies with drums, rattles, whistles and flutes – probably much like those played by Mexican and Central American Indians today.

Even as slaves, the Indians entertained their Spanish captors with their graceful dances, accompanied by percussion and song. Early Spanish versions of stringed

CULTURE

instruments – harps, fiddles, guitars and also mandolins – were added to gourds, sticks and whatever additional noisemakers could be harvested in the bush.

Fandangos and flamencos also crossed the ocean to be absorbed by the islands.

The mournful wail of the Moors and the folk melodies of Madrid mixed with the songs of the Arawaks, creating a distinctly new music which began putting down roots in the New World.

Where the French settled a similar alteration was performed on *quadrilles, gavottes* and contradances.

Slaves from Africa brought their own instruments or inventively recreated them in their new world – drums, usually in sets of three with different tones, such as the *marimba*, (concussion sticks), and *maracas* (rattles).

The Church, however, in its usually heavy-handed manner, looked down on

Above and right: Carnival fever does not discriminate on the basis of age, sex, national or ethnic origin.

the drum as a pagan relic. Perhaps, too, it sensed the dangers of free artistic expression amongst the slave class and sought to suppress it by all means. But the performers found that striking any hollow vessel with a bamboo stick, be it old cans or empty bottles, also resulted in music. Empty oil drums left over from World War II had an additional advantage: They could be given several tones by banging dents into the bottom. With a bit of technical ingenuity and a musical sense, this crude garbage of the so-called civilized world turned into a serious instrument. Today steel bands ply their trade not only in the Caribbean, but in other parts of the world too. The pans, as the drums are commonly known, give out a soft clanging sound, and their range is adequate for the performance of anything from the simplest folk dances to Chopin waltzes and Beethoven symphonies.

Another musical form that comes from Africa were such elements as response singing, which survives in today's Gospel choruses, the cocky improvisation

CULTURE

that developed into calypso and the Puerto Rican *plena*, and the persistent, hypnotic, and sometimes maddening repetition known musically as *ostinato*.

Indeed, Harry Belafonte, in spite of all appearances, did not create calypso, but he did do a great deal to popularize it, even though it may be in a somewhat bowdlerized version. Like the above-mentioned steel drum, calypso was born in Trinidad. The origins of its denomination remain unclear, with the best bet suggesting that the acclamation *kai-so* was the root of the term.

A calypso song may repeat a short, catchy phrase hundreds of times, a trait that some tourists find rather amusing, and others monotonous. African rhythms combined with stately old-world *gavottes* and *quadrilles* to become sensual new dances – the *merengue, bomba, conga, rumba, guaracha, bolero, beguine* and *danzon*. From *rumba* evolved *salsa,* and from Jamaica, via Ethiopia, came *reggae*. Curaçao's national dance, the *tuma,* appears to be simply a mixture between *rumba* and an Irish *jig*.

One particular African dance that survives today in one of its purest forms is the *big drum*, which is performed in Carriacou for almost every important ceremony from boat launchings to "stone" feasts. The latter celebrate the setting of a gravestone, an event that sometimes may take place months and even years after the burial of a loved one.

Steel band music, also called *pan* music, was born in Trinidad and has become a West Indian characteristic as far north as Bermuda. Reggae, born out of protest, has spread worldwide, but calypso can also be used as a form of political satire to influence West Indian voters. With their *impromptu* rhymes, calypso singers verbally gore politicians, tourists and everyone else. They give themselves exalted names like King Superior or Prince Worthy. The Mighty Sparrow, for instance, is famous world-

wide. It is not uncommon for a calypso singer to stop by a restaurant table, ask one or two innocent questions about a tourist's age or home town, then sing a hilarious bit of doggerel that describes him perfectly, without missing a beat or failing to find a word that rhymes, like the following :

You come far, fly DC-Tree
Island glad you visit we
You drink plenty rum,
You actin' naughty
You sixty-fi'
an' look like forty.

Every visitor will inevitably get a chance to try the world-famous *limbo*, a strutting, writhing dance in which the performers have to ease their way under a broom handle without touching either it or the ground with their fronts or backs respectively. After each round the broom handle is lowered just a few notches, naturally increasing more and more the chances of toppling over. The dance soon turns into an acrobatic feat, seemingly defying the laws of gravity.

CULTURE

Above: Some cultures are all-pervasive in the Caribbean. Right: These young women might speak a very old version of French.

Long after tourists have retired to nurse their pulled muscles, the locals will still be inching under bars that are only a few inches from the floor, often balancing a flaming torch in each hand to boot.

Fortunately, these touristy clichés have not displaced the more serious art. Originally limbo was not practiced to delight a group of whooping tourists, but rather to represent a dead person passing into the nether world. It is another African contribution to Caribbean culture, though the name is of Christian origin, suggesting the place where the dead are neither on earth nor in hell or heaven.

Traditional forms are still practiced, perfected and performed in our days by such groups as the Jamaica National Dance Theater Company, Les Grand Ballets de la Martinique, the Kibrahacha Dancers of Bonaire, the Folkloric Group of Guadeloupe and, finally, the Mayoumba Folkloric Troupe of Anguilla.

Limbo dancing is no longer restricted to the Caribbean, however, as a number of troups carry this art form to the far corners of the world. And travelers to East Africa will also have a chance to witness limbo performances in the dance's native land.

It was in Martinique that Cole Porter first saw the *beguine,* which is still performed here along with a host of other local dances such as the *ting bang*. Native dance groups also give performances aboard cruise ships, or on the docks to welcome passengers ashore.

In Dominica, the *korne korn-la* is performed on the second Saturday of the month, either at ScottsHead or Soufrière. The event includes native dances, conch shell blowing and culinary delights. In Bonaire, villagers celebrate the harvest with *simadans* in February. The Muslim New Year, celebrated in Trinidad, is a two-day affair that has already lost much of its original religious meaning. Folk events and noisy street carnivals mark National Day on the island of Dominica in early November.

The Friday night street dances at Gros Islet, in St. Lucia, are always spontaneous, genuine and gay events, despite the din of over-amplified recordings. "Jump-up" happenings could occur on any evening on any island – around a beach campfire or after a more formal program. They begin with a musician who comes down the street like the Pied Piper, collecting an ever-larger band of followers. West Indians come alive when they hear a beat, and their circle usually has room for the outsider. Local dances or concerts are generally advertised on crude posters stuck to telephone poles or in dusty shop windows. These informal notices will announce traditional events like the jazzy zouk music of Guadeloupe the liamuiga folk singers of St. Kitts and Nevis, or regular reggae, *compas* and *soca* festivals. Drama, pantomime and comedy are

CULTURE

performed in both English and Creole at the Lighthouse in St. Lucia.

Language

It was once joked that Britons and Americans are one people separated by a common language. Nowhere are variations of English more lilting and charming than in the West Indies, where most people speak a version of it, often in addition to a local *patois*.

Of course, English is not the only language spoken in lands that were settled first by Spain. Spanish remains the official language of Puerto Rico and Cuba in the Greater Antilles, and the Dominican Republic. In all local dialects, Spanish plays at least a small part. Seven million people speak Creole, an umbrella name for variations of French spoken in nations as far apart as Haiti in the Caribbean and Mauritius in the Indian Ocean. It is spoken throughout all the French islands, as well as in St. Lucia and in Jamaica, both English islands.

Papiamento, the language of the Dutch West Indies, has its origins in the Portuguese that was spoken in the slave markets of Africa. Its name derives from the verb *papaer,* which means to babble incoherently. As slavery diminished and was replaced by smuggling in and out of the South American mainland, it became useful to add Spanish words to the common vocabulary. Thus, with Dutch the official language, Spanish a working language, and the necessity to speak English in business and tourism, Papiamento evolved into an all-new mixture of African, Portuguese, Spanish, Dutch and French. It is heard more frequently the nearer one comes to the Spanish mainland, and even in some of the English and Dutch islands. The national word of welcome in the Dutch Antilles is a French-sounding *bonbini* and gratitude is expressed by a Teutonic *danki*. Although most islanders speak at least some English, they will beam with pleasure if a visitor spices up his or her language with an occasional Papiamento word.

CULTURE

The Aruban national anthem, for instance, illustrates this fascinating, and sometimes familiar-sounding language: *Aruba patria aprecia, nos cuna venera, chikito y simpel bo por ta pero si respecta.* Knowledge of Spanish or French becomes a prerequisite for understanding in this case, but even without full command of these languages, it is possible to get the overall meaning. The text translates as follows: "Aruba, be- loved home, our venerated cradle, though small and simple you may be, you are indeed esteemed." Papiamento, therefore, can be looked upon as some natural Esperanto.

For those with an ear for language, West Indian English will have lots of interesting auditory nuances. Very often, "v" and "w" are transposed, but not uniformly throughout the whole sentence, e.g.: "Ve went to the vell for water, get wery bushed ven we climb da hill."

Above: Indians arriving to the Caribbean in the centuries past brought their religion with them, and their descendants still practice it.

Objective and nominative cases also are transposed, as in "Him not good to we." In fact, the use of "we," when it should be "us," has become a sort of national fad – much as Americans slip in the occasional "ain't" to make a point. The "th" sound is very difficult for West Indians and usually sounds like a "t." A favorite island dance is the *ting bang,* and a classic calypso song rejoices that "she promise give me some dat ring ting ting." Finally, certain combinations of consonants always come out differently than they are spelled: "film" becomes "flim" and "ask" becomes "aks."

Language becomes a song on the tongues of some people, who usually put the accent on the last syllable and raise the tone of the last word in a sentence, like "Ve goin' to de mah-ket." If they are asking a question, the voice rises almost to a squeak, even in men.

Archaic words are also part of insular vocabulary, some harking back to Victorian and even Elizabethan times recalling without the shadow of a doubt in what century any given island was settled. "Is she a somber woman?" a West Indian may ask, when she wants to know if a woman is older and more sedate in her ways. In St. Barts (sometimes spelled Barths, pronounced Barts) a form of old Norman French is spoken.

On almost every island, an entire new vocabulary has developed, and it is interesting to listen for new words, turns of phrases, and names such as *oildown, fallback* or *goatwater* (all are stews), *mountain chicken* (frogs' legs), *salacos* (hats), *dunny* (money), or *rundown* (fish cooked in coconut milk).

But there is also an unspoken language. Women in the French West Indies and in St. Lucia wear madras scarves knotted into perky caps. Depending on whether there are one, two or three knots, the initiated will know at once if the woman is single, married or available. For example, a married woman sporting a cap with three knots would be a welcome sight for village gossipers.

And almost every major city in the Antilles has its own Oriental community. In Trinidad, where there are as many Asians as Afro-West Indians, the mix is one of the most vivid and varied human mosaics in the whole world. Happily, these differences altogether seem to have a lot more positive than negative results socially. Although the islands have their share of strife between white and black or Christian and Moslem, the people here have managed to live peacefully side by side in relatively close quarters.

Religion

The religious fabric of the Lesser Antilles is as colorful and complex as the islands themselves. It is also, in its current diversity, symptomatic of local history. On the one hand religion served the designs of the colonial masters. On the other hand it supplied the oppressed, the slaves that is, with hope and a common purpose, while at the same time maintaining their ties to Africa.

With the Spanish came priests and the heavy-handed, if not downright murderous, evangelism of the times. The English brought their Protestantism, usually in two or more bitterly contesting factions, and each surge of immigration brought fresh batches of religious refugees from a crowded and troubled Europe.

Jews came first from Europe and then also from Brazil. At one time, Sephardic Jews made up half the population of Nevis; the Jewish cemetery at Charlestown has gravestones dating as far back as 1690. The allegedly oldest synagogue in the Americas is Mikve Israel-Emanuel in Curaçao, founded in the 1630s. Portuguese, Dutch, German and French Jews – among them the family of Camille Pissarro, one major impressionist painter – were early settlers in the Caribbean and they have been a part of island life for centuries. Floors in the center of the synagogue at Curaçao are covered with sand in traditional Sephardic manner, a vivid reminder of the Jews' flight from Egypt centuries ago. The synagogue at Bridgetown, Barbados, dates to 1833, but its congregation to 1651.

The Lesser Antilles, especially the island of Barbados, became a stopover for Quakers who were fleeing persecution in England. At one time, five big meeting houses flourished on Barbados, and the faith spread from there throughout the West Indies. Governorship of the British Virgin Islands alternated several times between pacifist Quakers, who stopped the construction of forts and freed and educated their slaves, and non-Quakers, who beat their wives, built fortifications as fast as they could, and generally served as "Great Enemies and Despisers" of the Society of Friends.

Although their era actually ended by the 1760s, the Quakers returned to the islands more than once in the 1830s and

CULTURE

1840s, at the height of anti-slavery sentiment, to work for human rights. At Fat Hog Bay in the Virgin Islands, there are the remains of an old Quaker cemetery.

Laborers from the Middle East and the Orient brought their faiths with them as well. Earlier in this century, half the population of Trinidad were Hindu, Moslem or Parsee. Today, two of the liveliest festivals in Trinidad are the *Divali* Hindu Festival of Lights in late autumn, and *Hosein*, a joyous Moslem festival whose date is set according to the Islamic calendar. An East Indian population also remains on Guadeloupe. During their *Fête Annuelle*, they serve traditional curries.

Voodoo and a similar belief, *Obeah*, are associated more with Jamaica and Haiti than with the Lesser Antilles, but elements of both are encountered here on occasion. In native markets one sometimes comes across peculiar aerosol cans with strange labels and with rather exotic names such as "High Luck Winner". Called spray-on blessings, or *aerosols de benedicion*, they are sprayed around the house to banish bad spirits. Another religion similar to Voodoo, and found mainly on Trinidad, is *Shango,* a hybrid between African beliefs and Judeo-Christian creed – with a little Hindu mixed in.

Mainline religions were often layered atop lingering Arawak and Carib beliefs and African spiritualism, then veneered over with new religions such as Mormonism or Rastafarianism. The resulting mix usually is surprisingly harmonious and tolerant, except for some occasional problems such as the Moslem uprising in Trinidad in 1990.

The Caribbean has always been fertile ground for missionaries of all denominations, so that religion is very much a part of everyday life. Yet, it is often a religion far removed from the traditional faith as practiced in its homeland. A Baptist taxi

Above and right: Lacy carvings and simple constructions are some of the elements of traditional architecture in the Lesser Antilles.

CULTURE

driver may have a crucifix hanging from his rearview mirror, be listening to a Seventh Day Adventist preacher on the radio, and have a voodoo *dambala wedo* (snake symbol) on the windshield. Religion, like many other West Indies' charms, is a marriage of old and new, black and white, and gods and spirits.

Architecture

The most obvious – that is the most visible to the casual visitor – contribution to the cultural scene of the Lesser Antilles is architectural. Here the European nations played the most important and resilient role. Despite hurricanes, fires, sackings by pirates and men-of-war, a fair number of the old edifices still grace the cityscapes. Unfortunately, they do have to share space far too often with anonymous hotels built to accomodate the perennial flood of tourists, and hastily raised homes, but this apparently vicious contrast generally serves to better highlight their gracious and eloquent forms.

They stand like elegantly dressed visitors at a county fair, like a priest straying into a house of ill repute. The solid patrician symmetry of the French Empire style remains from those great days when Napoleonic France sought to expand its influence in the New World, quaint Dutch façades on Curaçao peer into the exotic colors of the Caribbean and the Virgin Islands still boast some remainders of the comfortable Danish Baroque introduced by their onetime owners.

The Lesser Antilles have few of the super-sized forts and monumental cathedrals built by the Spanish in the islands they colonized in the Greater Antilles. Still, many historic forts, churches and other architectural highlights do exist. One example for monumental architecture is the 17th-century Brimstone Hill, in St. Kitts. Built by the British and never surrendered in battle, it sprawls stonily over some 32 acres.

Among the many notable churches is the Cathedral of St. John the Divine, in Antigua, but almost every island has at

CULTURE

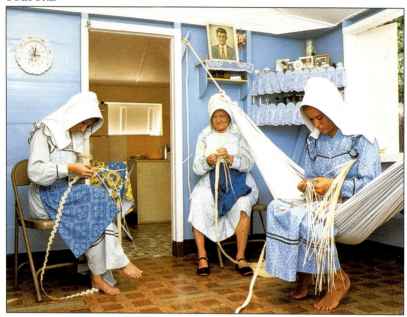

least one church of architectural interest – if only for its spartan utilitarianism. Many date back to the 19th or 20th century, St. John the Divine, for example, was erected in 1845. Sacré-Coeur Cathedral (1928), north of Fort-de-France, Martinique, on the road to Jardin de Balata, is a small and exquisite copy of the one in Paris. Also of interest is the baroque church at Case Pilote. It is the oldest church on the island, and a veritable wedding cake of dimpled angels. St. Peter's in Parham, Antigua, is one of the West Indies' loveliest, built in 1840 in Italian style. Curaçao's synagogue is the oldest in the New World and contains a very rare ritual bath. It was built in 1634.

One of the most interesting churches looks historic but was built in the 1930's. It is St. Mary's in Kingstown, St. Vincent. At the village of François, in Martinique, an obviously ultra-modern church contrasts in a fascinating way with the gingerbread-trimmed Hotel de Ville. Another landmark of architectural note is the dazzling Schoelcher Library *(Bibliothèque)* in Fort-de-France, Martinique. It was built at the Paris Exposition in 1889, shipped here in pieces, and reassembled.

In the Dutch West Indies, where streets are lined with the tall, narrow homes characteristic of old Amsterdam, some houses are trimmed with charming symbols such as flowers or birds, standing out in relief around the gutters or façades. The technique, called *floramiento de cas* in the native Papiamento *patois,* spread throughout the Dutch islands with bricklayers who carved the figures in clay while it was still damp. The pleasantly gentle pastel colors of many houses were meant – by government decree – to safeguard the inhabitants eyesight from the powerful combination of sun and whitewash. The best examples of West Indian Dutch style are found in Curaçao, which was settled and fortified by Dutch people determined to stand their ground in the

Above: Traditional costumes on St.Barts.
Right: Handicrafts against the sun.

CULTURE

New World. They dug in in 1634, installed Peter Stuyvesant as governor, and set about to protect the island with massive fortifications. Many of the oldest forts now house the best restaurants on the island, though Fort Amsterdam in Willemsted serves as office space for the local government.

The Protestant church facing the entrance of the fort is another fine specimen of baroque, specifically Dutch baroque, architecture. A later example of Dutch architecture stands behind the church on the Wilhelmina Plein, the *Stadhuis*, built in 1858 to house the government of the period. It exhibits the staid pomposity of its social and political position.

Usually any building referred to as a *fort* is worth investigating. The fort itself may be anything from a superb restoration to a pile of interesting rubble, but the panorama – like that from Fort George, in Port of Spain – will probably be one of the best on the island.

In Saba, fair-skinned, English-speaking descendants of Dutch and English settlers live in prim, whitewashed, fairytale cottages with lace curtains. Another fine example of Dutch West Indian style is the Olde Street Shopping Center in Phillipsburg, on Sint Maarten. Painted in pastels and decorated in airy fretwork and lattices, it is nowadays a smart mall and meeting place.

Until 1917, the Virgin Islands were a Danish possession yielding large and lucrative crops of sugar cane that enabled plantation owners to live well. They naturally made homes for themselves that kept alive the memory of their native Denmark, so that anyone strolling down the pretty streets of Christiansted or Frederiksted will experience a preview of any provincial town in Denmark. The Government House in the former, or Fort Christiansvaern are two particularly fine examples of this heritage.

Throughout the West Indies, many of the old greathouses have been turned into modern bed-and-breakfast inns or into restaurants. They are fine examples of plantation architecture, often restored to a

CULTURE

fare-thee-well. One of the most plush, both as a former plantation house and as a modern-day spa, is the *Plantation Leyritz*, in Martinique.

Arts, Handicrafts and Souvenirs

Paul Gauguin, who came to Martinique to live in a hovel and to paint for four glorious months before he went to Tahiti, is only one of the artists to have been inspired by all the blazing colors, blinding beaches and brilliant blue and turquoise seas of the Lesser Antilles. A museum in Carbet now commemorates Gauguin and his work. Other artists and writers who were inspired by the islands include Aubrey Davidson-Houston, Alex Waugh, Herman Wouk, Graham Greene, Somerset Maugham, Truman Capote, Anthony Trollope and Saint-John Perse (Alexis Saint-Léger), who won the Nobel Prize for literature in 1960.

Above: Friendliness and hospitality are very important social habits in the Antilles.

With the explosion in the number of cruise ships now calling in the Caribbean and the proliferation of modern duty-free shopping malls in dock areas, focus has unfortunately shifted to perfumes and porcelains and away from the meaningful and unique crafts made locally.

One of the most authentic products of the islands certainly is basketry made from native palms and grasses in centuries-old motifs. Some of the patterns go back to Africa. Every island also has its own painters, carvers and dozens of craft items that are not available on other islands. To those interested in folk art, it is these individual crafts that will prove to be the most exciting finds.

On market day in Castries, crude charcoal stoves are sold next to homemade pottery, primitive brooms and different kinds of hand-woven rush rugs. They are made by local people, usually for sale to St. Lucians, so they are very inexpensive. Nevertheless, these homely, everyday necessities are captivating and unique examples of folk art.

More upscale products in St. Lucia are the silk screen and batik fabrics at Bagshaw's, one of the most famous fabric houses in the Indies. Island themes and colors turn simple yard goods into works of art. Batiks made in St. Kitts at Romney Manor incorporate flowers and shells, as well as copies of ancient Indian petroglyphs to be found on the island. Also in Castries is the St. Lucia Artists Association, housed in a small *galerie* on the second floor of the Alliance Française Building. Artists also show at *Artsibit*, between Brazil and Mongiraud streets.

Furniture makers throughout St. Lucia work with local hardwoods, either using lumber or carving directly on a chunk of a limb or trunk. Nevis is known for its goatskin products. Pottery is made on many islands, including Barbados where leather work is also becoming popular. In Bequia, which was once a whaling center, hand-carved scale models of the old whalers are sold.

Works by local artists are displayed and sold at the Poisson d'Or, an expensive restaurant in Marigot, Sint Maarten, but it would be awkward to come as a browser and not a diner. The Lynn family runs a small art gallery at their home at Grand Case, also on Sint Maarten.

At the Carib reservation in Dominica, the descendants of the aborigines still sell dugout canoes made as they were before the arrival of Columbus. On a somewhat smaller scale, they also sell baskets and woven mats. The village itself, however, is not as interesting an anthropological adventure as one might be lead to expect. The Carib homes, as it turns out, are in fact rather ordinary looking.

Outside Basse-Point, in Martinique, at Leyritz Plantation, a doll-maker sells one-of-a-kind *poupées* made from local materials. *Doudou* dolls are another item made in the French West Indies. The Marché Rue Perrinon or La Savane are colorful street markets in Martinique. Some of the better jewelry stores on the island sell 18-carat gold *colliers chou,* or charming *sweetheart necklaces.*

At Roseau in Dominica, the tiny Tropicrafts factory makes palm straw goods for shipment throughout the region. At Kingstown, St. Vincent, a crafts center is housed in the old cotton gin. Fort Charlotte, in Kingstown, contains a series of paintings that tells the story of the Black Caribs, a tribal mingling of shipwrecked slaves and Carib Indians. At Port of Spain, Trinidad, local painters usually display their work at a market next to the Hotel Normandie.

Some islands have their own perfumeries, which utilize native flowers, spices and cocoa butter or coconut oil.

In some places, local handicrafts are sold through government cooperatives at markets set up especially for the tourist trade. One of these is Grencraft, in St. George's, Grenada. Handmade items are also sold through charity institutions, such as homes for the blind.

Local postage stamps make lasting and significant souvenirs, for as much or as little as one has to spend. For the serious collector, most larger islands have special philatelic offices where the more desirable collectible stamps are sold. One of the most impressive is the St. Vincent Philatelic Society, in Kingstown.

Recordings of local music also make authentic, lasting souvenirs. Except for a few international stars, most West Indian artists are not known outside their own region. So their tapes or LPs (CDs still are rare) are not available outside the small island or island group.

The West Indies do, of course, continue to attract modern artists and craftsmen from the outside world. Along with the expatriates have come the most up-to-date techniques and marketing skills, to blend with island materials and motifs. Superb woven goods, batiks, lead-free pottery, silkscreen, metalwork, coral jewelry and crafts of all kinds have been added to the shopping menu.

VIRGIN ISLANDS

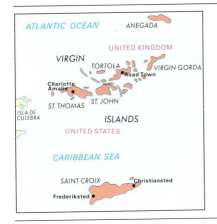

TURQUOISE SAILING GROUNDS

U. S. VIRGIN ISLANDS
BRITISH VIRGIN ISLANDS

On the map they are a mere sprinkling of tiny-dots, but as the traveler nears the islands by boat or plane they loom large, lovely and distinct against a foam-flecked sea.

It is said that Columbus named this archipelago for St. Ursula and her army of 11,000 virgins who were martyred in A.D. 238.

The Spanish never settled the **Virgin Islands**, leaving them open for French and English squatters who began occupying them in 1625. The French soon drifted away and, in 1650, the English were routed by the Spanish, who were in turn ousted by the French shortly thereafter. The story is a familiar one in the West Indies, where islands were grabbed at will by roving adventurers, and traded like pawns by European giants. In 1653, the flag of the Knights of Malta was raised over the islands. They sold out to the French, but in 1666, Denmark took possession of **St. Thomas** and **St. John**. In 1733, the Danes bought **St. Croix** and all three islands remained Danish for a period of 200 years.

Preceding pages: The Caribbean dream landscape, probably as Christopher Columbus himself saw it. Carnival provides a wild ambience. Left: The long and steep way up to the crow's nest.

Like the other Caribbean, the Virgins have only one climate – perpetual summer. Average temperatures usually range from 24 degrees centigrade in winter to 28 degrees in summer. The tradewinds almost always provide a cooling breeze; they just blow stronger in winter.

The Virgin Islands today are synonymous with yachting. Only very few other island groups offer so many coves, bays, beaches and sea gardens in such a concentrated area. Sailors can raise anchor, sail sheltered waters for only an hour or two, and find themselves in another harbor on another island. In fact, the Virgins are the yacht chartering center of the Caribbean, with large fleets of both bareboats and crewed ships.

Second only to yachting on the islands is scuba diving on coral reefs that boast more colorful sea life than an aquarium. Most hotels can arrange snorkel or diving trips, sometimes right on their own house reefs. If scuba will be the sole focus of your trip, request the Virgin Islands Dive Guide from USVI tourism.

Deep-sea fishing is another local speciality, although there is increasing evidence that, throughout the Carribean, the fish population is becoming overly and dangerously depleted by this alleged sport. Of course, few wish to spoil the fun with such thoughts, but those great, ro-

mantic days of Hemingway confronting mighty sea creatures on a one to one basis are passed. The activity itself has, to a considerable extent, degenerated into a something of a brutal game, though few would be ready to admit it. Today the sportsmen and -women are comfortably strapped in chairs atop a pair of mighty diesels and backed by the full weight of the latest in fishing technology, ready to haul in billfish, marlins, tuna and wahoo who, in turn, have less of a fighting chance than a bull in a Spanish arena. Lowering the limit weight in prize-fishing contests has only temporarily masked the extent of the problem.

There may be a gentle solution to the dilemma. Ever since Jacques Cousteau featured the whales of the Virgin Islands on television, more and more tourists have been coming here for whale watching. Humpback whales are particularly active from February to April; it is advisable to hire a boat with a skipper who knows the best places to spot spouting cows with their playful calves.

Although the Virgins are one island group, they are governed separately. Visitors should consider beforehand whether they want to go to the **American Virgin Islands**, called the **USVI**, the **British Virgin Islands**, known locally as the **BVI**, or to both groups.

Yacht Chartering

More charter boats can be found in the Virgin Islands than in any other part of the Caribbean. It is still possible to make arrangements on the spot and on the spur of the moment in certain anchorages with willing captains, but nowadays lots of travel agents represent a number of yacht charters. And there are also an increasing number of charter brokers who specialize in charter boats. The most up-to-date information is available from agencies like the Charterboat League, BVI Bareboats,

Above and right: The British and U.S. Virgins provide endless sand beaches and crystal clear waters for all aquatic activities.

VIRGIN ISLANDS

Conch Charters Ltd., Regency Yacht Vacations, Caribbean Sailing Charters Inc., Preferred Yachting Vacations, Virgin Island Sailing, Yacht Charters International, and others. Additional current listings can be found in newsstand magazines such as *Sail* and *Yacht Vacation*, or equally from Sunday travel sections of major metropolitan newspapers including (in the U.S.) *The New York Times, Washington Post, Boston Globe, Los Angeles Times, Miami Herald*. Further information is available at any of the tourist offices throughout the Virgin Islands.

Finding the right charter takes time and a bit of inquiring to assure the right boat, crew, safety standards, cuisine and locale. Many charter boats are privately owned, or are crewed by husband-wife teams, whose boat is both home and livelihood. It is best to deal with a charter broker who has already sailed on, or at least personally toured, the represented boats. Some are as spacious and formal as a good hotel. Others are equally intimate and informal. Some may turn out to be a vacationer's nightmare. If at all possible, one should correspond with former guests of the boat or the charter firm to ask about the state of the boat, quality of the crew, number of private baths, and so on.

Unless one is the holder of sterling sailing credentials, one will have to take a crewed yacht, or hire a capable captain to sail a bareboat. There are two provisioning options for those who will be bareboating (hiring a craft without a crew). One can take care of ones own supplies, by buying them in the islands, for example. The second is a full provisioning package of three meals a day, supplied by the charter firm. Another option is a compromise "split" plan in which some meals are provided aboard, some eaten ashore. The split plan is most popular; bringing supplies from home is the cheapest but most cumbersome – especially if plane changes and ferries are involved.

The different types of yacht charter include the following:

VIRGIN ISLANDS

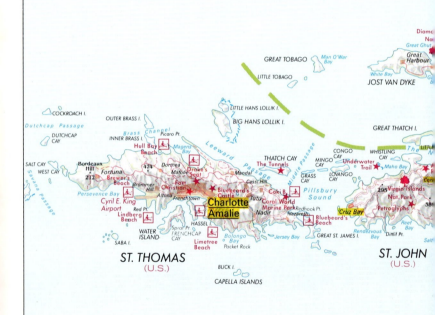

VIRGIN ISLANDS

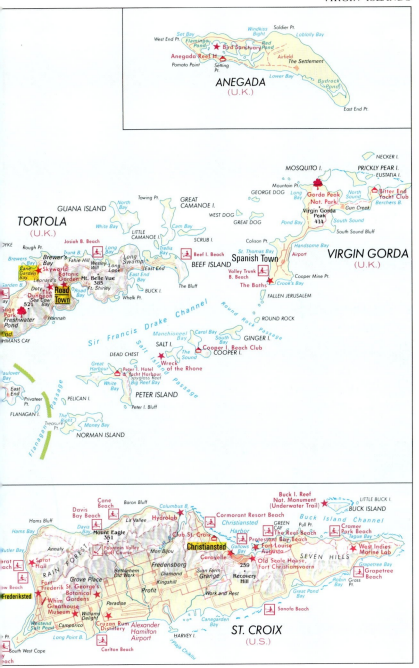

VIRGIN ISLANDS

Bareboat: If one has sailing experience and can meet the charter firm's requirements, one will be given a boat to handle independently. One then has to master all required tasks such as sailing, navigation, dish-washing, cooking, and swabbing.

Captained charter: A professional captain does the piloting, but the guests do the chores. Also available are charters with captain and cook.

Crewed charter: On a larger boat, the crew will consist of several people who do all the work and cater to one's every whim. On small boats, the crew will very frequently consist of a congenial couple, often live-aboards who have almost always a decidedly personal stake in treating their guests extremely well.

Flotilla charter: a bareboat that sails in company of other boats.

Learn-to-sail charter: This is a working cruise in which one lives aboard and meanwhile learns skills that will qualify one for future bareboating.

Live-aboard dive boat: If you want to devote your entire holiday to diving, take a fully-inclusive dive charter. Accommodations are on the spartan side, but meals are hearty and the diving unbeatable.

Powerboat charter: Different kinds of powerboats are frequently available for bareboating to people who are not yet accomplished in the fine arts of winching sheets, hauling yards, tuning rigging, reefing, battening and turning hard alee.

U. S. VIRGIN ISLANDS

In many ways, the USVI are positively as American as apple pie, yet they have a piquant Danish past that adds a unique patina to this highly popular Caribbean vacationing center.

Although discovered by the Spanish and originally settled by the British, these islands were in Danish hands until 1917 when the U.S. government, eager to fortify an outpost from which it could pro-

Above: Some of the smoothest sailing in the Antilles is off the Virgins' coasts. Right: Hair drying with solar power.

tect the Panama Canal, bought them for $25 million. Relations had always been cordial between the Danish islands and the United States. When the American republic declared its independence from Britain in 1776, one of the first foreign salutes to the stars and stripes came from **Fort Frederik** in St. Croix.

Denmark had offered the islands to the U.S. as early as 1869, but then the price of $7.5 million was too high for a country just recovering from a costly civil war. Even in 1917, when Washington paid the aforementioned $25 million, taxpayers were aghast. Yet, from today's point of view, the price, which figures out to about $300 an acre, was an absolute bargain.

Although the archipelago includes a sprinkling of cays, it is actually made up of three major islands, all of them named for saints. They are **St. Thomas** and **St. John**, close enough together to be considered part of the same vacation, and **St. Croix**, (pronounced *croy*). The name, meaning "holy cross" in French, goes back to the days of Spanish discovery, when Columbus christened it *Santa Cruz*. The French later took over and simply translated the name.

Most tourists routinely cross between St. Thomas and St. John by ferry, but St. Croix lies 40 sea miles away – a long ride by boat. The alternative is a rather expensive flight with the Sea Plane Shuttle.

Travelers can, in principle, choose among three very different holidays: St. Thomas with its bustling lifestyle, St. John known for its national park and remote camping and resorts, and St. Croix for its old-world charms.

Culturally, too, the islands are a blend of American casualness combined with a strong residue of European grace and a heavy African beat. One of the best places to see islanders in their own element is at a fish fry. These are generally announced at hotel receptions or posted in shop windows and on telephone poles. Posters are, by the way, the West Indian version of the jungle telegraph – along with local radio, they are as important as the newspapers for information on what

U. S. VIRGIN ISLANDS

is going on. Usually a *fry* is just a happy mixture of local food – including fresh seafood and a cornmeal dumpling called *fungi* – homemade music, friendly people and a drink called *maubi*.

St. Thomas and St. Croix have performing arts centers, but the program is more likely to be imported. Much more authentic in terms of local culture is a Quadrille: The Quadrille on St. Croix is the Emperor Quadrille, whilst on St. Thomas the people dance the North German Quadrille, both from the 18th century.

Shopping in the USVI

Known for a long time as one of the consumer capitals of the world for brand-name, duty-free goods, shopping in St. Thomas is no longer the bargain it once was, but still ranks among the best in the Indies. And there is also good shopping

Above: The colorful rooftops of Charlotte Amalie on St. Thomas. Right: Skilled workers have left their mark on houses.

in St. Croix, at both **Fredriksted** and **Christiansted**. The ports are still free, which means no duty and no sales taxes. Nowadays, it is still cheaper sometimes to buy expensive items such as jewelry, ceramics, porcelain or watches in the USVI and pay duty, but careful shopping is now required.

Customs regulations are a little different for each country. US residents, for example, can take back as much as $1200 in duty-free goods bought in the USVI, which is twice the allowance than in most of the Caribbean. Generally, stores are closed on Sundays, but when cruise ships are in port anything goes. Shops in hotels are a viable alternative. In most places hotel shops charge premium prices, but they are frequently branches of downtown stores selling the very same goods and charging the same prices.

St. Thomas

Flying into St. Thomas was once a fairly adventurous undertaking. Meanwhile,

ST. THOMAS

the runway has been extended to 7000 feet and a new terminal was opened. Besides the usual taxi service, St. Thomas has a bus service connecting Charlotte Amalie, Red Hook and Bordeaux.

Charlotte Amalie, St. Thomas' colorful waterfront, is a gaudy bustle of happy shoppers, blaring traffic, hustlers and street people. It is, too, one of the Caribbean's favorite ports of call for cruise ship. It consists of a thoroughly compact complex of narrow streets and alleys lined with shops that were once Danish warehouses. Today, more than a million people arrive by ship each year – more than twice as many as come here by air – and Charlotte Amalie lays out a full table to welcome them.

The streets themselves were laid out in pre-automotive Danish days, so they are incredibly narrow. The place to set out on foot after arrival by ship, bus, or taxi, is **Emancipation Square**. A full day is not too much time to allot to shopping, snacking, people watching, and dining in this area. Shops sell the usual duty-free specialties found in every cruise port, but even visitors not practicing the secular art of consumerism will have something to observe, namely the vibrant local scene and the old Danish architecture.

Also downtown is the **Visitors' Center**, in a building diagonally opposite the 19th-century **Grand Hotel**. There is another tourist office near the **West Indian Company Dock**. One sight to visit is **Fort Christian**, which was built in 1671 and is now a museum. The dungeons in this red brick construction were still in use until the 1960s! Another worth-while stop is at the stately **Lutheran Church**, which was built in the 1800s.

Just behind the church stands the **Hotel 1829**, built by a French sea captain, and east of it, the famous **99 Steps** (actually, there are 103) leading to **Crown House**, a magnificent old Danish mansion built for the governor in 1750. The sumptuous

crystal chandelier there is thought to have come originally from the palace at Versailles. The US governor resides these days in **Government House**, which was built in the 1860s. The two lower stories can be visited.

Nearby is **Blackbeard's Castle**, which was built as Fort Skytsborg by the Danes. Its name refers to the notorious Edward Teach, one of the most famous pirates who ever roamed the area. It should not, however, be confused with **Bluebeard's Castle**, on the eastern edge of town. Built as a watchtower for Fort Christian, it is thought to have been a onetime hideout for Bluebeard, another infamous pirate. It now serves as a hotel and restaurant.

European Jews were early settlers in St. Thomas, and their **synagogue** here, at the corner of Crystal Gade and Raadets Gade, is supposedly one of the oldest in the West Indies. It was built in 1833 and, in accordance with Sephardic tradition, its floors are strewn with sand in memory of the exodus from Egypt. The home of Camille Pissarro, son of a local Jewish

ST. THOMAS

merchant and one of the great French Impressionist painters, is now a shop and office complex on Main Street.

The rest of the island can be toured in an hour or two with a driver. While the Main Street shopping area at the waterfront is best seen on foot, the rest of the island is not. Hillsides are steep, traffic bad and sidewalks non-existent. The busses of the public transportation system connect Charlotte Amalie, Red Hook and Bordeaux. Cabs can be called from the hotel reception or hailed at the docks, or at Emancipation Square. As always, it is best to negotiate a fee in advance with the cab driver. There are, however, official cab rates that vary sometimes from taxi to taxi, but are roughly based on the destination and number of passengers. While rental cars and scooters are available and U.S. driver's license are accepted, driving and navigating around the

Above: The synagogue in Charlotte Amalie, one of the oldest in the world. Right: The underwater world is close at hand.

island are difficult. Driving is on the left side of the road.

During any island tour with a guide, one can stop to identify interesting local flowers and shrubs. Many of them, such as jasmine and periwinkle, will be familiar. Others, such as the thorny catch-and-keep, jumbi cutlass, nothing nut, pink shower, a thorny tree called the monkey-don't-climb and clashie melashie, are probably not so well known, at least under their unique local names. Dozens of types of orchids are found in the Virgins as well. Other curiosities include the "sensitive plant" from the mimosa family – its leaves fold up when approached – and the lovely little scarlet flower called jump-up-and-kiss-me. Frequently, a good guide will stop to pluck an island fruit such as a genip, mammee apple, or sea grape, which all grow luyuriantly in the wild. Bananas, tamarinds, soursop, coconuts, guava and passion fruit grow now and then in private yards. Breadfruit and coconuts were introduced, by the way, by Captain Bligh himself, who had collected them in the South Pacific.

Among birds to be seen here are frigate birds, also called man-o'-war birds, pelicans, delightful banana quit and colourful parakeets. Here, he mangrove cuckoo is called the dumb bird, and locals call the sparrow hawk a *killy-dilly*. Mockingbirds are everywhere, turning any walkway into a chirping concert hall.

Drake's Seat, with its legend (probably exaggerated) about Sir Francis sitting there to watch the sea, has an excellent view beyond the touristy bustle. The glimpse of **Magen's Bay** – one of the most famous honeymoon beaches in the world-shows that it is shaped like a heart. An equally good view can be had from the top of **St. Peter Mountain.** During World War II it was a lookout and radio center for the Allies.

Practically all tours end up at **Coral World** on **Coki Beach**, a stunning tourist attraction built over a beautiful living

ST. THOMAS

reef. In the main building, a spiral staircase leads down inside a gigantic cylinder and suddenly arrives on the reef itself. In the spacious air chamber, one can observe life on the ocean floor as it goes on undisturbed. Other displays on the five-acre grounds include: a **Touch Pond,** where everyone can actually touch certain sea creatures; the **Baby Shark Pond,** with young sharks; the **Sea-Turtle Pool;** the **Reef Tank,** featuring sharks, barracudas and mantas; and the **Marine Gardens Aquarium** with 21 salt-water pools for exotic fish. Fish feeding time is at 10 a.m. and 11 a.m. daily. A guided tour of the park is given daily at 3 p.m., but visitors are free to roam around at will any time. The complex has an all-day admission fee that allows one to leave for a refreshing swim at Coki Beach and then return. plan at least half a day to enjoy the sights.There are several gift shops, snack bars and excellent restaurants available here. Coral World is open 365 days a year.

A particularly inuiting experience is an underwater safari. Atlantis Submarine and Looking Glass both operate two submarines off the coast south of St. Thomas. Passengers are taken down to a depth of about 100 feet and guided on a close-up exploration of submarine fauna and flora.

St. Thomas' beaches are a story in themselves: Coki and **Brewer's Beach** have shaded picnic tables and water-sports equipment for rent, **Hull Bay** has surfing on the north shore, **Limetree Beach** lies in a picturebook cove, **Lindberg Beach** is known for its bath house, and finally there are the famous Magens Bay, **Morningstar Beach** and **Sapphire Beach**. **Bluebeard's Beach** is popular with windsurfers on weekends. Private property rights in the USVI, by the way, apply only from the high-tide line up, so that everyone has a right to enjoy any beach without fear of trespassing. Other activities on the island, in addition to those offered by hotels and resorts, include parasailing, fishing, windsurfing, boating and day sailing, diving, golf and tennis.

DIVING

Diving in the USVI

A good choice of diving boats, guides and the latest equipment are available in the USVI. Information is usually held at the disposal of the guests at hotels. Even if the hotel does not offer a scuba package as such, it will put one in touch with a good diving shop, divemaster and boat.

One resort that even specializes in dive packages is **Bolongo Bay**, in St. Thomas, home of the St. Thomas Diving Club. Other dive packages are offered for instance by the Caravelle in St. Croix, The Buccaneer in St. Croix, Club St. Croix, Sapphire Beach Resort in St. Thomas, The West Indies Inn, St. Thomas; and aboard the Triworld, a 58-foot trimaran.

A number of dive packages in St. Croix are also offered by the Cormorant Beach Club, Hotel on the Cay, King Christian Hotel, Pink Fancy Hotel and Chenay Bay Beach Colony through one central reservation desk. For specifics on the packages offered by the various operators, one can either contact the individual establishments, or ask for details from tourist offices. It is not a bad idea to consult in good time with a well-informed travel agent for the latest on special discounts, particularly off-season bargains.

Packages are available for every level of skill, from simple beginner lessons and refresher courses to top level professional courses. Special underwater still and video cameras are available for rent, and some of the dive shops even do their own photo processing on the spot.

Among the sites most popular with scuba divers are by name: **Buck Island**, which is the United States' only underwater national park and a particularly attractive spot for both snorkelers and divers; **Frenchcap Cay**, off St. Thomas, where one can explore an 80-foot undersea pinnacle; **Sprat Point**, just off Charlotte Amalie; and **The Tunnels** at Thatch Cay. Because the wreck of the *Rhone* in

Above: The waters around the Virgins are ideal for scuba divers and snorkelers. Right: Always a comfortable breeze for sailors.

the BVI is such a popular site with divers, it is often included in dive trips that begin and end in the USVI.

Coki Beach is suitable for night diving. During the day it is crowded with cruise ship passengers but at night the magnificent reef here becomes the sole domain of divers and glittering tarpon. The underwater world in the Virgins is an Eden of living creatures. There are corals the size of houses and sea fans as big as apple trees, swaying with the current and seeming to pose in soft yellows and lavenders for the divers camera.

Wreck diving is always exciting in the Indies, not merely because some of the ships are centuries old and frozen in time, but because any sunken ship, such as the Barges, which sank before World War II, now provides underwater shelter to huge colonies of reef fish. The wreck of the freighter *Cartensor Senior* lies in three pieces off **Little Buck Island**. It was sunk on purpose, to form an artificial reef. Dive guides come here to feed fish regularly, assuring an unending show for their guests. **Packet Rock**, off Bolongo Bay, is notorious for the great number of wrecks it claimed. One of the wrecks, the *HMS Warwick*, dates to Victorian times. There is not too much left of the ship itself, but divers occasionally find small artifacts on the sea floor here. Remains of the *Major General Rogers,* a U.S. Coast Guard buoy tender, can still be seen off St. John, some 45 feet below the surface. It is home to huge schools of fish. Lots of wrecks, including the 177-foot freighter *Rosaomaira* and the tugboat *Northwind,* lie off Frederiksted. For wall diving, one can explore the *Salt River,* where the bottom plunges 1000 feet. Black coral grows here at a depth of about 80 feet.

St. John

Ferries run frequently between St. John and St. Thomas for only a few dollars. Even if one does not have time to disembark, the round trip itself actually offers the commodities of almost any delightful sightseeing cruise.

St. John is as unspoiled as St. Thomas is packed with people. Ferries are met at **Cruz Bay** by tour guides who offer island safaris in open-air jitneys or plain taxi service around town. They are a true bargain for a quick look at the island. For a longer stay it might be better to rent a jeep, scooter, or car. St. John, two-thirds of which is a national park, is one of the few places in the Caribbean with legal and comfortable camping facilities. At **Cinnamon Bay Campground**, located on a national park beach with a famous underwater snorkeling trail, it is possible to rent a rustic cottage, or a site with or without a tent, but making a reservation months in advance is essential. A private campground, **Maho Bay**, offers luxury beachside camping, watersports rentals and a good restaurant.

Park rangers present free programs Saturday and Sunday at Cinnamon Bay, describing island history and marine life.

ST. JOHN

Every Tuesday at 9 a.m., rangers lead a wading walk along the coral flats and mangrove lagoons. Beginner snorkelers can tour the **Underwater Trail** with a ranger.

An interesting way to visit the island is by boat. **Coral Bay** is one place to drop anchor, with a modest offering of drinks and snacks. The **Hurricane Hole** berthing spot is usually void of poeple. Leaving **Caneel Bay**, with the exclusive vacation resort **Caneel Bay Plantage**, you sail by Hawk's Nest Bay to reach **Trank Bay**, one of the most beautiful bathing spots.

Every tourist visits the ruins of **Annaberg Plantation**, with its big windmill. The former housing of the slaves has been partly restored. On Wednesdays and Fridays, from 10 a.m. to 1 p.m., demonstrators are on hand to show how medicinal plants were prepared and used, and how weaving, baking and terracing were done in colonial times. They also demonstrate charcoal making, which was once upon a time an important industry among freed slaves.

Visitors with a little more time can hike one of the trails in the plantation on their own, or sign up for a ranger-guided hiking tour. The route follows the old road of the sugar cargoes, down a steep and rugged mountainside trail that leads to a stunning beach.

St. Croix

St. Croix differs somewhat from the other Virgin Islands. It is the largest of the islands and its topography is not as rugged and mountainous. Consequently, it is the golfing center of the archipelago. It is agricultural, serene, uncrowded, affluent and has the most and best historic sites of the three major USVI. And it has its own special "out-island:" **Buck Island Rift**, a national park and a snorkeler's and diver's paradise, is well worth

Above: Sailing is one important source of income for islanders. Right: Tourism changed the face of many an island, such as St.Croix.

ST. CROIX

a day's excursion out of Christiansted (*Buck Island Reef Natural Trail*).

The island has two major settlements, and is steeped in tidy, sunbaked Danish charm. Both offer duty-free shopping, lots of cool and informal bars where one can relax with a rum swizzle, excellent restaurants, and just enough Yankee mannerisms to let one know that this is still U.S. territory.

Christiansted could just as well be an 18th-century Danish village, opened up to the tropical trade winds and transported brick for brick to a palm-fringed paradise. Prim arcades shade the walkways, leading past shops boasting a tempting array of wares, quaint boutiques and some hidden courtyard restaurants. In the course of a brief walk one can see the **Old Scale House**, which was built in 1856 and once served weigh the wares passing through the port. It now harbors the Visitors' Bureau. 18th-century **Fort Christansvaern**, with its dank dungeons stands nearby. Its ramparts offer a spectacular view of the town.

Most of the waterfront has been declared a historic district, and the fort and other historic buildings are administered by the National Park Service, so it is no problem to find a park ranger who can answer all questions.

Near the fort is the **Steeple Building**. The old warehouse, built in 1749, is now the post office and customs office. A small museum exhibiting artworks of the Arawak and Caribs has been placed inside. Opposite stands the oldest Lutheran Church on the Island (1753), with a small museum. Standing in Company Street, one can easily imagine **Apothecary Hall** in the days when it was a pharmacist's home and shop. From here one can go on to the corner of **Queens Cross Street** and **King Street**, and look at the 18th-century **Governor's House**. It is an office building, but no one is likely to complain if visitors come inside to look at the stately staircase leading to the former ballroom. Right besides the Lutheran church, there is also a Neo-Gothic Anglican church and a Moravian church built in the 1850s.

FREDERIKSTED

Although **Fort Frederik** has always been guarding Frederiksted since 1752, St. Croix' second city has had an entirely different look ever since the city was ravaged by fire in 1878. As all of the restoration work was done in the style of the times, there is a definite Victorian theme, gingerbread and all, to the numerous buildings that were constructed then. Any rebuilding after that, including the large-scale restoration of buildings lost in hurricane Hugo, has also tended towards styles of the 1800s.

Frederiksted is easily accessible from Christiansted by taxi-van. An extended, pleasant walk through the city leads to the old defensive fort, which nowadays houses a museum, and then onward along a couple of narrow streets to a Moravian church built in 1774, a Lutheran church that was erected two years later, and an Anglican church dating back to 1812.

Above: St. Croix, a veritable paradise for golfers. Right: Close encounters of this kind are not all that rare in the Virgin Islands.

Yet another church, Catholic St. Patrick's, was begun in the 1840s.

For centuries, an enormous banyan tree used to be the most significant landmark at **Fisher Street**, but dreadful Hurricane Hugo, which devastated St. Croix in 1989, uprooted and mangled it. Countless funds poured in from all over the world to trim the tree and replant what remained. Fishermen still come to clean their day's catch nearby. It is a really picturesque scene, but only without a camera, as the fishermen do not take kindly to having their picture taken.

Visitors are encouraged to rent a car or jeep, and pry themselves away from the beaches long enough to see some of the historic sites. Driving around (do not forget to stay on the left side) is a pleasure in itself. Roads are predominantly spacious and well-marked and around every corner one comes across an old windmill, or a breathtaking view of the sea, or both.

Whim Greathouse, situated near Frederiksted, is the only estate left of some 300 that once flourished here when sugar was king. The elegant greathouse has been meticulously restored and magnificently furnished with lots of antiques from the 18th century. Even hurricane Hugo hardly disturbed this serene landmark. Each day, the traditional *Cruzan johnny cake* is made in Whim's cookhouse, and the scent steals out across the twelve acres to mingle with the smell of the flowers, trees and grasses that have grown here for centuries. A couple of hours should be allowed for a tour of the house (the guides do an excellent job), grounds, out-buildings and gift shop. The plantation is open every day.

One will encounter other greathouses while touring the island. Some are private homes; some have been turned into well-furnished restaurants or guesthouses. A favorite with tourists is **Sprat Hall**, which dates back to 1650 and where guests are now served dinner in what was once the ballroom.

St. George Village Botanical Garden is built around remnants of what used to be a Danish workers' village when the whole complex was a busy estate in the mid-19th century. Useful maps are available at the entrance and one is left free to wander around the grounds at will. There is a rain forest walk, an orchard, ruins of the original rum distillery and the cane pressing works, a working smithery, and a replica of an Arawak hut. The largest Arawak Indian settlement on St. Croix occupied this site a long time before the Spanish arrived. However, the gardens were severely damaged by hurricane Hugo, and it might be many years before new trees mature, but nature is a quick recoverer in these parts so there is even now much to be seen here day in and day out. It is open daily; a donation for the garden's general upkeep is requested.

The **Cruzan Rum Distillery** offers sampling tours on a regular basis. The local rum is also bottled for other companies under labels that are kept secret, so it is likely that the taste is familiar. Cruzan Rum is one of the best buys and best tastes on the islands. The duty-free allowance for Americans returning to the United States is six bottles as long as at least one bottle is of Virgin Island origin. The local distillate is either white- or amber-colored, 80 or 151 proof. Easy-to-carry boxes of six bottles are available at the airport if one did not have time to buy rum in town.

A rather unique way to see the island is on horseback. Mounted guides lead one along country trails, pointing out places of historical interest, identifying local flowers and shrubs. A special package is available out of St. Thomas that includes the round trip flight to St. Croix, a day's ride and an overnight stay at Sprat Hall.

If one is staying in a hotel or guest cottage that does not have a beach, the host will have information about beach clubs. Other beautiful beaches include **Cramer Park**, **Davis Bay**, **Sandy Point**, **Protestant Bay**, **The Reef**, **Sprat Beach**, **Cane** or **Grapetree Bays**, and the palm-fringed beach off the **Cormorant Resort**.

Island etiquette

Two things should be kept in mind when packing for a trip on the Virgin Islands. First, that the USVI are more affluent than most of the other islands of the West Indies. Local people themselves dress well, especially in business settings. Fashionable summer-wear is often seen at the resorts, but only rarely must gentlemen wear jackets at dinner.

Secondly, adequate respect is due to natural West Indian modesty. Very revealing bathing costumes should be worn only on tourist beaches. It is illegal to wear bathing suits and other scanty clothing while walking around.

BRITISH VIRGIN ISLANDS

The Virgin Islands were first described by Christopher Columbus, who claimed

Above: One of Mother Nature's Caribbean gifts, the "Traveler's Tree." Right: The soft sell true to the islands.

everything for Spain, but it was Sir Francis Drake who put this area on the British map. On one of his many raids on the Spanish, he fought his way through the Virgins. The **Drake Channel** is a permanent reminder of his deeds.

Development was slow. The islands were tiny, untillable and most difficult to defend. However, by 1756, with cotton and sugar prices soaring in Europe, planters were eager to try their luck, and they brought their seeds and slaves over and began cultivating the land. As piracy was flourishing throughout the Caribbean, the English needed a centrally-located spot to establish their court to try enemy captains. They chose Road Town on Tortola, which became a center for political intrigue and all the inherent wealth and venality that go with it. British presence in the Virgin Islands was permanent from then on.

Prosperity was to last less than a century. Beet sugar, produced in Europe, became a cheap and popular alternative to imported cane sugar. Anti-slavery senti-

BRITISH VIRGIN ISLANDS

ments were rumbling in England, while slaves in the islands became increasingly rebellious. Slaves throughout the British islands were in fact officially freed in 1834, decades before emancipation took place in the Danish islands (Virgin Islands today), so Tortola became a magnet for slaves who had managed to excape from nearby St. John.

A hurricane destroyed the sugar crop in 1819, and it never recovered. Nor was it ever replaced by any other cash crop that was as lucrative as sugar cane. By 1850, all but 500 of the white residents had fled the islands. Only in recent years, with the development of tourism, have the British Virgins seen any hope for a return to their former prosperity.

As a nation of many islands, the BVI is in fact kept together by its scheduled ferries, host of water taxis, charter boats and rental boats. Planes serve Tortola (Beef Island) and Virgin Gorda, as well as Anegada, Anguilla, Antigua, St. Croix, San Juan, St. Kitts, Sint Maarten, Dominica, the Dominican Republic, San Juan in Puerto Rico and Virgin Gorda and St. Thomas. Options in both sightseeing and transportation are manifold. The water is, of course, the British Virgin Islands main asset, so most visitors come here for the sailing, deep-sea fishing, scuba diving and underwater photography, or beaches.

There are camping facilities at Anegada, **Brewer's Bay** (Tortola) and **Little Harbour** on **Jost Van Dyke**. Sailing can be learned in the school at the Bitter End Yacht Club or at the **Offshore Sailing School**, and boardsailing specialists are the **Boardsailing BVI School**, and the school at **Trellis Bay** on **Beef Island**. There are many outfitters for watersports, and resorts that specialize in them.

Tortola

Tortola, the largest island in the BVI, is only 12 miles (20 km) long, three miles (4.5 km) wide, and has a population of about 14,000. Those who arrive by sea will probably check in at **Road Town** or **West End**. For those who want to tour

OUT ISLANDS

the island, there will be taxis on hand to meet all ferries here, and also all flights into the airport at Beef Island. The fare should be agreed upon in advance. Bicycle and scooter rentals are also available in Road Town, and there is a privately organized bus service as well as sightseeing tours.

Tortola still has the overall sleepy air of an out island, even though Road Town is the capital of the BVI and a major center of the yacht chartering business. The city, of course, thanks to these two factors, does have a certain pace to it.

Touristic interest centers on the boating, beaches and diving. Sightseeing points include the **Botanic Garden** in Road Town, and the **Mount Sage**, a National Park surrounding a 1700-foot (527 m) peak known locally as "the rain forest" in the southwest of the island.

Fort Recovery, a stronghold built by the Dutch in 1660 on the coastal road to West End, is now a ruin of historic value. As for the few foundation walls of Dr. William Thornton's mansion nearby, they are basically only for the trivia-famished: Thornton was the architect of the Capitol in Washington D.C.

Another popular day tour is to **Cane Garden Bay** with its bars, restaurants and rum distillery. Those, however, who are touring the island by taxi, may choose to stop for lunch at **Skyworld** or **Mario's Mountain View Restaurant**, which is famous for its food as well as its breathtaking panorama.

Out Islands of the BVI

In all there are 50 to 60 islets, cays and rocks that makes up the BVI. Some of them are privately owned. Many are too remote to visit unless one is cruising aboard a charter boat. Here, in alphabetical order, are some points of interest:

Right: The Virgin Gorda Baths are extremely interesting geological formations.

For years **Anegada** was a vicious siren that seemed to lure unwary skippers and then scour their ships to sawdust on its cruel reefs. The only coral island in the British Virgin Islands, it is only 28 feet above sea level and is surrounded by a reef strewn with wrecks. Today, a population of 250 people make their living here by fishing, guiding and operating the 12-room Anegada Reef Hotel, which is a Mecca for divers.

Cooper Island: Except for the regular staff of the Cooper Island Beach Club, where the guests can lunch on a famous shrimp and swordfish dish, this island is uninhabited. Pulling into **Manchioneel Bay**, one should watch out for the eponymous trees bearing a small, green, apple-like fruit. Their fruit and sap are so poisonous that people have been blinded temporarily exclusively by breathing some smoke from a manchioneel bonfire.

Jost Van Dyke is said to be named for one of the Dutch pirates who roamed this area, but it was settled by one of the many Quaker families that came here in the early 18th-century to grow sugar cane. One of them was the aforementioned William Thornton. The island, which is served by ferry from West End, has excellent beaches and a few fine places to eat. Little Dix Bay was developed as a luxury resort by Laurence Rockefeller.

Norman Island: It claims to be the "Treasure Island" that Robert Louis Stevenson made famous. Snorkelers particularly love exploring the three caves south of **Treasure Point**. The southernmost cave is the one said to have held the enormous pirate treasure.

Peter Island is the exclusive domain of discriminating vacationers and visiting yachtsmen, who are requested not to hang their laundry from the lifelines while at anchor, lest they offend guests ashore. **Dead Chest Island**, off Peter Island, is said to be the inspiration for *Yo ho ho and a bottle of rum*. Legend says that infamous Blackbeard stranded some

of his men here leaving them only a cutlass and a bottle of rum. Peter Island can be reached by ferry directly from Road Town.

Salt Island, as its name suggests, produces salt. The three ponds operate on the same principle as they did 200 years ago. Ten people live on Salt Island, among them is Clementine Smith, who won the British Empire Medal some years ago for her local conservation efforts.

Virgin Gorda, largest out island of the BVI, was once a copper mining center and capital of the island group. In its heyday early in the 19th century, it was home to 8000 people. That number has been reduced to about 1500. The island is laced with hiking trails, and much of it has been declared a nature conservation area. The ruins of the old mines are interesting, but **The Baths**, a geological treasure, is unique. Gigantic rocks piled up along the coast forming a network of caves with warm, shallow salt water ponds. Most hotels will arrange a day trip to Virgin Gorda from Tortola or St. Thomas.

Diving in the BVI

Some 200 shipwrecks litter the sea floor of the BVI, and the persistent diver can explore many of them. Dive trips can be arranged at all hotels. Points of interest include the wreck of the *Rhone,* where scenes for the movie *The Deep* were filmed. The 310-foot Royal Mail steam packet went down at Salt Island during a hurricane in 1867. Today, encrusted in coral, and home to what seem to be a billion fish, it lies in water about 80 feet deep. Another wreck can be found in 60 feet depth of water north of **Beef Island**.

Spyglass Reef, off Peter Island, is the place for tube sponges. At **Paint Walls**, off the south end of Dead Chest, are formations of coral and schools of reef fish. The underground landscape off the *Indians* is made up of canyons, grottos, and coral reefs in a deep dive at **South Bay**, off **Mosquito Island**, one can see enormous mushroom-shaped coral heads. Diving trips are available for all possible levels of skill.

UNITED STATES VIRGIN ISLANDS

Accommodations
(Area code 1340)

Note: Reservations for St. Croix accommodations can be made toll-free from the U.S. mainland at Tel: 1-800/524-2026. Hotel associations maintain counters at the St. Thomas and St. Croix airports, but it is best to make reservations from your home, well in advance. AP = three meals daily, MAP = breakfast and dinner.

LUXURY: **Bluebeard's Castle**, Box 7480, St. Thomas, Tel: 774-1600, Fax: 774-5134. MAP available. A classic luxury hotel with shuttle service to Magens Bay, restaurants, bars and entertainment. **Caneel Bay**, St. John, Tel: 776-6111, Fax: 6938280. Large complex (171 rooms) surrounded by 7 bays; pool, 3 restaurants.
Elysian Bay Resort, Box 51, St. Thomas, Tel: 775-1000. Watersports and health club. **Marriott Frenchman's Reef**, Box 7100 St. Thomas, Tel: 776-8500. Full resort facilities. **Morningstar Beach Resort**, Box 7100, St. Thomas, Tel: 776-8500. **Stouffer Grand Beach Resort**, Box 8267, St. Thomas USVI 00801, Tel: 775-1510. The only four-star resort in the U.S. Virgin Islands. **Virgin Grand Beach**, St. John, Tel: 776-7171. Sprawling 264-room resort on quarter-mile beach, big pool. **Westin Carambola Beach Resort**, St. Croix, Tel: 778-3800. Full luxury resort with a world-class golf course, tennis, aquatic sports, beach, pool, elegant restaurant.

MODERATE: **Cormorant Beach Resort**, St. Croix, Tel: 7788920. Cozy, hospitable hideaway on a picturebook beach. CBP Plan includes breakfast, lunch and all drinks to 5 p.m. Dinner optional. Freshwater pool, tennis, croquet, hammocks. **Mark St. Thomas**, Blackbeard's Hill, St. Thomas, Tel: 774-5511. Restored 200-year-old Danish house. Pool. **Ramada Yacht Haven**, Charlotte Amalie, Tel: 774-9700. Near the harbor. Cable TV, pools, AC, restaurants, free shuttle to beaches. **Sprat Hall Plantation**, St. Croix, Tel: 772-0305. A taste of old-fashioned living.

BUDGET: Complete lists of apartments, self-catering cottages, condominiums, guest houses and rental agents offering private homes can be obtained from the tourist offices (see below).
Caravelle, Christiansted, St. Croix, Tel: 773-0687. In the historical part of town, near the harbor; popular Restaurant, diving on Buck Island. **Heritage Manor**, Box 90, St. Thomas, Tel: 774-3003. European-style manor house with historical flair in the town center. Pool.

OTHER ACCOMMODATIONS: A large number of crewed yachts in all price categories are available as an alternative to hotel accommodations. For a larger vessel, consider the *Sir Francis Drake,* a three-masted topsail schooner with 13 cabins and one luxury suite (main office in St. Thomas).

Restaurants

Most hotels have excellent restaurants; cuisine on St. Croix and St. Thomas includes West Indian, French, Chinese, Italian. Reservations generally required.
LUXURY: **Baywinds**, in the Stouffer Grand Beach Resort, Tel: 775-1510. **Café Normandie**, Frenchtown, St. Thomas, Tel: 774-1622. Closed Mon. **Beach Terrace Dining Room**, Caneel Bay, St. John, Tel: 776-6111. Dressy dining (jackets for gentlemen); extravagant menu and Sundays a West Indian buffet. **Mark St. Thomas**, Blackbeard's Hill, Charlotte Amalie, St. Thomas, Tel: 774-5511. **Raffles**, Compass Point, St. Thomas, Tel: 775-6004. Dinner to live piano music, Gershwin and Cole Porter. **Sprat Hall Plantation**, St. Croix, Tel: 772-0305. **Sugar Mill**, Caneel Bay Resort, St. John, Tel: 776-6111. A la carte lunch and a legendary dinner buffet in an old sugar mill.

MODERATE: **Agave Terrace**, in the Point Pleasant Resort, St. Thomas, Tel: 775-4142 or 776-5694. Famous for Sunday brunch. Terrace restaurant with view over the hills, cosy bar, live music. **Chez Jacques**, Frenchtown, St. Thomas, Tel: 776-5797. Closed Tues. Lamb, paté, home-made baguettes, top wines. **The Point**, Cabrita Point, St. Thomas, Tel: 776-2922. **Smugglers**, in the Stouffer Grand Beach, Tel: 7751510. Rich buffet and table service, Calypso singing.

BUDGET: **Eunice's Terrace**, Smith Bay, St. Thomas, Tel: 775-3795. Native specialties such as *old wife, fungi,* conch, lobster, sweet potato, peas and rice, fried plantain. **Panchita's**, upstairs in the waterfront market, St. Thomas, Tel: 776-8425. Tex-Mex prepared by restaurateurs from San Antonio. *Tacos, quesadilla, fajitas, burritos.* **Victor's Hide Out**, off Rt. 30, Tel: 776-9379.

Access

Service to the Virgin Islands from San Juan is by American, LIAT and Virgin Air. Nonstop to St. Thomas/St. Croix is from New York on Delta and from Miami on Eastern or Midway. Passports are needed for entry. A number of lines run ship service to the Caribbean islands from Miami.

Emergencies

Dial 915 for police, 921 for fire, and 922 for ambulance. These numbers do not require a coin.

Seasonal Events / Festivals / Sports

Carnival on St. Thomas is after Easter with parades and costumed groups, for info: 776-3112. **St. Croix Jazz and Arts Festival**, in October for two weeks. **St. Croix Festival**, from mid-December to Jan. 6.

GUIDEPOST BRITISH VIRGIN ISLANDS

SAILING: for one day: Charteryacht League, Homeport, St. Thomas, Tel: 774-3944.

DIVING: Numerous diving centers on every island offer diving programs and underwater safaris.

Tourist Information

ST. CROIX: Visitors Bureau, Scale House, Waterfront, Christiansted, Tel: 773-0495; **Custom House Building**, Strand Street, Frederiksted, Tel: 772-0357.

ST. JOHN: Division of Tourism, Cruz Bay, P.O. Box 200.

ST. THOMAS: Information bureau at the airport and at the harbor Charlotte Amalie, Tel: 774-8784.

USVI Tourist Information, 1270 Avenue of the Americas, New York NY 10020. USVI Tourist offices are also located in Atlanta, Chicago, Los Angeles, Washington, San Juan and in London, Great Britain.

BRITISH VIRGIN ISLANDS

Accommodations
(Area code: 809)

Note: Because of the difficulty in reaching some of the more remote hotels, it is best to make reservations with sufficient advance. Some, but not all, properties can be reserved through the BVI Tourist Board (see section on Tourist Information). A booking agent specializing in all BVI arrangements, on land and sea, is Best Vacations Imaginable, Tel: 494-6186. Mailing address P.O. Box 306, Road Town, Tortola, BVI.

LUXURY: **Bitter End Yacht Club** P.O.Box 46, Virgin Gorda, Tel: 494-2746. Lodgings on land or water, yacht atmosphere, day trips, diving, boutiques, restaurants. **Drake's Anchorage**, P.O. Box 2510, North Sound, Virgin Gorda, Tel: 494-2254. Nature preserve, twenty-eight-person resort on private island, French cuisine. Beaches. **Guana Island Club**, Tortola, Tel: 494-2354 or write P.O. Box 32, Road Town. AP, no credit cards. **Little Dix Bay**, c/o David Brewer, P.O. Box 70, Virgin Gorda, Tel: 494-5555, Ultra-exclusive l02-room resort. **Marina Cay**, P.O. Box 76, Road Town, Tel: 494-2174. Private island, 10 rooms, all watersports, restaurants, bar, dining MAP. **Peter Island Resort and Yacht Harbour**, P.O. Box 211, Road Town, Tel: 494-2561. Private island, exclusive resort. Rooms, villas, AP. Marina, restaurant. **Sunset House**, P.O. Box 263, Road Town, Tel: 494-2550. MAP hide-away with pool, jacuzzi.

MODERATE: **Anegada Reef Hotel**, Tel. or Fax: 495-8002. Fish, swim, explore coral reef on remote island. Diving or fishing packages, AP. No credit cards. **Frenchman's Cay Resort Hotel**, P.O. Box 1045, West End, Tortola, Tel: 495-4844. Villas with kitchen. Freshwater pool, beach, restaurant. **Moorings/Mariner Inn**, P.O. Box 129, Road Town, Tel: 494-2332. Overlooks marina. **Olde Yard Inn**, P.O. Box 139, Virgin Gorda, Tel: 495-5544. Cosy hotel with a library, boutique. Film showings in the evening. **Prospect Reef Resort**, P.O. Box l04, Road Town, Tel: 494-3311. Rooms with Kitchenette, Villas, pool, air-conditioning, water sports, boutiques. **Sebastian's on the Beach**, Road Town, P.O. Box 441, Tel: 495-4212. 26 rooms, beach, restaurant with beach grill. **Sugar Mill Hotel**, P.O. Box 425, Road Town, Tel: 495-4355.

BUDGET: **Maria's by the Sea**, P.O. Box 206, Road Town. Pool, restaurant, bar, kitchenettes, AC. **Guaveberry Spring Bay**, P.O. Box 20, Virgin Gorda, Tel: 495-5227. One- and two-bedroom houses on the beach. No credit cards. **Rudy's Mariner Inn**, Great Harbour, Jost Van Dyke, Tel: 495-9282. Chummy hotel with beach bar, restaurant, nature trails. AP.

Restaurants

Note: It is important to make reservations; even the best restaurants are small and not ready for unexpected guests. In many hotels you'll also find good restaurants. The yacht harbors often have gourmet takeaways.

C&F Restaurant, Purcell Estate, very popular with the locals as well as visitors, Tel: 494-4941. **Mario's**, Palm Grove Shopping Centre, Tel: 494-3883, West Indian specialties. **Drake's Anchorage**, North Sound, Virgin Gorda. Tel: 494-2254. Crepes, baked dolphin in curry sauce with bananas, sometimes a serenade by a native band. **Skyworld**, Tortola, Tel: 494-3567. Dizzying view from a mountaintop. Classic and West Indian cuisine, **Sugar Mill**, Tortola, Tel: 495-4355.

Access and Local Transportation

Ferries serve the BVI from St. Thomas and St. John. Air service is from San Juan, St. Croix, and St. Thomas. Airlines include Air BVI, Eastern, and American. LIAT provides regular service between the BVI and St. Kitts, St. Maarten, and Dominica.

Formalities and Currency

Canadian, American and British citizens need proof of citizenship such as a passport, voter registration card, or birth certificate. Others need a passport, and in some cases a visa.

Currency is the US dollar. Hotel tax is 7%, departure tax US$ 10 by air and US$ 3 by sea, and stamp duty on checks and travelers checks is l0%. Cruising permits for yacht charterers range from 75 cents to US$ 4 per day. BVI temporary driving permit is US$ 10.

Tourist Information

BVI Government Tourist Board, P.O. Box 134, Road Town, Tortola, Tel: 494-3134.

ANGUILLA AND ST. MARTIN / SINT MAARTEN

SEASIDE IDYLLS AND CRUISES

ANGUILLA
ST. MARTIN / SINT MAARTEN

ANGUILLA

As little as ten years ago, Anguilla island was the perfect example of isolated, out-of-the-way Caribbean. Indeed, there was simply not much here besides a few small hotels, a large amount of wild brush and the islanders' goats strolling across unpaved roads at will. Those who visit the island today will still encounter the goats, yet even though Anguilla has been discovered by the world at large it is still not overrun by tourists. Still, even with increased emphasis on tourism, the island hardly qualifies as a touristy or as a crowded place. The cruise ships have not arrived yet and, thanks to the petite proportions of the harbor, they are not likely to appear on the horizon anytime in the near future. One of the region's most beautiful white sand beaches is here, and some of the hotels and resorts are the most expensive in the whole world. It's no small wonder, then, that the general price level of the island is well above average.

Anguilla has been as quiet through its history as it is now. Even Christopher Columbus, who managed to set foot on

Preceding pages: Sailboats of every shape and size flock like sheep to the peaceful coast at Baie Nettlé, St. Martin.

so many islands of the Caribbean, did not feel the need to take a closer look here. According to some stories, he sailed by in 1493, named the island after the Italian word for eel, because of its long, narrow shape, and then sailed on. Others deny that Columbus was ever involved in naming the island, pegging it rather on the French *anguille* or Spanish *anguila,* also words for eel.

Regardless of the exact European origin of its name, a new era began in 1650, when British settlers from St. Kitts came over, and then continued on to explore the Virgin Islands. In the following century and a half passed, the French attacked a few times but were rebuffed, and a small group of Irishmen landed on the island to settle. In 1825, though, Anguilla lost a little of its isolation when England attached it to the neighboring islands of St. Kitts and Nevis to form one single crown colony. The Anguillans were far from thrilled with this enforced union, but it was not until 1967 that the island boiled over. In that year the British combined the islands of St. Kitts, Nevis and Anguilla into one state with the main government based in St. Kitts. The islanders promptly seceded from the union. Fearful of an outbreak of violence, the British sent a peace-keeping force, which turned out to be unneccessary. But five

ANGUILLA

years later the British amended the administrative arrangement, re-adopting Anguilla as a colony. Then, in 1980, the island was finally granted a separate constitution and elected representatives began looking after island affairs. Standing on its own, the island at that point decided to take a serious look at its tourism potential.

A Swimmer's Paradise

The capital of this densely populated island (7000 people for 35 square miles) is **The Valley**. Since this is not a place famed for its tourist sights, most people try to orient themselves by the harbors, bays and beaches. For more than anything else, Anguilla is appreciated for the bountiful and pristine beaches of its entire coastline. On the southeast side of the island is **Sandy Hill**, where the fishermen ply their trade, and where one can buy fresh-caught fish right off their boats. Or else one can snorkel in the clear waters there. Farther west is a cluster of magnificent beaches ideal for lounging around. These include **Rendezvous Bay**, with its view of the neighboring island of St. Martin, **Cove Bay**, **Maunday's Bay** and **Shoal Bay West**. The latter two have the added attraction of sumptuous resorts.

On the north coast, **Barnes Bay** is a top spot for windsurfing and snorkeling, **Sandy Ground** is for scuba diving, while **Shoal Bay East** is regarded as one of the prettiest beaches in the entire region. On this long, developed beach are facilities for diving, sailing and fishing.

The sea is what determines life on Anguilla. Boat races are the national sport on the island, and they are in all classes. Carnival sweeps over the island at the end of July or beginning of August. The usual way of celebrating the Festival for both natives and visitors is with boat races, fancy dress parades, shows, calypso festivals, beach picknicks and barbecue parties.

Above: Shoal Bay, Anguilla. Right: This feat requires amazing body control.

There are not many outings worth tearing oneself away from the beach for. One of the few would be **Wallblake House** at **Cross Roads**, a plantation house built in the late 18th century by an English settler. A museum depicting island history has been lodged in the house.

Sports

The little island has no less than 33 beautiful beaches and bays along its coastline, and no vacation resort fails to offer a complete range of water sports. **Tamarian Watersports**, in the village of Sandy Ground is an international training center for divers. Its shop offers all equipment for diving or snorkeling for sale or for rent. **Shoal Bay Watersports** rents out boats and water skis. **Enchanted Island Cruises**, **Princess Soya Cruises**, **The Mariners** and **Tall Boy's Big Bird Two** all provide boats and yachts, and organize cruises of one day or more. For more land-based activities, such as tennis, there are courts available around the island. The **Coccoloba Resort** has two courts, and so does the **Carimar Beach Club**, the spectacular **Cap Juluca** and the **Cinnamon Reef Beach Club**. The super-deluxe resort of **Malliouhana** offers three courts, as do the hotels **La Sirena** and **Sonestra Beach Resort**.

Shopping

Since this island is small and still rather quiet and undeveloped, the shopping opportunities, for those interested, are not that great. Guests at the luxury resorts such as Malliouhana will find high-priced boutiques offering resort-wear if the apparel they brought should not prove chic enough for the other guests. Otherwise, local crafts, such as baskets, hand-crocheted mats, wood dolls and shawls are available at the **Anguilla Arts and Crafts Center** in The Valley, or at **The Au Revoir Gift Shop** in **The Quarter**.

Nightlife

If one is looking for an island with a thrilling nightlife, Anguilla is not the venue to opt for. But there is music to be heard most nights in restaurants, hotels and clubs. Usually on Thursday nights, a traditional group called the Mayoumba Folklore Troup performs at the expensive luxury hotel **La Sirena**. Traditional music can also be enjoyed at **Pimm's**, the restaurant at Cap Juluca in Maunday's Bay, and at the Coccoloba Plantation in Barnes Bay. A livelier place to see and be seen is **Johnno's Beach Bar**, at **Sandy Ground**, or the **Dragon Disco**, in **South Hill**, where music and dance go on long into the night.

ST. MARTIN / SINT MAARTEN

Definitely, 37-square-mile (88 sq. km) **St. Martin/ Sint Maarten** is an oddity with its two separate cultures, French and Dutch. It is the smallest piece of land in the world to be shared by two sovereign

ST. MARTIN / SINT MAARTEN

powers. It may also be one of the most developed. People do not come to this island in pursuit of its rustic beauty. For that disappeared long ago in the frenzy of construction that still continues apace. Cranes are part of the landscape.

People come to this place because they know they will have a range of choices in accommodation and activities, or because they have heard it is pretty (albeit from people who last visited the place 20 years ago), or because it is easily accessible. Nonstops from international destinations land daily at Juliana Airport, on the Dutch side of the island. Those visitors looking for a little more charm can board a small plane or ferry for a day trip to more evocative places, such as St. Barts or Anguilla. Indeed, one of St. Martin/Sint Maarten's major advantages is that it is at least conveniently located; the other islands are just minutes away.

Above: Keeping a cool attitude in the midday heat. Right: The old courthouse of Philipsburg now functions as a post office.

History's Confusion

Like so many other islands in this region, the story of St. Martin / Sint Maarten surfaces with the journeys of Columbus. But it owes its name to the faulty navigation of seafarers who came after the great explorer.

As legend has it, Columbus discovered the island on the feast day of St. Martin of Tours in 1493. He did not, however, name this particular island "St. Martin." By all accounts, he most probably gave that name to the nearby Nevis. But the names Columbus gave to some of the islands were jumbled by later navigators, and this meant that, by 1516, this particular island appeared as St. Martin on the charts.

Even though Columbus claimed the island for Spain, the Spanish never got around to officially taking possession of it. The French, starting off from their settlements in Guadeloupe, occupied the north, while the Dutch claimed the south. In the 1640s the Spanish pushed the

ST. MARTIN / SINT MAARTEN

Dutch off their side and a protracted struggle between those two colonial powers ensued. 80 years later, the Spanish finally gave up their bid for control. They felt overextended in the Caribbean, it seems, and so they voluntarily raised their camp and retreated.

In the meantime, the Dutch, somewhat optimistically, concluded an agreement with the French to divide up the island between the two of them. In 1648, so another local legend has it, a Dutchman and a Frenchman started out back to back and walked along the coast of the island until they met again. The border was drawn straight from this point and the territory in each of the halves was assigned to the respective countries. That the French ended up with a larger section of the island (21 square miles to the Dutch 16) has been attributed to the fact that the Dutchman had shorter legs.

For the next century, neighborly relations were not exactly smooth. Tensions grew, culminating in the annexation of the French St. Martin by the Dutch in 1793. The official explanation was that the English posed a threat to the entire island and the Dutch were merely defending it against them. They continued to hold sway over the French side of the island until political roles reversed in Europe. Backed by its stronghold in Guadeloupe, an increasing powerful France was able to take over the entire island without Dutch resistance. In 1801 the British really did invade the island, but were ousted again within a year. Finally, in 1802, the French and Dutch worked out an amiable arrangement again, reaffirming the boundaries decreed in the original walking contest of 1648.

Relations have been completely peaceful ever since, though they've also been competitive. Watching the Dutch develop their side of the island (the Dutch were the ones to build the international airport, for instance) the French decided to get busy themselves and follow suit. Tourism began to boom in the 1960s.

It was the Dutch who began expanding their infrastructure on a large scale, such

ST. MARTIN / SINT MAARTEN

as building an international airport. The French then decided to get into the game, and followed their neighbors' example.

Touring Across Borders

The first thing to note about the island is: Both sides are duty free ports, which means that no taxes are paid on imported items, so it should stand to reason that prices on those items will be lower. In many cases that is true, which is why one will see cruise ship passengers swarming the shops lining Front Street in Philipsburg. Shoppers should be aware of the prices of items they are interested in, however, and spend some time shopping around. Not all shopkeepers keep prices low, and in some cases the prices can even be higher than back home.

Starting on the Dutch side, the major town is **Philipsburg**, instantly recogniz-

Above: The panoramic view of the harbor of Marigot, St. Martin. Right: Typical golden sundown scene, balm for the eye.

able by the plethora of shops found along **Front Street**. Large numbers of cruise passengers often swarm through the streets of Philipsburg in search of bargains. The entire international range of consumer goods are available here, designer clothing, Swedish crystal, Finnish pottery, French jewelry and perfumes, German cameras, Italian leather and, of course, West Indian handicrafts. So the town is usually pretty crowded. The back streets are correspondingly less so.

The bay of Philipsburg known as **Great Bay** has a number of sights, notably remains of ancient fortifications. There is the over 300-year-old **Fort Amsterdam**, for example, which was built by the Dutch on top of the ruins of a former Spanish fort. It stands on a spit of land between Great Bay and **Little Bay**. **Fort William** stands on top of Fort Hill, to the left of Philipsburg. At **Point Blanche**, across Great Bay, one will also discover the ruins of Fort Bel-Air.

Heading west, one arrives at **Maho Bay**, just past **Juliana Airport**, an area

ST. MARTIN / SINT MAARTEN

that is so Americanized, it looks like any ordinary beach town in the U.S. **Mullet Pond Bay**, and the vast **Mullet Bay Resort** are next, where one finds a golf course and more crowds.

Westward and then north across the French border, one reaches **Baie Longue**, a mile-long stretch of beach that some consider to be the prettiest on the island. Not far from here is **Baie Rouge**, a more isolated beach, where nude bathing is common. The **Baie Orientale**, on the northeast side of the island, has the most popular nude beach.

Soon after the **Pointe du Bluff**, comes **Marigot**, the capital of the French side, and an enchanting mix of Gallic sophistication and West Indian color. There are not quite as many shops here as in Philipsburg, but the restaurants are excellent and abundant.

Every Saturday morning, vendors set up stalls in **Market Square**. During the rest of the week, one can also inspect fortifications erected here by the French. On a hill overlooking Marigot is **Fort St. Louis**, built in 1786. A good place to stop off along the main road to the east of Marigot is **Paradise Peak**. At 1500 feet (480 m) above sea level it is the highest point on the island and an excellent spot for a grand view or for taking photographs.

Farther up the coast is an even more dense concentration of restaurants in the tiny town of **Grand Case**. It is called the "restaurant capital of the Caribbean" and no one needs to wonders why. Every type of cuisine is offered here, with much of it served against the romantic backdrop of scenic ocean views.

Heading west one reaches an area known as **French Cul-de-Sac**, one of the most spectacularly scenic parts of the island. Dramatic green hills contrast with the red roofs of the houses. But again, the scenery is often marred by the ugly interference of builders' cranes.

Farther south is **Orleans**, the oldest settlement of the island, also known as the **French Quarter**. It is small, picturesque and is mercifully not yet destroyed by construction. South of Orleans

ST. MARTIN / SINT MAARTEN

on the coast is **Oyster Pond**, an important spot in island history, although it may not look like it at first. The marker commemorating the event in question is on the other side of the island, but nevertheless, this is reputed to be where the Frenchman and the Dutchman began their famed walk around the island in 1648.

Heading south and back to Philipsburg, one passes the relatively deserted **Guana Bay Point** on the island's east coast, from which one can see a few desolate islands and, farther off in the distance, the island of St. Barts.

Sports and more

Like all of the islands, St. Martin / Sint Maarten takes full advantage of its surrounding waters to offer all conceivable sorts of aquatic activities. **Bobby's**

Above and right: The Caribbean nature is generous, and the Caribbean's nature is very musical as every visitor will notice.

Marina and **Great Bay Marina** on the Dutch side both offer daily sailing trips. The 45-foot ketch *Gabrielle* is also available for individual tours as is the catamaran *Bluebeard II*, which is based in Marigot and frequently sails around Anguilla to the small island of **Prickly Pear**. Sailboats can be rented from **Caribbean Watersports**.

Because of the rich reefs and ultra clear water, snorkeling and scuba diving are popular pursuits. They can be arranged through a number of shops. **Watersports Unlimited**, **Ocean Explorers** in Simpson Bay, **Maho Watersports** in Mullet Bay Resort, **Little Bay Watersports**, **St. Maarten Diving and Watersports** in Great Bay, **The Grande Case Beach Club** and the **Le Galion Beach** all offer excursions for a fee. Maho Watersports also has a diving helmet for rent, which allows you to walk around the sea bed. The best places to enjoy such submarine activities are **Cole Bay**, **Ile Pinel**, **Cay Bay** and Maho Bay.

Anyone looking for the pleasures of fishing will be in for a good time. Fishing tours lasting anywhere from a few hours to several days can be chartered for the right fee. The waters around the island is full of wahoo, tuna, barracuda, marlin and other favorites (though in the entire Caribbean basin over-fishing has been raising critical voices). The two marinas mentioned above on Sint Maarten and the **Marina de Lonvilliers** in Anse Marcel on the French side offer such tours.

The beach enthusiasts have 37 top beaches to choose from. Baie Orientale, as mentioned, has the leading nude beach. On the French side of the island skimpy or absent beachwear is accepted all over the place. Not on the Dutch side, however. The amenities of the French beaches are excellent.

Golfers have somewhat limited options. Mullet Bay has the only golf course and it is restricted to hotel guests and island residents. It might be possible to ar-

ST. MARTIN / SINT MAARTEN

range admission through one's hotel. Tennis players, however, have it much better. There are about 50 courts on the island, with the largest concentration at the Mullet Bay Resort. The large hotels (La Belle Créole, La Samanna, Le Galion, Maho Beach, and Great Bay) all have their own courts. Even if you are not staying at one of them, you can rent a court for a fairly low fee.

Nightlife

Nighttime activities differ on the French and Dutch sides, with scenes on the Dutch side being more crowded and raucous. One of the most popular pastimes over on this side is going gambling in casinos, of which there are eight, mostly in hotels such as the Grand Bay Beach Hotel, the Divi Little Nay Beach Hotel, Pelican Resort and Treasure Island. The largest casino is **Casino Royale** at the Mullet Bay Resort. One should not be misled by the name, however; this place is as far from the grand old European casinos in style as it is in distance. It is rather like the Las Vegas spots, with lots of lights and hoopla.

If gambling once loses its charms or finally becomes too costly one can head for one of the island discos. **Studio 7**, a popular hangout for both locals and the hordes of tourists staying at nearby Mullet Bay Resort, is right above Casino Royale. If this establishment becomes too dark and claustrophobic, which is certainly possible, one can go next door to the open-air **Chéri's Café**, where dancing is to live bands just about every day of the week. Chéri's also has the best hamburgers on the island, just in case you get hungry.

Jazz is the fare every evening at the **Grand Café Europe**, situated above the Maho Beach Hotel.

The French side is a bit more sophisticated and discreet. Locals tend to favor **L'Atmosphère**, a disco at the Port La Royale Marina, or **Le Privilège** at Anse Marcel. A younger crowd frequents the **Night Fever** in Colombier.

GUIDEPOST ANGUILLA

ANGUILLA
(Area code: 1264)

Accommodations

LUXURY: **Cap Juluca**, a Moorish fantasy, with stark white domes and arches, a privacy-seeking hedonist's dream. Box 240, Maunday's Bay, Anguilla, Tel: 497-6666. **Malliouhana**, with awe-inspiring bluff-side location and sumptuous decor. Box 173, Mead's Bay, Anguilla, Tel: 497-6111. **Cove Castles**, stark white luxurious villas. Shoal Bay West, Box 248, Anguilla, Tel: 497-6801. **Coccoloba Hotel**, less elegant, more facilities. Box 332, Barnes Bay, Anguilla, Tel: 497-6871. **Cinnamon Reef Beach Club**, luxury villas, more fun. Box 141, Little Harbour, Anguilla, Tel: 497-2727. **Mariner's**, cottage colony, with great restaurant on the beach. Box 139, Sandy Ground, Anguilla, Tel: 497-2671. **Carimar Beach Club**, private villas. Box 327, Meads Bay, Anguilla, Tel: 497-6881. **Anguilla Great House**, West Indian bungalows surround a large manor house. Box 157, Rendezvous Bay, Anguilla, Tel: 497-6061.

MODERATE TO BUDGET: **Sonestra Beach Resort**, Rendezvous Bay, Tel: 497-6999, Fax: 497-6899. **Rendezvous Bay Hotel**, historic, Anguilla's first, pre-boom hotel. Spacious and simple. Box 31, Rendezvous Bay, Anguilla, Tel: 497-6549. **Cul de Sac**, tiny inn on a man-made beach. Box 173, Shaddick Point, Anguilla, Tel: 497-6461. **La Sirena**, apartment complex with bay view. Box 200, The Valley, Anguilla Tel: 497-6827.

Restaurants

Pimm's at Cap Juluca. Enjoy the spectacular view while dining on sophisticated seafood and desserts. Maunday's Bay, Tel: 497-6666. **Malliouhana**. Five star, elegant atmosphere, mainly French cuisine. Mead's Bay, Tel: 497-2731. **Cinnamon Reef Beach Club**. Elegant, but fun, native Anguillan specialities. Little Harbour, Tel: 497-6871. **Roy's**. A good old-fashioned pub serving roast beef, fish and chips. Crocus Bay, Tel: 497-2470.
Mariner's. Basic restaurant on the beach, serving fresh seafood. Sandy Ground, Tel: 497-2671. **Lucy's Harbour View**. Fresh seafood with panoramic view over Road Bay. South Hill, Tel: 497-6523. **Johnno's**. Casual in the extreme, delicious barbecued chicken, ribs and fish. Live music on weekends. Sandy Ground, Tel: 497-2728. **Uncle Ernie's Shoal Bay Beach Bar**. A beach shack with tables, good barbecued ribs and chicken, low prices.

Festivals

Anguilla honors the *Queen's Birthday* on the second Saturday in June. Holidays are *Constitution Day* (August 6) and *Separation Day* (December 17). *Carnival* is celebrated with parades and a regatta end of July/ first week of August.

Access and Local Transportation

Visitors arrive either at the small **Wallblake Airport** by plane from nearby islands, or at **Blowing Point Harbour** by ferry from St. Martin. Air service is with on Air Anguilla, American Eagle, LIAT, Tyden Air or WIN Air. Taxis are available at either stop, and cabbies act as guides. A good guide is Mack's Taxi, Tel: 497-2855.

Formalities and Currency

American and Canadian citizens need a passport, or a photo I.D. along with a birth certificate, voter's registration card, or driver's license. All other citizens must have a passport. A temporary drivers'-license costs US$ 6.
The Eastern Caribbean Dollar (EC$) is legal tender, exchanging at a fluctuating rate currently around 2.68 EC$ to 1 US$. Credit cards are not generally accepted, traveler's checks and US dollars are accepted in many establishments.

Tourist Information

Anguilla Tourist Office, The Valley, Anguilla, British West Indies, Tel: 497-2759.

ST. MARTIN / SINT MAARTEN

Accommodations
Dutch Side
(Area Code 599)

LUXURY: **Oyster Pond Yacht Club**, romantic inn for a quiet getaway. Box 239, Philipsburg, Tel: 522206. **Caravanserai,** small, discreet luxury near the airport and the jet noise. Box 113, Philipsburg, Tel: 552511. **Belair Beach Hotel**, all suites on Little Bay Beach. Box 140, Philipsburg, Tel: 523362. **Pointe Pirouette Villa Hotels**, villas in four separate locations. Box 484, Philipsburg, Tel: 544207. **Treasure Island Hotel and Casino** at **Cupecoy**, sprawling complex with (too) much action. Box 14, Philipsburg, Tel: 543219.

EXPENSIVE: **Mullet Bay Resort**, 600 rooms and the island's only golf course. Box 309, Philipsburg, Tel: 542801. **Pelican Resort & Casino**, suites and studios, great views. Simpson Bay, Box 431, Philipsburg, Tel: 542503. **Divi Little Bay Beach Resort & Casino**, large rattan-furnished beachside villas. Box 61, Philipsburg, Tel: 522333. **Maho Beach Hotel & Casino**. Maho Bay, Tel: 552115.

MODERATE TO BUDGET: **Mary's Boon**, informal, family style inn, also too close to the airport. Box 278, Philipsburg, Tel: 544235. **Passangrahan**

Royal Inn, on Great Bay Beach. Box 151, Philipsburg, Tel: 523588.

French Side
(Area code: 590)

LUXURY: **La Samanna**, the pacesetter for luxury. Box 159, Marigot 97150, Tel: 875122. **L'Habitation de Longvilliers**, elegant. Box 230, Anse Marcel, Tel: 873333. **La Belle Créole**, quaint, sometimes inept or rude service; spartan decor, but big rooms and good facilities. Box 118, Marigot 97150, Tel: 876600.

EXPENSIVE: **Grand-Case Beach Club**, spacious apartments on beach. Box 339, Grand-Case 97150, Tel: 875187. **Alizea**, small, luxurious, overlooking ocean. Mont Vernon, Tel: 873342.

MODERATE TO BUDGET: **Heavea**, small, romantic guest house, Grand-Case 97150, Tel: 875685. **Le Royal Louisiana**, charming city hotel. Rue du Général de Gaulle, Marigot 97150, Tel: 878651. **La Résidence**, Rue du Général de Gaulle, Marigot 97150, Tel: 877037. **Club Orient**, basic prefab chalets on clothing optional beach. Baie Orientale, Tel: 873385.

Restaurants
Dutch Side
(Area code: 599)

Oyster Pond Yacht Club, elegant . Oyster Pond, Tel: 522206. **Le Bec Fin**, sophisticated French on Front Street, Tel: 522976. **Café Royal**, simple fare in pretty garden. Palm Plaza, Front Street, Philipsburg, Tel: 523443. **West Indian Tavern**, funky, historic place. Stay with the simpler food. Front Street, Philipsburg, Tel: 522965. **La Rosa**, romantic, Sicilian cuisine. Front Street, Philipsburg, Tel: 523832. **Le Bibloquet**, 5-course *prix fixe* menu. **Point Blanche**, unlisted phone number which is given to good customers.

French Side
(Area code: 590)

Le Poisson d'Or, romantic, on waterfront in Marigot, fresh fish. Off Rue d'Anguille, Tel: 877245. **La Vie en Rose**, experimental menu, solid desserts. Blvd. de France, Marigot, Tel: 875442. **Le Tastevin**, waterfront café great seafood and desserts on Grand-Case's main street, Tel: 875545. **Auberge Gourmande**, Burgundian fare, Tel: 875545. **La Nadaillac**, serious French food, overlooking Marigot Bay. **Galerie Perigourdine**, Rue d'Anguille, Marigot, Tel: 875377. **Bistrot Nu**, casual place, fabulous seafood. Rue de Holland, Marigot, Tel: 877739. **Jean Dupont**, elegant French, at Port La Royale marina. Tel: 877113.

Access and Local Transportation

American visitors to Saint Martin/Sint Maarten arrive at **Juliana Airport**, on the Dutch side. Service is provided by American Airlines, BWIA, or LIAT. Inter-island hops arrive at either Juliana or **L'Esperance Airport**, on the French side, with service on Air Martinique, WIN Air, Air Guadeloupe, or Air St. Barths. Ferries arrive at the dock in Marigot, and, less regularly, at Philipsburg from the neighboring islands.

Taxis are available at all entry points. Taxi service is readily available, too, from either Juliana Airport on the Dutch side and the Marigot ferry stop on the French side. Rates are not fixed so out on the island, between standard stops, you will have to negotiate a fee with the driver.

Buses run between Philipsburg, Marigot and Grand Case, price US$ 1.50. Rental cars available at the airport, but because of a deal with the taxi union, car rental agencies can only give you a car at your hotel.

Festivals

Both sides celebrate the French-Dutch friendship with a National holiday on November 11 with parades and festivities at the border. Carnival takes place on the French side before Ash Wednesday and on the Dutch side during the last two weeks of April.

FRENCH SIDE: July 14: *Bastille Day*. July 21: *Schoelcher Memorial Day* (in remembrance of the abolition of slavery). The *Heineken Regatta* in March is an event for sailors.

DUTCH SIDE: A colourful *Carnival* a is celebrated at the end of July, and the *Trade Winds Regatta* takes place in spring.

Formalities and Currency

Visitors need a passport in most cases, although Americans can get by with a birth certificate or voter's registration card. A room reservation and proof of ongoing or return travel arrangements are required. There is a departure fee of US$ 10.

Currency on the Dutch side is the Netherlands Antilles Florin (NAF), which exchanges at a fluctuating rate currently around 1.80 NAF to 1 US$.

On the French side the currency is the French Franc, currently exchanging at around 6 FF to 1 US$. US dollars, credit cards or traveler's checks are widely accepted.

Tourist Information

DUTCH SIDE: Sint Maarten Tourist Information Bureau, Walter Nisbeth Road, Philipsburg, Tel: (00599) 522 337, Fax: 522 734, and at the airport.

FRENCH SIDE: **St. Martin Tourist Information Office**, Marigot Pier, Tel: (00590) 875 326.

ST. BARTS

BEACHES AND DIVING DELUXE

ST. BARTHÉLEMY

SABA

ST. EUSTATIUS

ST. BARTHÉLEMY / ST. BARTS

St. Barts, or **St. Barths** – no one on the island would ever refer to it by its full name St. Barthélémy – is a unique place.

Even arriving here can be quite an experience. Those who come in by air will probably never forget it; it is like earning a traveler's "red badge of courage". The tiny plane comes in low, between two mountains, with little clearance on either side. Just as a large cross on top of a hill and a graveyard down below it come into view, the plane touches ground and the runway comes to an end almost immediately, directly in front of a beach. It has already happened that pilots, who mistakenly overestimated the length of the runway, have landed in the water.

As one moves about the island, a special flair crops up again and again. St. Barts is an exclusive island, a popular spot among celebrities, and it is easy to see why. The whole scenery, with its tropical lushness and mountainous terrain, is more appealing than in many other parts of the Caribbean. The accommodations nestled in the hillsides, overlooking

Preceding pages: The basic pleasure of feeling the warm, powdery sand on one's feet. Left: Gustavia, a definite hint of traditional Swedish quaintness.

perfect beaches, are luxurious, charming and private, with service equal to the best available anywhere, and not the lackluster performance too often found in even good hotels in the Caribbean. Parallel to the accomodations, the food is sensational. All of the people here seem beautiful and thin and to be wearing designer clothes. Simply put, this place is chic. It is also expensive. But, often, so are places with less to offer. Most do not mind the expense, and they aim to return.

Columbus discovered St. Barts in 1493 and named it for his brother, Bartholomeo. Carib Indians, who occupied this island and others, were able to maintain themselves here longer than elsewhere. French colonists from St. Kitts, however, were wiped out shortly after their arrival in 1656. In 1694 another group of settlers arrived from Normandy and Brittany, but they did not hold the island for very long. As it was an agriculturally backward island, with no sugar industry, the French decided to give it to Sweden in exchange for trading rights in Sweden. That was in 1784. The Swedes built the capital of Gustavia and turned the island into a prosperous port. Natural disasters hit hard, with hurricanes and earthquakes causing many residents to flee. In 1878, however, France regained control, the Swedes having been quite willing to rid

ST. BARTS

themselves of this costly piece of useless real estate. Today, the island is tied to France, and its citizens are descendants of the Norman and Breton settlers who came here three centuries ago. In some parts of the island, the residents still dress in the style of those times, oblivious to modern age and the scanty bikinis (or lack of them).

Getting Around the Island

St. Barts is only eight square miles (22 sq. km), but there is so much here it seems larger. Also, barring the great restaurants and the superlative beaches, there is not that much to actually visit on the island, though a day trip is certainly worth the investment.

Most visitors begin a tour in the southwestern part with a visit to the capital, **Gustavia**. One can easily spend a day here. Gingerbread buildings house boutiques, with open air cafés interspersed between them. The picturesque harbor, with an 18th-century anchor as decoration, is packed with luxury yachts.

Among the special sights to see are the **Swedish Town Hall**, which dates back to the Swedish days, and the **Bell Tower**, whose church was destroyed in a hurricane, and to the north **Fort Gustave**.

St. Barts has duty-free status, so it is obviously a place to buy jewelry, imported liquors and European fashions. However, shopkeepers set high prices. For passionate window-shoppers, the streets of Gustavia are nevertheless full of possibilities, among them **Alma and Samson**, **Stéphane & Bernard**, or **Vali Baba**.

Just a little way northwest of Gustavia lies the fishing village of **Corossol**, where one can still witness the origins of the island's population. Locals often use old French dialects and the older women wear large starched white bonnets, the *quichenottes* or *calèches* from 17th-cen-

Above: The monied crowd keeps to its secluded villas on St. Barts. Right: Bliss can be something as simple as a little shadow.

tury France. Women weave straw hats and bags, displaying them on the side of the road. They dislike conversation, though, and do not take to having their pictures taken at all. The **Inter-Oceans Museum**, near Corossol, displays quite a collection of interesting seashells.

North of the town of **Colombier**, with its bay **Anse de Colombier**, is **Anse des Flamands**, a nice beach with a historic note. On top of the hill is the crater of the extinct volcano that created the mountainous terrain. Rounding the corner, one comes to **St. Jean**, the island's most populous spot and most famous beach. St. Jean also has concentrated shopping especially at the St. Jean Commercial Centre or Villa Créole Shopping Center, a cottage complex in the West Indian style. Up the road, to the east, is **Lorient**, site of the first French village named after a town in Brittany, and farther on, **Marigot**, a good beach for fishing and snorkeling. Past the next settlement of Grand Cul-de-Sac is the **Toiny Coast**, which looks more like France than the Caribbean, with steep slopes and craggy rocks. Around the next bend is **Grande Saline**, a quiet beach, and **Anse du Governeur**, a beach with a view of neighboring islands.

Sports

Lying around on unspoiled beaches is the main pastime here. Topless is accepted, total *au naturel* is not. Yachting is also extremely popular. Day-long trips can be arranged through the **Yacht Charter Agency**, or **La Marine Service Boat Rental**. Small boats can be rented through the luxury **Guanahani Resort**, or the **Tom Beach Hotel**. Scuba diving and snorkeling are popular at some beaches and most hotels rent gear. Agents that arrange day sails usually also arrange diving trips. If one happens to be at **St. Jean Beach**, the **Pelican** can accommodate all diving needs.

Fishing is also popular but can be dangerous. Many fish are toxic because of the oxidation of seaweed in the water south of the island. For that reason, fish-

SABA

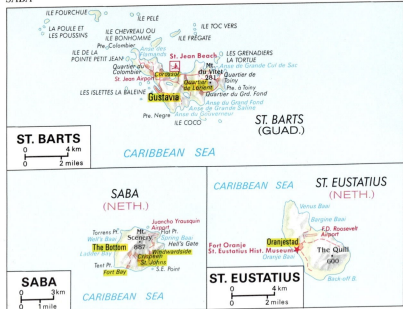

ermen recommend having your catch checked by the experts. They themselves fish only north of the island. The same companies that offer sailing trips can provide a boat for fishing. The *Bertram*, a ship for deep-sea fishing, is also available for business.

Windsurfing is gaining popularity, so places to rent boards can be found on an increasing number of beaches along the Anse des Flamands, St. Jean and Grand Cul-de-Sac. Lessons are given at St. Barts Wind School, Wind Wave Power at St. Barths Beach Hotel, Grand Bay Watersports at the Guanahani and Atlantis Windsurfing at Grand Cul-de-Sac.

Tennis players will have no problem finding courts, for golfers, though, the island is too small and rocky for a course. For tennis courts, one might try the Guanahani Resort, the Sports Center of Colombier, Le Flamboyant Tennis Club, the St. Barths Beach Hotel, or Manapany.

Right: Houses cluster to the steep, volcanic slopes of the island of Saba.

Nightlife

Nights are spent in stylish surroundings, in accordance with the elegant flair of the whole island. Discos, such as **La Licorne** and **Autour du Rocher**, both in Lorient, are the exception rather than the rule.

Jazz lovers watch the sun set to soothing sounds at **L'Hibiscus**, in Gustavia. Pop fans head to the bar at the **Yacht Club** in Gustavia. Dancers opt for **Pearl's Club**, at the Jean Bart, in St. Jean. Sailors prefer **Le Select**. Romantics linger over after-dinner drinks high atop **Lurin**, at Castelets, or at any of the island's other restaurants.

SABA

If the flight into St. Barts can make one's heart skip a beat, the plane trip into **Saba** can stop it altogether. This is a tiny island atop a volcano, with sharp peaks crammed into a small space. The only flat part of the island, the landing strip, is in-

credibly small. Angling in to land here takes precision, strong nerves and a special training. Once one has recovered, though, a very calm feeling takes over. Saba, a story-book place, untouched by time and still isolated, despite the rampant tourism all around it. The islanders call it the "Unspoiled Caribbean Queen" – and they are right. Even its early history seems to have predestined it to being an out-of-the-way hideaway.

Columbus first saw the island in 1493 but did little about it. It was only in 1623 that a small group of ship-wrecked Englishmen landed but found neither people nor any worthy natural resources.

In 1635 a Frenchman claimed it for France. In 1640 a Dutch settlement took root, but English, Spanish and French battled the Dutch for it. In all, the island changed colors twelve times before finally raising Dutch colors in 1816.

Once the Dutch won firm control, they started building. The five-square-mile island is so mountainous that no point is directly accessible to any other point. 800 stone steps were built to create a village in a valley known as The Bottom, which serves as the island's capital. More steps were necessary to build the towns of Windwardside, Hell's Gate, Fort Bay and St. John's. **The Road** was completed between 1933 and 1947. Other conveniences came later. Television made it here in 1965, all-day electricity in 1970. But there are reasons for the island's slower pace. Islanders would have it no other way.

Stalking Saba's Sights

Using **The Road**, a land version of the terrifying flight in, and starting at **Flat Point**, the airport, one spirals past Hell's Gate and banana plantations and tropical foliage before getting to **Windwardside**, the island's second largest village. There are lots of tiny houses and even tinier shops here, as well as the majority of the island's inns. Recommended at this point is a visit of the L. Johnson Memorial Museum, the erstwhile dwelling of a sea-faring captain. Nearby, 1064 steps lead to

SABA

the summit of **Mount Scenery** (2838 ft/887 m), which is, exactly as its name conveys, a mountain top from which to survey the exhilarating view.

Heading downward towards The Bottom, you pass the village of **St. John's** before arriving at the bowl-shaped valley situated 820 feet (250 m) above sea level. At the other end of town is a lookout point with steps leading down to **Ladder Bay**, one of the settler's first landing points. Taking The Road to the end you finally comes to **Fort Bay**, site of a small harbor and another early landing point. Keep in mind that the island's supplies used to be carried up and down these steps. A well-tended path leads to **The Bottom**, the island's main town, whose streets are lined with typical Dutch houses.

Above: Saba's Underwater National Park is one of the world's most beautiful places to dive. Right: A harmonious and welcoming entrance is a sign of hospitality.

Sports

Saba has no beaches. Hiking is popular and the newly-formed Conservation Foundation has created trails for all levels of skill. One hike leads up to Mount Scenery. Another takes you to the sunrise at Hell's Gate or sunset at Fort Bay. Saban lore is kept alive by Bernard Johnson, who works at the Chinese Family Restauran. Horticultural information is provided on hikes with Anna Keene, at the **Weaver's Cottage Under the Hill** in Windwardside.

The other popular sport in, or rather off, Saba is diving. The entire coast and its waters have been declared the **Saba Marine Park**, and are protected accordingly. The area is totally unspoiled, and diving is restricted to specific areas, for example at **Torrens Point**, **Big Rock Market**, **Tent Reef**, or **Diamond Reef**. Dives can be arranged through the **Saba Deep Dive Center** in Fort Bay, **Sea Saba Dive Center**, in Windwardside, or **Wilson's Dive Shop**, in Fort Bay.

Nightlife

When the sun slowly goes down and the body yearns for a completely different kind of activity, there is Saba's nightlife, which is not that bad for this David of islands. One can indeed dance till the morning hours at **Guido's Disco** in Windwardside, or **Lime Time** in The Bottom. Those who just want to lounge around are better off at the **Captain's Quarters** or at the bar at **Scout's Place** in Windwardside.

SINT EUSTATIUS / STATIA

Flying into **Statia** (as it is commonly called) is an experience few forget. Less terrifying than descending into Saba, one is better able to enjoy the view. A prominent sight is **The Quill**, an extinct volcano reaching up over 1,800 feet, where a rain forest with thick, wild foliage has sprouted. Unfortunately, for those who love the old, quiet Statia, the island has become noticeable busier in recent years. Though still out of the way, it is step by step coming out of isolation. One important reason is the abundance of archeological artifacts. Numerous students converge here regularly to study pre-Colombian sites. Another are cruise ships. It has become a weekly port of call. But, only purists will get too upset about this. Statia is still the kind of place where one can leave it all behind.

Statia's history is basically Dutch; it was settled by citizens of the Netherlands in 1636. But like neighboring Saba, English and French fought the Dutch for control and it changed hands no less than 22 times before permanently becoming a Dutch possession in 1816. Interestingly, the island's history is not just tied to the countries of Europe. It played also a part in the development of the United States of America. During the Revolutionary War, when the British blockaded the colonies, supplies were slipped to the colo-

nists through neutral Statia. Ben Franklin routed his mail through the island. In 1776, a war ship, the *Andrea Doria*, flying the new American flag, sailed into the harbor and was received by a 13-gun salute, the first by a foreign nation, that earned Statia the nickname "America's Childhood Friend". This tribute angered Britain, which declared war on Holland in 1780, and attacked and sacked the island. Ten years later, after the French ousted the British and returned the island to the Dutch, it regained its position as a rich trading port. In the 1800s trade diminished and a wealthy Statia is now but a distant memory.

A One-Town Island

Oranjestad, Statia's only town and, therefore, its capital, is an architectural curiosity. Built on cliffs, it is split level, with an **Upper Town** and Lower Town separated by the cliffs. In the Upper Town, one can see **Fort Oranje**, dating back to 1636, and boasting having fired

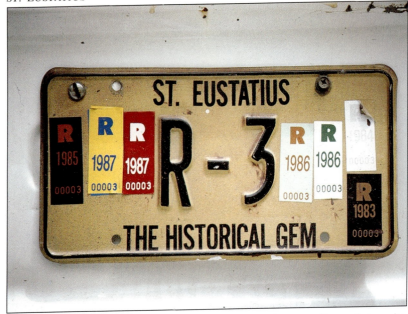

the first salute to the new American state in 1776. Generally, Fort Oranje is still in excellent shape, considering the numerous shellings it has suffered during the past centuries.

Nearby is the **St. Eustatius Historical Museum**, which has been established in a very beautifully restored 18th-century house (Van Tonningen Str. 12). It displays pre-Columbian finds.

Also worth seeing in the Upper Town is the remains of the **Synagogue** built in 1738 and the **Dutch Reformed Church** dating to the year 1775. Two more carefully revamped houses from the colonial era are the old **City Hall** in Fort Oranjestraat, and the **Three Widows' Corner** on Kerkweg, which has a pretty tropical garden. **Fortstraat** is the connecting street to the Lower Town. Unfortunately, what was once a thriving settlement in the 1700s is now almost completely abandoned.

Above: Statia, though small, was indeed a vital link in European-American relations.

Nightlife is not really much to write home about in quiet St. Eustatius. Locals patronize the **Cool Corner**, in Oranjestad, or finish up the evening relaxing to music at the **Golden Era Hotel**.

Thanks to its dense and interesting vegetation, one of the most popular excursions —especially for the hardy souls— is to **The Quill**, (1968 feet/600 m). The climb can be achieved with or without local guides.

Diving is worthwhile around remnants of 200 sunken ships. Snorkeling will provide views of coral and fish. *Dive Statia* provides equipment and instruction. Beaching is also popular, but the beaches here are not what one usually associates with the Caribbean.

Smoke Alley Beach on Statia is, as its name conveys, a beige and volcanic black sand beach. On some beaches, notably **Crooks Castle**, north of Oranjestad, an exciting thing to do is search for blue glass beads, which were minted as currency by the Dutch West Indies Company in the 1600s.

GUIDEPOST ST. BARTS / SABA / ST. EUSTATIUS

ST. BARTS
(Area code: 590)
Accommodations
LUXURY: Check the selection of luxury villas at Sibarth Rental and Real Estate, BP 55, St. Barthélémy, Tel: 276238. Hotels include **Guanahani**, Box 109, Grand Cul-de-Sac 97133, Tel: 276660. **Hotel Manapany Cottages**, Anse des Cayes 97133, Tel: 276655. **François Plantation**, Bungalows, Colombier 97133, Tel: 277882. **Castelets**, Box 60, Mt. Lurin 97133, Tel: 276173.
EXPENSIVE: **El Sereno Beach**, BP 19, Grand Cul-de-Sac 97133, Tel: 276480. **Filao Beach**, Box 167, St. Jean 97133, Tel: 276484. **L'Hibiscus**, Rue Thiers, BP 86, Gustavia 97133, Tel: 276482.
MODERATE: **Village St. Jean**, Box 23, St. Jean 97133, Tel: 276139. **St. Barths Beach Hotel** and **Grand Cul-de-Sac Beach Hotel**, Box 81, Grand Cul-de-Sac 97133, Tel: 276273.

Restaurants
Castelets, romantic, sublime French food, Morne Lurin, Tel: 276173. **La Toque Lyonnaise**, sophisticated, El Sereno Beach Hotel, Tel: 276480. **L'Ananas**, perfect fish, Rue Sadi Carnot, Gustavia, Tel: 276377. **La Gloriette**, casual beachside café, Grand Cul-de-Sac, Tel: 277566. **Club Lafayette**, Grand Cul-de-Sac, Tel: 276251. **Le Relais**, good Creole food, Petit Cul-de-Sac, Tel: 277300. **Le Marine**, casual restaurant, fresh fish, Rue Jeanne d'Arc, Gustavia, Tel: 276450. **Chez Francine**, St. Jean Bay, Tel: 276049.

Access and Local Transportation
Visitors arrive at either **St. Jean Airport**, via Windward Islands Airways, Air St. Barthélémy, Air Guadeloupe or Virgin Air, or by cruise ship or daysailer at **Gustavia harbor**. For rental cars: Henry Greaux represents Hertz, Tel: 276021. St. Barth Car represents Avis, Tel: 277143. Caraibes Car Service represents Europcar, Tel: 276487.

Formalities
Most visitors need a passport, although Americans and Canadians can get through with a photo ID or a birth certificate.

Currency
Currency is the French Franc, valued at approximately 5.8 FF to 1 US$. US dollars, credit cards and traveler's checks are widely accepted.

Tourist Information
Office de Tourisme, Quai du Général de Gaulle, Gustavia, Tel: 278727.

SABA / SINT EUSTATIUS
(Area code: 599)
Access and Local Transportation
Air travelers arrive at the **Yrausquin Airport** on WIN AIR. Travelers by sea from Sint Maarten arrive at **Fort Bay Saba**. Cruise ships tie up in Oranjestad / St. Eustatius. Taxis stand at both locations. Rental car agencies are near the airport.

Formalities and Currency
Americans need proof of citizenship (no driver's licenses). Residents of Great Britain need a British Visitor's Passport. Everyone else needs a passport, and all need ongoing tickets.
Official currency is the N.A. Guilder, currently exchanging at around 1.80 NAF to 1 US$, but greenbacks, or traveler's checks are widely accepted. Credit cards may be harder to use.

SABA
Accommodations
Inns here are charming and moderately priced. **The Captain's Quarters**, Windwardside, Saba, Tel: 462201. **Juliana's**, apartments, Windwardside, Saba, Tel: 462269. **Scout's Place**, B & B. Windwardside, Saba, Tel: 462205. **Cranston's Antique Inn**, The Bottom, Saba, Tel: 463218.

Restaurants
Captain's Quarters, simple Creole, Windwardside, Tel: 462201. **Scout's Place**, simple continental, Windwardside, Tel: 462205. **The Serving Spoon**, West Indian, The Bottom, Tel: 463225.

Tourist Information
Saba Tourist Board, Windwardside, Tel: 462231, Fax: 462350.

SINT EUSTATIUS
Accommodations
LUXURY: **Old Gin House**, gracious, Box 172, Oranjestad, Tel: 382319. *MODERATE:* **The Golden Era**, Box 109, Oranjestad, Tel: 382345. **La Maison sur la Plage**, Box 157, Zeelandia, Tel: 382256.

Restaurants
Old Gin House, **Mooshay Bay Dining Room**, Lower Town, Oranjestad, Tel: 382319. **L'Etoile**, Prinseweg, Upper Town, Oranjestad, Tel: 382299.

Access and Local Transportation
Air travelers arrive at **Roosevelt Airport** on Windward Islands Airways or LIAT. Cruise ships anchor below Oranjestad. Taxis and rental cars are available.

Formalities and Currency
Americans need proof of citizenship in form of a passport, birth certificate or voter's registration card. All other nationalities need a passport.
US dollars are widely accepted, exchanging at around 1 US$ to 1.75 NAF.

Tourist Information
St. Eustatius Tourism Foundation, Fort Oranjestraat, Tel/Fax: 382433.

ST. KITTS

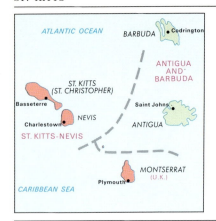

CARIBBEAN CHARMS OF YORE

ST. KITTS

NEVIS

MONTSERRAT

Note: As the book goes to print (October 1997), Soufrière on Monserrat is in full eruption. The extent of the catastrophe is unknown. All information appearing in this book refers to pre-eruption times! (The editors)

The islands of **St. Kitts**, **Nevis** and **Montserrat** conjure up images of the Caribbean as it was 30 years ago. All three share a British heritage. St. Kitts-Nevis is an independent nation, but Montserrat remains one of the few British colonies left in the Caribbean. All three offer old West Indies charm, small, gracious hotels and inns and some of the Caribbean's most dramatic panoramas. The trio are part of the British Leeward Island group which also includes Antigua, Barbuda and Anguilla. An aviator once said that these islands look like "a fleet of cockleshells set afloat in the sea." St. Kitts is the largest of the three and for this reason has the most developed tourist facilities.

ST. KITTS

St. Kitts is the largest island and the one with the best tourist infrastructure. The early settlers, the Caribs, also found

Preceding pages: As long as no breezes or hurricanes are blowing, of course, the sea can be used as a mirror.

the local nature particularly enchanting. They called **St. Kitts** *Liamuiga*, or "fertile isle." In 1493 Christopher Columbus spotted St. Kitts, naming it *San Cristóbal* (Saint Christopher), for either himself or the patron saint of travelers. He sailed on, leaving the island and the Carib Indians undisturbed.

The British anglicized the name of the island almost as soon as they arrived in January, 1623, when Sir Thomas Warner established the first English colony in the West Indies. They were warmly received by the Caribs. St. Kitts is proud of its other title, "Mother Colony of the West Indies", which it earned by sending out colonizing parties to other islands.

In 1625, both the English and the Indians welcomed a French party seeking refuge after a skirmish with a Spanish warship. The peace ended a year later when the Caribs, fearing the growth of the European colonies, planned to drive out the foreigners. The British and French, though, discovered the plan and killed the 200 Caribs on the island along with 2000 others who had come to their aid. They then settled down to growing tobacco and sugar cane and sending out colonists to other islands. Periodical fighting broke out between the two, although a treaty partitioned the island in a strange manner. The French got both

ST. KITTS

ends and the English the middle. To protect their territory the British set out to build a fortress at **Brimstone Hill**. Construction started in 1690 and the fort took some 100 years and thousands of slaves to build because of its site and its enormous size. Its name is derived from the faint smell of sulfur that always lingers in the air. The fort commands a spectacular view of Nevis, Montserrat, Saba, Statia, St. Martin and St. Barts. The view reportedly drew "an astonished reaction" from Queen Elizabeth II during her October, 1985, visit, when she declared the entire area a national monument.

The British believed its vantage point 750 feet (230 m) above the Caribbean made it completely impregnable. However, the French attacked the British in 1782, before the fort was completed. The 950 British and Scottish soldiers fought a tremendously brave battle against more than 6000 French troops before surrendering. As a mark of respect the French allowed the British to march from the fort in full formation with colors flying. A year later the British retook the fort and accorded the French the same respect.

The treaty of 1783 restored both fort and island to Britain once and for all. The islanders were free to concentrate on sugar cane. As the demand for sugar declined, St. Kitts fell asleep as far as the world was concerned. She only woke from it in recent times, when development began on a larger scale and the nation of St. Kitts-Nevis eventually gained independence in September 1983.

The Fertile Isle

St. Kitts is shaped like a primitive cricket bat and has a fat end that is dominated by rain forests, mountain ranges and sugar cane fields. The island is 23 miles long (36 km), five miles wide (8 km). The central part consists of a rugged mountain range whose highest point is **Mount Liamuiga**, formerly called

Above: Brimstone Hill, the Caribbean's Gibraltar. Right: More than food for thought.

ST. KITTS

Mount Misery, at 3792 feet (1185 m). Hardy visitors can make the eight-hour excursion to the peak. A Land Rover will take visitors part of the way and then a guide should be hired. After that, it is a long, steady climb to the lip of the crater.

Basseterre is the island's capital and only town. Its French name is traced back to the days of French occupation, but the town today is very British-looking. Except for a couple of new banks it has not changed much over the years.

Goats still wander through town. The main square is called the **Circus** and its centerpiece is the **Thomas Berkeley Memorial**, an ornate Victorian Clock Tower with four faces and a fountain in its base. Another square is **Independence Square**. A park has taken the place of the old slave market.

Basseterre boasts some fine examples of West Indian architecture in the islands. Another landmark is the Anglican **Church of St. George**, which has been plagued by disasters since its construction back in 1670. The actual structure dates to 1868. Its steeple was toppled by an earthquake in 1974. A number of old books and maps dealing with the West Indies are exhibited in Court House, as well as pre-Columbian rock paintings and ancient stonemason's tools.

Sightseeing on the island is easy. One can drive around the island in just about two hours but should take more time to relax and enjoy the views and historic sights. The main road follows the shoreline around the island, running parallel to a narrow-gauge sugar cane railroad that hauls the cargo to the refinery near the airport.

Situated just outside Basseterre is the **St. Kitts Sugar Factory**, which provides a look into the island's history with tours on advance notice. The best months for visiting are February to July, when cane is actually being ground and one can observe the entire process from raw cane to bulk sugar.

Privately owned **Fountain Estate** sits high on a hill north of town. It was the home of Philippe de Longvilliers de Poincy, who served for 20 years as governor of the French Antilles. The royal poinciana, or flamboyant tree, was named after him.

Next stop is **Old Road Town**, site of the first permanent British settlement in the West Indies and serving until 1727 as the British capital of the island. At the **Wingfield Estate** nearby, interesting Carib **petroglyphs** (stone carvings) chiseled into a small cluster of boulders.

After driving through a tropical rain forest the next site is **Romney Manor,** an older estate house and home of **Caribelle Batik Factory**. Visitors are invited inside to watch how the colorful cloth is made. Customers can order clothing and wall hangings.

Middle Island Village is where Sir Thomas Warner, leader of the original British landing party, is entombed under a marble slab in the yard of **St. Thomas Church.**

NEVIS

Soon after comes what has been nicknamed the "Gibraltar of the West Indies," the fort **Brimstone Hill**, whose turbulent history was already described earlier on in this chapter. Inside its massive defensive walls, which are seven to 12 feet thick and still bristling with old cannons, are the remains of a hospital, store rooms, kitchens, a cemetery and a fresh-water cistern. Although the fort was badly damaged over the centuries, the main fortifications have survived. The entire **Prince of Wales Bastion**, dedicated by Prince Charles in 1973, was meticulously restored and consists of a visitors' center, souvenir shop and restaurant.

Dieppe Bay, a gently curved piece of seaside real estate, lies all the way in the north of St. Kitts, is a pleasant spot for swimming and picnicing. The sands are volcanic gray to black.

Monkey Hill is a 1319-foot (402 m) knoll west of Basseterre, named for the island's population of black-faced velvet monkeys, originally imported by the French and left behind when their masters moved on. The view from the top is worth the trip and with a little luck one might spot a monkey or two.

Frigate Bay, southeast of Basseterre, was developed for tourism in order to preserve the rest of the island. It is the site of a number of hotel and condominium projects and an 18-hole golf course. The area boasts two beaches, one on the Atlantic, the other on the Caribbean side.

NEVIS

Nevis was also sighted and named by Christopher Columbus, for a change, on his second voyage in 1493. He named the circular island *Las Nieves*, Spanish for "snow," because of the snow-white clouds clinging to the mountain that dominates the island. The next seafarers to arrive were Captain John Smith and his English crew in 1607. They were en route to settle the Jamestown colony in

Above: The Black Rocks near Dieppe Bay testify to the volcanic origins of St. Kitts.

Virginia but stayed in Nevis long enough for the captain to note, "here we found a great poole, wherin bathing ourselves we found much ease." They also found time on Nevis to pursue a group of mutineers and hang them.

Permanent colonization took place in 1628, when English Captain Anthony Hilton arrived with 80 planters. In the 17th and 18th centuries Nevis was more prosperous than St. Kitts and was nicknamed "the Queen of the Caribbees." The island has always appealed to the English aristocracy.

Alexander Hamilton, who made his way into history as one of the framers of the American constitution, was born in Nevis, in 1755, in a Charlestown estate house. Admiral Lord Nelson, then Captain of His Majesty's Ship *Boreas*, was headquartered in neighboring Antigua but favored Nevis as a fresh-water stop, where he eventually married Frances Nisbet. Their best man was the Duke of Clarence, who was later to become King William IV of England. The wedding took place at Montpelier Estate, now site of an exclusive inn.

The "great poole" that Captain John Smith recorded was to become famous for its hot sulphurous springs and curative waters. **The Bath House**, an imposing place on a hilltop, was built at the end of the 18th century. The stately ruins still stand overlooking **Bath Village**, which at one time was a luxurious spa. Five mineral baths have been restored and are now open for visitors (information at the tourist office). There is talk that the massive hotel which is still standing may be restored as well.

Eventuallly, Bath Village became the most important spa in the British West Indies, attracting more than 4000 tourists each year, and one of the most popular winter refuges of English people of fashion in the early 19th century. Gertrude Atherton, in her novel *The Gorgeous Isle*, wrote of the Bath House: "... the whole effect being that of an Eastern palace with hanging gardens, a vast pleasure house, designed for some extravagant and voluptuous potentate."

Life in Charlestown, the island's vivid capital, usually revolves around the mid-morning arrival of the ferry from St. Kitts, two miles (3 km) away. Otherwise, it is the *Culturama*, celebrated in late July and early August with dances, calypso shows and special events. The town dates from 1660 and is a miniature West Indian port. A self-guided tour of Charlestown can easily be done in an hour. Not far from the spot of Alexander Hamilton's birth stands the **Historical Museum** of Nevis, which is also known as the **Alexander Hamilton Museum**. It has exhibits on Hamilton and island history and culture.

St. Paul's Church was first built in the 17th century and has been restored and rebuilt several times since. In the cemetery is the tomb of John Huggins, builder of the Bath House, who died "on the 6th day of December, 1821, aged 58..." **St. Thomas Church** at the other end of town was first built in 1640 and has been restored over the years after earthquakes and hurricanes. There is also the old **Jewish Cemetery**. At one time Sephardic Jews coming from Brazil made up a quarter of the population of Nevis.

Outside of town, the main road that circles the island offers views of island life when sugar and cotton were king and Nevis was Queen of the Caribees. It is worthwhile to make a stop at **St. John's Church** in **Fig Tree Village**, just a few miles from town. The record of Lord Nelson's marriage to the governor's niece Frances Nisbet is in the church register. Tombstones in the mossy old graveyard date back to 1682. Montpelier Estate, which nowadays serves as a hotel, was the setting for the wedding. Right by **Morning Star Plantation**, the **Nelson Museum**, opened in 1992, contains a

NEVIS

large collection of Nelson memorabilia. Among other items, is a faded letter written by Nelson with his left hand, after he lost his right one. There are also paintings depicting Nelson's romance with Lady Hamilton, and porcellain, pictures, books and dining chairs from the admiral's flagship *Victory*. There is also a grandfather clock that was deliberately and permanently stopped the moment Queen Elizabeth II entered the museum on February 22, 1966, one of the biggest events in the recent history of Nevis.

Near Montpelier is the **Clay Ghaunt Estate** with the **Eva Wilkin's Studio**. Everybody, including Prince Charles, heads for her studio. Wilkin, now in her 90s, is the artist laureate of Nevis. In 1977, she received a Jubilee Award from Queen Elizabeth commemorating the death of Queen Victoria. She has also been made a Member of the British Empire, still the greatest honor, short of knighthood, that Great Britain bestows on commoners. Her paintings are usually of Nevisians. Wilkin tells the people who rent most of her 200 acres: "If they don't pose for me, I'll raise their rent. It's now the same as it was 20 years ago, $10 per acre per year. I'm not making any money from it. That's why I still paint." Wilkin's studio is on a promontory that gives it one of the best views on the island of Nevis. Her paintings and prints are on sale here and sometimes one may be fortunate enough to meet the artist herself.

There are ruins everywhere on Nevis and one of the most impressive is doubtlessly the **Eden Brown Estate**, built in the 18th century by a wealthy plantation owner as a generous wedding present for his lovely daughter. Nothing is left but a substantial foundation, some thick walls and a set of steps with a large landing. One could easily imagine guests being announced here when arriving for dinner or a ball, but only one single party was ever held in the house, the night before

Above: An Antillean beauty, perhaps Miss Nevis 2000. Right: Hardy Caribbean fishermen go out and truly give it all they've got.

the daughter's wedding. An argument between the groom and a guest led to a duel. Both men died. No one ever lived in the house after that. According to legend, the bride's sobbing can be heard just before sunrise each day.

Pinney's Beach, almost 4 miles long (6 km) is the island's best beach, although some of it was simply washed away by hurricane *Hugo* in 1989. The reef-protected waters are clear and fine for swimming. **Nevis Peak**, a 3152-foot (985 m) mountain, is ideal for day hikes. Numerous monkeys live in the luscious vegetaion along its sides. They were introduced by the French and are thought to number over 8000 by now. The sunset is best experienced near Salsa and Merengue in the **Beachcomber** next to the beach-side Four Seasons Hotel.

MONTSERRAT

*Please note: As we go to print (October 1997) the future of **Monserrat** is unclear owing to a full-scale eruption by the Soufrière volcano. All information is naturally based on pre-eruption data.*

Montserrat, the least developed of the trio of islands was sighted by Columbus in 1493 and named *Santa María de Montserrat* for the famous monastery near Barcelona, Spain. It was not until the early 1600s that Irish settlers colonized it, when the English shipped out a band of reluctant colonists who had been captured after a rebellion. Montserrat was also a place of refuge for Irish settlers who fled their new homes in St. Kitts due to religious persecution. The strongest Irish influence is found in names of places on the island and the surnames of many of today's residents. By 1648 there were more than 1000 Irish families living in Montserrat. The island was captured by the French in 1644, restored to England in 1668, retaken by France in 1782, and then ceded to Britain in 1783. The island, unlike most of the neighboring, has chosen voluntarily to remain a British Crown Colony. The Irish nicknamed Montserrat the "Emerald Isle" because of

MONTSERRAT

the vibrant plant life and the densely forested mountains.

The English and Irish transformed Montserrat into a farm and plantation island. Slaves were imported, but the terrain was too rugged for the kind of agriculture planned by the colonists. Though it produces enough fruit and vegetables for its own needs, the island essentially remains undeveloped.

Recent history has been tough on the little island. In 1989, Hurricane Hugo destroyed 95 per cent of habitations. And volcanic activity since 1995 culminated in a full-scale eruption in August 1997 that did extremely heavy damage. What happens next (as we go to print) is unknown, even whether Monserrat can ever be inhabited again.

The flag of the island is the British Union Jack, but the official badge is the Irish *Lady with the Harp*. The Shamrock can be seen on the center gable of Gov-

Right: The sulphurous emanations of Galways Soufrière perfume the land.

ernment House, and is on the stamp for passports. The island marks March 17, St. Patrick's Day, as a public holiday because of a slave rebellion on that date.

It is not that unusual to spot for instance Ringo Starr, Paul McCartney or Stevie Wonder. For hidden in the lush northern hills is a state-of-the-art recording studio launched by George Martin, the former producer of the Beatles.

The capital, **Plymouth**, is tidy and well kept with a West Indian flavor of yesteryear. It is a small town of 3,000 people and easy to tour in about an houranda-half. Barring the previously-mentioned St. Patrick's Day, the town and island explode with activity during Christmastime, which is celebrated with parades and masquerade parties. It is best to start with **Government House**, a Victorian structure complete with remarkably well maintained lawns and gardens. **St. Anthony's Church**, the island's oldest, was originally started in 1632 and redesigned and rebuilt several times during the following centuries. The tamarind tree out-

MONTSERRAT

side is more than 200 years old. On Richmond Hill is the **National Trust Museum** housed in an old sugar mill and displaying a collection of artifacts, some of which date back to Carib times. Saturday morning is market day.

From Plymouth a road leads down the southwest coast and then cuts inland to **Galway Soufrière**, a 3000-foot (almost 900 m) active volcanic range. From a newly built lookout, you can peer at hot sulphur springs that bubble up from its innards. The crater allows experts to monitor volcanic activity under the island.

Chances Peak, at 3002 feet (914 m), is the highest point of the volcano. The climb can be difficult and hazardous, so it is advisable to arrange for a guide before starting out. On a clear day, though, when the views are memorable, you will appreciate having made the effort.

Near the town of Morris is the **White River Valley**. Its main attraction, the **Great Alps Waterfall**, is at the end of a difficult one-mile hike through dense rain forest. It is a small waterfall, dropping 70 feet (22 m) into a shallow pool of clear water, but most impressive during the rainy season when the tumbling cascade splashes over a mossy and moist ravine. Swimming is best in the rocky pool below the falls. For the energetic, another cascade, **White River Falls**, is located farther up the valley.

To the south near **Old Fort Point** stands the *Radio Antilles* transmitter, beaming 2000 watts of power between Cuba and Venezuela. Visiting is allowed if someone happens to be around.

Rendezvous Beach is on the far northwest coast of the island and the only white sand strand. It is reachable only by boat and is a popular spot for picnics, romantic getaways and the like.

Monserrat also has its fair share of fine diving spots. Pristine coral reefs can be found at **Pinnacle Rock**, **Lime Kiln Bay**, **Woodlands Bay** and **Little Bay**. Boats are also available for all sorts of activities, be that deep-sea fishing, sailing around the island, surfing, water-skiing or snorkeling.

ST. KITTS / NEVIS / MONTSERRAT

Please note: As we go to print (October 1997) the future of *Monserrat* is unclear owing to a full-scale eruption by the Soufrière volcano. All information is naturally based on pre-eruption data.

Access and Local Transportation
BWIA flies directly from the USA to St. Kitts. There are also direct charters from several US cities and Toronto during the winter season. LIAT flies from other Caribbean islands and also to Nevis from St. Kitts (as does the Nevis Express).
Several cruise lines including Chandris Fantasy, Cunard, Norwegian and Windjammer make St. Kitts a port of call. The state-run ferry makes one or two round-trips daily between St. Kitts and Nevis except on Thursdays and Sundays.
There is no non-stop service from the USA or Canada to Montserrat. Most visitors fly in from Antigua, although flights are also available from St. Kitts to Montserrat on Montserrat Air Services. Reservations are handled through LIAT.
ST. KITTS: The easiest way is by taxi, which are unmetered. Be sure to settle the price before starting out, even though set prices are usually officially posted. There is bus service between island villages but it is infrequently used by tourists.
Car rental is easy to arrange and costs about 40 US$ and up a day plus a St. Kitts driver's license, which costs EC$ 50 and is valid for three months. Some companies include the local license and offer free pick-up and drop-off. Driving is on the left.
NEVIS: Rates are fixed for taxis and published in the various tourist guides. Be sure to confirm whether the fare is quoted in EC$ or US$. There are buses between villages, but few tourists use them because schedules are sketchy.
Car rentals are mostly mini-mokes, baby British jeeps, which can negotiate the rocky island roads. Average rate is about 30-45 US$ a day. You will also need a Nevis driver's license for about 12 US$. Driving is on the left.
MONTSERRAT: Taxi rates are standardized by law. Standard rates for car rentals are about US$ 20-45 a day. A temporary driver's license is needed and available at the airport or at the police station for about US$ 12.

Formalities and Currency
Proof of citizenship or a ticket of return or ongoing transportation are required for citizens of the USA, Canada or the U.K. Citizens of other countries need a passport. The currency of St. Kitts-Nevis and Montserrat is the Eastern Caribbean Dollar (EC$), called *Bee Wee* by most locals.

The current exchange rate is about 2.68 EC$ to 1 US$. US dollars are accepted in most places. Credit cards are generally accepted in hotels but may not be in restaurants or small shops.

Festivals
Carnival on St. Kitts and Montserrat is held around New Year.

Tourist Information
St. Kitts Department of Tourism, Pelican Mall, P.O.Box 132, Basseterre, Tel: (869) 465-2620, (869) 465-4040, Fax:(869) 465-8794.
Nevis Tourism Bureau, Main Street, Charlestown, Tel/Fax: (869) 469-1042.
Montserrat Board of Tourism, P:O:Box 7, Plymouth Church Rd. Tel: (664) 491-2230, Fax: (664) 491-7430.

ST.KITTS
(Area code: 1869)
Accommodations
EXPENSIVE TO MODERATE: **Jack Tar Village St. Kitts Resort & Casino,** the largest hotel on the island with 242 rooms, is the centerpiece of the Frigate Bay development. All-inclusive rates cover everything from sports to meals and cocktails. **Frigate Bay Beach Hotel** is a five minute walk from the Caribbean side of the bay. Set on a hillside 64 one- and two-bedroom apartments. **Ocean Terrace Inn** is one of the island's best inns overlooking Basseterre harbor. The 54 rooms include 8 one- and two- bedroom apartments. **Fairview Inn** was originally an 18th century great house of a wealthy French plantation owner set on the rise of a hill. The manor house has rooms in the main building and others in cottages in the rear garden.
Golden Lemon Inn and Villas was created by Arthur Leaman, former decorating editor of *House & Garden* magazine. Next to the Great House Leaman has added 16 villas of one- and two- bedrooms, each with its own pool and furnished with antiques. The inn has gardens and courtyards, a tennis court, small black sand beach and superb food. **Rawlins Plantation** is a small, family owned inn set on a former plantation among the remains of a sugar factory. A 17th century windmill has been converted into a suite complete with a private bath and sitting room.

Restaurants
St. Kitts restaurants feature local specialties such as turtle stew, crab back, turtle steaks, creole fried fish as well as continental fare. **Georgian House** is a restored colonial house in the heart of Basseterre serving a mix of continental and West Indian fare. Romantic atmosphere and fine food. Dinner only. **Patio**, in Frigate Bay, provides a leisurely dining experience in a private home. Only dinner is served and

GUIDEPOST ST. KITTS / NEVIS / MONTSERRAT

reservations are essential as each dish is prepared to order and space is limited. **Ballahoo** is in the heart of Basseterre on the second-story of a Victorian building with lots of gingerbread. Its wide veranda is one of the coolest places in town. Open for lunch and dinner except Sunday. **Fisherman's Wharf** in Basseterre is a casual place at the water's edge where seafood and steaks are served at the picnic tables. On Wednesdays and Fridays there is a popular seafood buffet. **Golden Lemon** is a must for visitors touring the island. Reservations essential. Lunch is served in a lush, tropical setting under a breadfruit tree, dinner in an elegant candle-lit dining room. The menu changes daily and the food is delicious. **White House** offers dining outdoors or indoors in the original dining room of an 18th-century greathouse. Reservations are essential at this inn about three miles north of Basseterre.

NEVIS
(Area code: 1869)

EXPENSIVE TO MODERATE: Nevis specializes in character inns, many of which have been adapted from long-abandoned sugar plantations. The 17th-century **Old Manor Estate** is located on what was a working sugar plantation until 1936. The great house is the longest continually lived in house in all the West Indies. Today the estate is renowned for its gracious hospitality. The pool was created from a 150-year-old cistern. **Nisbet Plantation Beach Club** is the former home of Frances Nisbet who married Lord Nelson. The present main building on the former coconut plantation was rebuilt on the foundations of the original 18th century great house. There is half a mile of sandy beach, one of the island's best. **Zetland Plantation** is another former plantation which lies 1,000 feet up the slopes of Mount Nevis. There are views of both the Atlantic and Caribbean and nearby Antigua and Montserrat. Plantation suites (cottages) are scattered about the 750 acres. **Hermitage Inn** is said to be the oldest all-wood house in the Antilles, built in 1740. Rooms are filled with antiques. Besides the main house, there are ten units in five buildings designed like small plantation houses. Many contain huge, four-poster beds. **Golden Rock Estate** was a sugar estate built in 1815, high in the hills. The original windmill has been turned into a deluxe honeymoon suite or accommodations for four or five. There are 15 double rooms spread throughout the gardens. **Montpelier Plantation Inn** is situated 700 feet up the slopes of Mount Nevis with 16 rooms in cottages. The main house has been set on the foundations of the ruins of the great Montpelier estate. The **Hurricane Cove Bungalows** are a good alternative to the plantation hotels. **Pinney's Beach Hotel** is a 48-room resort hotel on the island's most spectacular beach. The **Four Seasons Resort** has 196 rooms and suites and has all the amenities of a luxury hotel, including a golf course.

Restaurants

Nevis grows much of its own food which is offered in unusually high quality. There are very few restaurants but the small inns provide superb dining. Some notable inns for dining include the **Old Manor Estate**, **Hermitage Plantation** and **Montpelier Plantation Inn**. **Pinney's Beach Hotel** offers some fine local cuisine for those who are spending a day at the beach.

MONTSERRAT
(Area code: 1664)

Please see note top left !

Today there are five hotels, villas and condos for rent. **Villas of Montserrat** offers deluxe villas from two-bedrooms to three- and four-bedroom deluxe accommodations. There are 65 units in the island's largest villa complex. **Shamrock Villas** features 20 one- and two-bedroom apartments overlooking the sea, 400 yards from the beach. There is also a freshwater pool and tennis court.

Vue Point Hotel features 28 separate cottages, 12 double-bedrooms in connected units. There are two lighted tennis courts and the island's most complete water sports setup. **Egret House**, Woodlands Beach, Plymouth, Tel: 491-5316. **Flora Fountain Hotel** is centrally located in Plymouth. It is built around a circular courtyard with 18 rooms. It is less popular with tourists because of its location and lack of sports facilities.

Restaurants

Montserrat grows some of the best fruits and vegetables in all the Caribbean. *Mountain chicken* or legs of the large frog native only to Montserrat and nearby Dominica, is a local delicacy. **Belham Valley Restaurant** is the premier dining establishment of the island. The setting is tropical romantic in a former private home on a hillside overlooking Belham River and the valley. Open for dinner. **Vue Point** is another elegant establishment which offers fixed-price dinners. The Wednesday night barbecue is an island event. **The Iguana** is set in a tropical garden. Dinners include mountain chicken, fresh tuna, kingfish creole, red snapper. Desserts are often freshly made ice cream. **Blue Dolphin Restaurant** offers good local food and fresh fish dishes are the specialty of its fisherman owner. It is on the outskirts of Plymouth. **The Oasis** is on the ground floor of an 18th century stone house. Food is simple but very tasty. The owner often performs magic for the guests and blows up balloon-shaped animals.

117

ANTIGUA

A BEACH FOR EVERY DAY

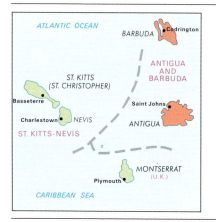

ANTIGUA

BARBUDA

Antigua, the largest of the Leeward Islands, claims to have one beach for every day of the year, including leap years. While some may quibble about the exact numbers, there is no doubt that Antigua is blessed with a necklace of beautiful white sand beaches that attract thousands of visitors. Everyone has a favorite. It was probably Half Moon Bay that the late American artist Georgia O'Keefe found so appealing on her 1975 visit to the island. She had a special fondness for "a lovely white sandy beach, a crescent with palm trees outlining the coast. She enjoyed walking that beach collecting seashells, and when it got hot she would sit under the palm trees in the shade..."

Antigua, Barbuda and Redonda form the independent nation of Antigua and Barbuda. The nation became independent from Britain on November 1, 1981, although the islands had associate status within the British Commonwealth since 1967. Redonda is an uninhabited rocky islet of less than one square mile. Barbuda, sparsely inhabited, lies 30 miles north of Antigua. It is 62 square miles (160 sq. km) of wilderness, surrounded by wide beaches, protected by coral reefs.

Preceding pages: Everything goes during carnival. Left: Admiral Nelson understood the strategic value of English Harbour.

ANTIGUA

Antigua was discovered by Columbus in 1493. He named the island after *Santa Maria la Antigua* of Seville. The accepted pronunciation has always been English and therefore it is "An-TEE-ga" with a hard "g." The island was first colonized by English planters from St. Kitts in 1632. After a brief period of French occupation in 1661, it was formally turned over to England by the Treaty of Breda in 1667. It has remained British ever since. During the next 200 years, the British built forts on the shoreline and a major naval installation at English Harbor, always expecting the French to try to make a comeback. They never did.

According to *The Romance of English Harbour*, the first reference to English Harbor was in a letter dated December 9, 1671, when Sir Charles Wheeler, Governor of the Leeward Islands, urged the Crown to consider it as a seaport for the British fleet because of its deep and huge bay. By 1704, the harbor was home for the fleet, which set out from here on raids and forays over the next 100 years, a period of constant struggle for power between British, Spanish, French and Dutch explorers, settlers and pirates.

This, then, was the site chosen by the British in the mid-18th century to be their

ANTIGUA

main naval base in the Leeward Islands, safe from marauders and hurricanes, a place to bring men-of-war for careening and their crews for carousing.

The only remaining Georgian naval dockyard in the whole world achieved its greatest fame when the man who was to become Britain's most celebrated naval hero, Captain Horatio Nelson, was headquartered here for four years in 1784-87. Nelson's stay was not a happy one. He alienated local merchants by trying to strictly enforce the Navigation Act, by which Britain sought to close all its West Indian ports to American shipping.

Nevertheless, Nelson's command of the Leeward Squadron was, a smart career move for an ambitious naval officer. During his time, the Antillean islands ranked higher in importance than the North American colonies. Sugar was king. It was so lucrative that the British government spent a fortune on the dockyard to maintain the might of the Royal Navy and discourage the French or any other would-be invaders.

From the windows of his home, Nelson could look out and see his frigate, the *Boreas*, being overhauled. But Nelson did not view his stay in quite the same way as the tourists who flock here some 200 years later. "I am alone in the Commanding Officer's House, while my ship is fitting, and from sunrise until bedtime I have not a human creature to speak to," he complained to Mrs. Nisbet, a widow from Nevis whom he met in 1785 and was to marry two years later.

One of Nelson's close friends was the captain of *HMS Pegasus*, Prince William Henry, the Duke of Clarence and later George IV. He served as best man at Nelson's wedding to Frances Nisbet.

As naval vessels grew larger and the skirmishes in the West Indies diminished, Antigua's importance as a naval base receded and the yard was officially abandoned in the early 19th century. By the 1950s the old dockyard was in an ad-

Right: Hot rhythms are also part of the musical scene on Antigua and Barbuda.

vanced state of disrepair. It was rescued by a group of dedicated Antiguans and expatriates who formed an organization known as the *Friends of English Harbour*. The Canadian government has contributed about two million dollars toward the restoration and the cosmetic improvement of the area. Utility cables have been buried and antique street lighting has been added.

Most Antiguans today are descended from Africans once brought to the island as slaves to work in the sugar cane plantations. Slavery was abolished in 1834, but sugar cane nevertheless remained the mainstay of the island's economy until the present century.

Nowadays, most Antiguans live off the tourist industry, while the country experiences the usual tribulations of any young, modern nation trying to find a new economic means of survival.

St. John's

Antigua's 108 square miles are composed of the same limestone and volcanic formations that have created the islands throughout the Caribbean. On the social side, centuries of British domination are apparent in language and manners as they are in the fortifications of the Dockyard area. Cricket is a national passion and virtually the entire country comes to a halt when an important cricket match is on.

The capital of the country is the city of **St. John's**, situated on the northwest side of the island. It has a population of about 30,000, or nearly half of the island's inhabitants. More than half of the country's hotels are just minutes away by car. The new deepwater harbor, where, during the winter months, cruise ships dock almost every day, is about a mile from the center of St. John's. The town is so small, it can easily be seen in a day.

The Anglican **St. John the Divine Cathedral** dominates the town from its hilltop position at Church Lane. It has had a

disastrous history. This Anglican cathedral was begun in 1845 to replace a stone building started in 1745, which had been destroyed by an earthquake. The first church on the site was built in 1683. The figures of St. John the Baptist and St. John the Divine, erected at the south gate of the present church, are said to have been taken from one of Napoleon's ships and transported to Antigua in a British man-of-war. The twin towers and structure were badly damaged by another violent earthquake in 1973. The pitch pine interior was finally restored. The towers and the southern section have since been restored, but renovating the northern section is an ongoing project hampered by lack of funds.

Antigua's newest shopping and entertainment complex, **Heritage Quay**, is a multi-million-dollar center featuring a variety of duty-free shops, a casino, and a vendor's arcade in which local artists and craftspeople display their wares. Restaurants offer a wide range of cuisine and great views of St. John's harbor. Another

ANTIGUA

*Above: A startling yellow poui in full bloom.
Right: Another era comes alive in Admiral's House in Nelson's Dockyard.*

good spot for shopping and strolling is **Redcliffe Quay**. At one time Redcliffe Quay was a slave-trading quarter. After the abolition of slavery, the quay was filled with rum shops and merchants peddling various wares. It has recently been redeveloped and contains a number of interesting restaurants and shops, some of which are housed in former warehouses.

The Old Court House, on Market Street, now houses the **National Museum** and the **Archives**, a voluminous collection of Antiguan historical documents. The **Police headquarters**, situated on **Newgate**, is primarily noteworthy because it used to be the arsenal.

On Fridays and Saturdays the marketplace is bustling with local people. Its location at the south end of town is somewhat off the tourist path. About half a mile to the northwest is **Fort James**. It was built as a lookout point for the city and harbor. Its ruined ramparts, built in 1703, overlook the bay and its guns still point out to sea.

Touring the Island

Outside of town is **Fig Tree Drive**, a 20-mile circular drive across the main mountain range. The road passes through lush tropical hills and several small fishing villages along the beautiful southern coast. It winds through the remains of a rain forest, then passes thatched villages and hamlets with little churches, goats and children and fields of mango, avocado, breadfruit, guava and – typical for Antigua – black pineapple trees. Banana trees, by the way, are locally referred to as fig trees.

Antigua is only 12 miles north-to-south by 15 miles east-to-west, but one could spend days following coiling coastal roads that lead to places like **Lignumvitae Bay**, **Standfast Point**, **Rendezvous Bay**, **Nonsuch Bay**, or **Indian Town Point**. Each small village has a church that reflects the history of the area. One of the more famous is **St. Barnabas Church** in the village of Liberta. It is known in the area as the **Chapel of Ease**. The church was built more than 100 years ago of Antiguan green stone. **Green Bay** was built by the Moravians in 1845 for the emancipated slaves, and the **Spring Gardens Church**, built in 1755, was also erected for their benefit. Prior to that time they worshipped under an old tree. Another enchanting church is in **Parham**, built in 1840 in Italian style.

East End is ruggedly beautiful and isolated. It is home to **Indian Town**, one of Antigua's national parks at the northeastern point on the island. Over the centuries Atlantic breakers have lashed the rocks, carving a breathtaking natural bridge known as **Devil's Bridge**. It is surrounded by blowholes with foaming surf. It is also the site of an archeological excavation of Carib Indian remains. A newer

sight is **Potworks Dam**, the largest manmade lake on the island. It has shrunk because of a prolonged dry spell in recent years, but still provides for most of the island's water supply.

On any island with more than 300 beaches, watersports and beachcombing invariably have to be the main attraction. **Dickenson Bay** is one of the best beaches and probably the most populated: there are local vendors selling dresses, jewelry and crafts, as well as relaxed sunbathers, waterskiers, windsurfers, parasailors and sailors. There are also several dive operations here. Major hotels can book visitors on the 108-foot "pirate ship", the *Jolly Roger*. It sails along the coast and offers sun, fun, rum drinks and lunch along with a pleasant stop for snorkelers.

English Harbour

The climax of an island tour is without a doubt a visit to the old British navy station **English Harbour** at the southwesternmost point of Antigua. The restored harbor and wharf buildings around **Nelson's Dockyard** line the protected bay.

The restoration of the ancient naval base, however, has not created a lifeless museum but in fact a lively center for sailors, history buffs and anyone who enjoys lounging in a four-poster canopy bed in a building that once housed 18th-century engineers.

The engineer's office has been rejuvenated as the 22-room **Admiral's Inn**. It stands on the site where Admiral Nelson strolled about when ever his *HMS Boreas* was in port. Pop-star Madonna stayed here in a corner room with a big canopy bed. The terraces and lawns sweep right down to the water's edge. The storehouse for copper and timber is now the **Copper & Lumber Store Hotel**, with 14 suites. The suites, really apartments, have an 18th-century flair with all the comforts and amenities of the 20th century. They are named after ships that fought in the Battle of Trafalgar: *Boreas, Collingwood, Agamemnon* and *Britannia*.

Canvas is still stitched in the Sail Loft. The white clapboard **Admiral's House** is now a museum of Nelson memorabilia and a gift shop. Nelson himself never actually lived here, but it does contain what might have been his bed, a four-poster of gilded ivory-colored wood. In the museum guest books are the signatures of modern-day British royalty: "Philip, 1964", and "Margaret, October 21, 1981", and "Elizabeth R."

It was Prince William Henry, Duke of Clarence and friend of Nelson, who built **Clarence House** on the hill opposite the dockyard so that he could escape the heat and bustle. Later on, Clarence House hosted one of his descendants, Princess Margaret, who stayed here on the occasion of her Caribbean honeymoon. Nowadays it serves as the country residence of the Governor and is open to the public if no official guests are staying there.

In 1985, the dockyard and the surrounding countryside, an area of about 15 square miles all told (about 40 sq. km) was declared a national park. It includes Falmouth Harbour, Cobb's Cross and **English Harbour Town** just north of Nelson's dockyard. The ridge of hills above the town was fortified in 1787 by General William Henry Shirley and came to be known as **Shirley Heights**. Along the road to the summit of Shirley Heights, there are fortifications, barracks and powder magazines for the troops that guarded the dockyard from potential invaders. The Antigua Historical Society has identified all the ruins and published a complete map of the facilities along the route. Its restaurant provides light refreshments and a stunning view of the harbor. It also presents occasional dinner/theater evenings with buffets of local fare and plays by Caribbean writers.

An Interpretation Center was opened on Dow's Hill, where the turbulent history of the country is presented in grand style.

English Harbor is still a place of bol-

Above: The bobby's helmet is only one item recalling Antigua's closeness to England.

lards and hawsers, capstans and anchors, chandlers and carpenters, in its modern role as home port to one of the Caribbean's largest charter yacht fleets. The best time to see the dockyard is during *Antigua Sailing Week* in late April beginning of May.

Sailing Week is a time for serious and off-the-wall competition and festivities. Desmond Nicholson, archeologist and director of the museum, and Howard Hulford, owner of the Curtain Bluff Hotel, originated the event toward the end of the 1960s with the intention of extending the winter season a bit with a "little boat race." Sailing Week is now heralded among the ten best yacht races in the world. More than 100 boats compete in the race, which traditionally begins on the last Sunday in April. The regatta consists of five races, ranging from about 15 to 30 miles in length, with overnight stops at three different anchorages around the island. This helps to spread the action around the island rather than concentrating it entirely at English Harbor, the traditional center of yachting.

There are massive beach parties after each race. Locals and visitors alike join in as steel and reggae bands, food tents and assorted vendors converge for a night of merry-making. Shirley Heights provides an ideal vantage point for several races.

But not every day is devoted to serious racing. Tuesday is *Lay Day,* an excuse for nautical fun and games. *Dockyard Day* on Saturday brings the activities to a close with another afternoon of silliness known as the *Non-Mariner's Race.* Entering vessels must not cost more than $25 to build and must never have been in the water before the start of the race.

Saturday evening is a classy finale to the week – *Lord Nelson's Ball,* one of the social events of the year. The Governor-General himself hands out the awards at the ball which is traditionally held at the Admiral's Inn.

BARBUDA

Barbuda is one of the last frontiers of the Caribbean. The Spanish called the island *Dulcina*. Most people will immediately think of Bermuda or Barbados whenever it is mentioned. But Barbuda, a small coral island, is one of the most undeveloped islands in all the Caribbean and hence a special tip for serious scuba divers. Its 62 square miles of scrub and miles of pink sands are just 15 minutes away by small plane from Antigua.

The main town, **Codrington**, is named after Christopher Codrington, who was once the governor of the Leeward Islands. He is believed to have deliberately wrecked ships on the reefs circling the island.

He received Barbuda in 1691 from the British Crown in return for "one fat pig per year, if asked." According to legend, Codrington used the island as a breeding station for strong slaves suited for sugar cane plantation life in the West Indies. Whatever the real story, a large number

of residents still bear the name Codrington. The family also fished and farmed the island for almost 200 years in order to provide supplies for their plantations located on Antigua.

Most of the island's 1200 residents live in, and somewhere around, Codrington. For the most part, the rest of the island is unmarred by development. A drum and siphon constitute the gas station. Left mostly to themselves over the centuries, Barbudians have evolved their own special system of common land use.

The **Frigate Bird Sanctuary**, one of the largest in the world, is two miles by boat from Codrington's pier. From a small skiff puttering in and out of the mangrove bushes, visitors can watch male frigate birds with their scarlet neck pouches puffed up like bright balloons as they swoop and soar to woo the female birds. The mangroves stretch over miles in the Codrington Lagoon.

Above: On an excursion to the Frigate Bird Sanctuary in the Codrington Lagoon.

Other curiosities of the island include the mighty **Martello Tower**, a fortification dating to the 19th century.

Hunters and fishermen are attracted to Barbuda as it has some fallow deer, guinea fowl, pigeon and even boars. Those interested in fishing for bonefish and tarpon can negotiate trips with owners of small boats.

Barbuda is basically a day trip from Antigua although there are three hotels to stay overnight and only one resort, **Coco Point Lodge** (on the southern tip of the island). The latter seems to make a fetish out of its remoteness. Guests return year after year. Secrecy and privacy are what this place is all about. It has its own airstrip and guests can fly in and be drinking a rum punch on the beach 15 minutes after landing alongside a private two-and-a-half mile (4 km) beach. Barbuda means natural beauty and a serenity that is hardly equalled in the Caribbean.

About three-quarters of a mile away from Coco Point Lodge is another luxury resort complex named the **K-Club**.

ANTIGUA AND BARBUDA
(Area code: 1268)
Access and Local Transportation
American Airlines and BWIA fly direct to Antigua from New York and Miami daily. Air Canada and BWIA fly direct from Toronto. BWIA also flies from Baltimore and Miami and twice a week from London. British Airways flies non-stop from London four times a week. LIAT provides air links to 20 other Caribbean islands. LIAT also has daily flights to Barbuda (15-minute flight). Air and boat charters are also available to Barbuda.

Antigua is a very popular cruise-ship stop during the winter season when as many as 40 cruise ships dock at Deepwater Harbour each month. However, cruise stops continue throughout the year.

On Antigua taxis are always available at the airport, in St. John's, at Deepwater Harbour and at the hotels. Printed information on taxi rates is available in the tourist offices and in hotels. It is always best to agree with the driver on the fare before you set out. Drivers are also unofficial tour guides. Taxis for touring can be hired by the hour or the day. Public transport does exist, but it's not very reliable.

Car rental is the best way to get around. Driving is on the left. You must have an Antiguan driver's license which can be obtained at the airport or the police station in St. John's for about 12 US$ with a valid US license. Rates for rental cars are about 50 US$ a day and 270 US$ a week. During holiday times you should remember to reserve a rental car before arriving. There are a variety of rental firms including Budget, Carib Car Rentals, National, Hertz, Sunshine, and Village Car Rentals.

Formalities and Currency
Citizens of the USA and Canada need proof of citizenship (passport, birth certificate or voter's registration) plus an onward or return tickety. Citizens of other countries need a passport.

The official currency is the Eastern Caribbean Dollar (EC$), called *Bee Wee*, valued at about 2.68 EC$ to 1 US$. Banks exchange at the day's rate. Credit cards (VISA, AMEX, Diners) and traveler's checks are accepted at hotels and many shops and restaurants.

ANTIGUA
Accommodations
EXPENSIVE: **Jumby Bay** is a super luxurious private-island resort for a maximum of 76 guests who enjoy two lovely beaches, water sports, tennis and all food and drinks for between US$ 990 and 1650 per day for two in the winter season. There are no clocks, telephones or radios; Tel: 462-6000, Fax: 462-6020.. **Curtain Bluff Resort** is clubby. Tennis courts and a resident pro, yacht for day sails, two beaches and water sports. Men must wear ties after 7 p.m. Tel: 462-8400, Fax: 462-8409. **St. James' Club**, private yacht club, two big pools, beaches, riding, nightclub/disco, casino.

MODERATE TO BUDGET: **Halcyon Cove Beach**, Dickenson Bay Beach, Tel: 462-0256, Fax: 462-0271. **Hawksbill Beach Resort**, Tel: 462-0301, Fax: 462-1515, lovely beachfront site, water sports, pool and tennis. **Royal Antigua**, Tel: 462-3733, Fax: 462-3732; casino, water sports, tennis courts. **Admiral's Inn**, 200-year-old hostelry in the heart of Nelson's Dockyard. Most of the dockyard's social life is centered here. No beach, but the hotel will transport guests across the harbor to one nearby, Tel: 460-1153, Fax: 460-1534. **Copper & Lumber Store Hotel**, unique setting in Nelson's Dockyard. Rooms with 18th-century furnishings and kitchens. No sport facilities but transport to beach. Tel: 460-1058, Fax: 460-1529

Restaurants
Julian's, international and local cuisine at the heart of St. John. **Pascal's French Restaurant**, an elegant French restaurant, Five Island. **Dubarry's** in Barrymore Hotel in St. John's features lobster and other seafood. **L'Auberge de Paris** on Dickenson Bay spezializes in French and West Indian cooking. **Latherfield Restaurant** on Hodges Bay about eight miles northeast of St. John's occupies a yellow-and-white Victorian house and an American-born chef serves up unusual dishes such as *California cioppino,* a fish stew. **Pavillion** features Antiguan lobster or the catch of the day. It is about three miles south of St. John's. **Shirley Heights Lookout** was the 1790s lookout station for advance warning of unfriendly ships heading toward English Harbor. It is now a romantic restaurant. Specialties include pumpkin soup and grilled lobster. Friday is Caribbean night when a buffet of local and Caribbean dishes is served. There is also live entertainment. On Sundays there is a barbecue with hours of entertainment from 3 p.m. to midnight. **Crabb's Pier 5** overlooks a particularly opulent marina and serves lunch and dinner.

BARBUDA
Accommodations
EXPENSIVE: **Coco Point Lodge**, Tel: 462-3816, Fax: 462-5340; open from November 15 to May 1. Rates include air transfer from Antigua and three meals a day. K-Club, Tel: 460-0300, Fax: 460-0305, open from Nov. 15 to Aug. 30.

Tourist Information
The **Antigua Department of Tourism**, Box 363, St. John's, Tel: 462-0480. Also at the V.C. Bird Intl' Airport, Heritage Quay and at the ship terminal in St. John's, and corner Thames and Long Streets.

GUADELOUPE

BEACHES, FORESTS AND VOLCANOES

GUADELOUPE
DOMINICA

If there were an official and objective system of rating the West Indies, Dominica and the two beautiful French islands that flank it, Martinique and Guadeloupe, would rank at the very top. Located at the easternmost arc of the archipelago, where the Windwards and Leewards meet, these volcanic islands certainly rank among the most beautiful in the Caribbean in terms of landscape.

GUADELOUPE

Columbus sighted Guadeloupe, which the Caribs called *Karukera* ("land of beautiful waters") in 1493, on his second voyage. He named it after *Santa Maria de Guadelupe de Estremadura*, fulfilling a vow he had made to the monks at a monastery in Spain after surviving a storm.

Only on his third voyage, in 1496, did Columbus set foot upon one of the islands, which he named after his flagship *Maria Galanda*. The French began colonization in 1635 and imported the first slaves 15 years later. Guadelupe was annexed by Louis XIV of France in 1674, and, for the sake of French spelling, an "o" was added to its name. Maria Galanda became **Marie-Galante**.

Left: The French sense of style has come over the ocean to the island of Guadeloupe.

Although Guadeloupe was occupied by the English between 1759 and 1763, Louis XV ceded lands in Canada to England in 1763 in exchange for restoration of his West Indian holdings. During the French Revolution, Guadeloupe's own reign of terror under Victor Hugues resulted in execution or exile of plantation owners and in the emancipation of the slaves. Under the Consulate and the Empire of Napoleon I, slavery was restored, and in 1815, France salvaged this overseas possession out of the Congress of Vienna that, at least temporarily, restored the Bourbon monarchy. In 1848, Victor Schoelcher finally freed the slaves permanently. Indentured laborers from India soon replaced them, but Guadeloupe never again truly prospered with an agricultural economy.

In 1946, Guadeloupe became an overseas department of France, administered by a prefect and an elected legislature, and represented in Paris by two senators and four deputies. French subsidies have kept the local economy going. Today, however, there is a substantial radical movement pushing for independence.

The island is shaped like a tilted butterfly, with a narrow strait called La Rivière Salée separating Grande-Terre, the northeastern "wing," from Basse-Terre, the southwestern one.

GUADELOUPE

PARC NATUREL

Grande-Terre is flatter and still a lot more agricultural, with sugar cane, bananas and livestock as main products. The coast is largely made up of white sand beaches. Grande-Terre has been referred to as a tropical Normandy. Basse-Terre is more mountainous and more scenic. It is also known for its dark sand beaches.

Pointe-à-Pitre on Grande-Terre, near the Rivière Salée, is Guadeloupe's largest town, prime business center and air gateway. Basse-Terre, the town which is the namesake of the butterfly's other wing, is Guadeloupe's administrative capital. It is also the prettier town, with a greater concentration of old buildings and a picturesque location between Soufrière and the sea.

Around Basse-Terre

Pont de la Gabare, the bridge over the **Rivière Salée**, is the spot where most chose to begin a tour of this "butterfly wing." The expressway forks at the **Baie-Mahault**. The road heading north passes first through **Lamentin**, which lies in the midst of an extended sugar cane area. To find out more about the sweet business, stop at the **Compagnie Fermière de Grosse Montagne**, an operating sugar refinery, and, give or take a few extra miles, you may want to take investigate the spirits at the **Musée du Rhum** to the northwest of **Ste. Rose**, which documents the rum industry on the island.

The road proceeds along hundreds of turns down the western coast. The black sand beaches and recondite bays give the landscape here a very special touch. **Basse-Terre**, the capital of Guadeloupe, is in the lower southwestern corner. It's a pretty town, founded in 1640, and still showing a great deal of colonial architecture. The **jardin botanique** (botanical gardens) is one of the attractive sights in town. A historic place of interest is Fort St. Charles, a massive fortified construction over the **Rivière du Galion** that has

been guarding the southern part of town since the time of its founding.

A well-improved road leads through pretty landscapes to Trois-Rivières, where the **parc archéologique des Roches Gravées** begins. Many rock carvings (petroglyphs) done by Arawak Indians about 1000 years ago can be seen in this open-air museum.

The next town on the way is **Bananier**, the hub of the local banana industry. A little road to the noth leads into the Parc Naturel to the **Chutes du Carbet** that tumble down three levels on the eastern slope of the Soufrière volcano.

Besides its fine bays for swimming, **Capesterre-Belle-Eau** has a large Hindu population that does its worship at the **Temple de Changy**. And to the north of Petit-Bourg begins the **Route de la Traversée**, which crosses the Parc Naturel to reach Mahaut on the west coast.

Above: The beach at Deshaies is shadowed by a row of palm trees. Right: Few still wear traditional costumes.

Parc Naturel

The centerpiece of **Basse-Terre** and one of the highlights of the West Indies is **Parc Naturel**, 74,100 acres of tropical splendor, scenic uplands, pristine lakes, rushing waterfalls and rain forests. Once-abundant raccoons, agoutis and iguanas have been nearly extinguished, but it is hoped that these species will regenerate within the park.

Soufrière, a 4813-foot (1467 m) volcano, is the highest point on Guadeloupe and the park's main attraction. The volcano's latest eruptions in 1956 and 1976/77 left a legacy of steaming fissures, fumaroles and sulphur vents. Both craters are still smoking, a sign of activity.

The rather difficult road to the summit begins at the parking lot **Savanne à Mulets**. In addition to the main visitor center, interpretative stations give some interesting information about the volcano, the flora and fauna, the rain forest, coffee cultivation and even the sea, which can be seen from the park's

NEARBY ISLANDS

heights. Two waterfalls grace the parc, the **Cascade aux Ecrevisses**, which tumbles into a cool pool, and the aforementioned Chutes du Carbet.

Grande-Terre

Guadeloupe's busy commercial center, **Pointe-à-Pitre,** on **Grande-Terre**, was leveled by an earthquake in 1843. It was rebuilt, but visited by a variety of other natural catastrophes, including fires and standard Caribbean hurricanes. Today's city is an eclectic mix of semi-old, semi-new and brand new construction.

The heart of Pointe-à-Pitre is **Place de la Victoire**, the original market square and now a busy and attractive park, recently refurbished and replanted. There are old buildings with typical wrought-iron balconies and antique charm and a fine church, **Basilique de St. Pierre et St. Paul**, completed in 1847 and nicknamed the "Iron Cathedral" because of its framework of bolted iron ribs to protect it from destruction by hurricane or earthquake.

Office buildings, a couple of active markets, a busy harbor and two interesting local museums, the **Musée Schoelcher** and the **Musée Saint-John Perse**, named after the winner of the 1960 Nobel Prize for Literature, complete the Pointe-à-Pitre picture. The new Centre des Arts et de la Culture, is a dynamic addition to cultural life in Guadeloupe, as is the Librairie Générale, a bookstore and gallery specializing in the works of local artists and writers.

A drive along the coastal road of Grande-Terre brings ample rewards, quaint villages, lively resorts, startlingly beautiful coastlines, swamps of mangroves and sheltered beaches and bays. **Gosier**, a little town on the southern coast of Grande-Terre, is into Guadeloupe's main resort strip, and **St. François** is coming along in that direction. In addition to endless acres of sugar cane,

Grande-Terre offers some points of interest. The **Fort Fleur d'Epée** is the ruins of an 18th-century fortress. **Ste. Anne** and **St. François** are also much appreciated vacation areas on the southern coast. The mansion called **Zevallos** is located on the eastern tip. Also worthwhile are the first colonial capital at **Le Moule** and an Arawak village called **Morel**, recently uncovered by archaeologists. The **Musée d'Archéologie Précolombienne Edgar Clerc** in **La Rosette** has exhibits from this era.

Idyllic Islands

Excursions to the nearby islands of **Marie-Galante**, south of Grande-Terre, and **Îles des Saintes**, a cluster of eight little islands south of Basse-Terre, are rewarding sidetrips. Marie-Galante is a tranquil oasis where sugar cane remains king and distilleries still produce potent rum (and where there also is a small rum museum at the prize-winning **Distillerie Poisson**). For touring by moped or bicycle Marie-Galante's 59 square miles are just ideal. One should make a stop at **Château Murat**, an 18th-century manor and one of the French West Indies' best-preserved wind mills and a sugar refinery. The area abounds in natural beauty, including the **Gueule du Gouffre**, a rocky abyss on the Atlantic coast; **La Grande Barre**, a green highland which divides the island into two plateaus; and the **Trou au Diable**, a sea-level grotto which can be visited with a guide.

Only two of the eight Îles-des-Saintes are inhabited – mainly by fishermen and their families. The largest is **Terre-de-Haut**. Its jagged shoreline comprised of rocky coves and quiet bays is a playground for watersports enthusiasts of any kind. The island's leading curiosity is **Fort Napoléon**, built in the early 19th century, long after the last shots were exchanged between the French and English.

Beaches

Guadeloupe beaches excel in quantity as well as quality. Most public beaches are free, though some levy a parking fee or a small charge for use of the changing facilities. Beachfront hotels and motels always do. Most hotel beaches are topless (optional, of course), but modesty is encouraged at village beaches. Guadeloupe has a handful of nude beaches, of which **Pte. Tarare** is the most popular. **La Créole Beach** in Gosier is referred to as the Riviera of Guadeloupe, which flatters the rocky French version as this one here is a beautiful strip of beach with fine white sand and small hotels (the largest has just 186 rooms). Excellent beaches are also found at **Port Louis**, **Le Moule** and **Petit-Canal**. Basse-Terre's unique dark-sand beaches are breathtaking, whereas Marie-Galante's honey-hued sand beaches and turquoise water are spectacular and secluded. **Anse Canot**, **Vieux Fort** and **Capesterre** are the best beaches in the area.

Sports

Water is the dominant factor here, with deep-sea fishing, sailing, waterskiing, etc. Guadeloupe was also one of the first Caribbean islands to catch surfing fever. **Pigeon Island** is considered one of the world's ten top diving spots, according to the late marine biologist Jacques Cousteau. If you've had enough of the salty water for a while, you can go climbing in Parc Naturel, and there is also an 18-hole golf course, 41 tennis courts, horse races and cock fights.

Cuisine

Guadeloupe is not different to its political status, a tropical version of a distant French province, where the **patois** is Creole, the cuisine is an adaptation based on local ingredients, but where the Gallic background still stands out sharply, even in a multi-cultural society with strong African and East Indian roots. The business and bureaucratic pace is that of provincial France, where offices and shops close for a civilized lunch hour, and wine is the beverage of choice with meals – truly an anomaly within this original home of rum.

French cuisine, both classic and *nouvelle*, is abundant on Guadeloupe, but its native distinctive Creole creations are memorable. Among the characteristic dishes are *palourdes* (tiny clams in a herb-flavored broth), *crabe farci* (land crabs stuffed with a spicy filling) and *colombo* (goat curry, whose name as well as its seasonings obviously give away its Asian origin). Others include *blaff* (fish poached with lime and garlic), *cribiches* (fresh-water crayfish), *migan* (breadfruit with lemon juice and salt pork), *christophenes* (a delicate green squash) and *oursins* (sea urchin).

Right: Dominica is frequently also called "Rainbow Island", and not without reason.

Music and Nightlife

If Guadeloupe's cuisine and language display a dominant French tenor, its music takes more after its African roots. *Gwoka* is a traditional form of African music that accompanies daily activities, while newer *zouk* combines European instruments and melodies with the potent beat of drums, drawn from the African *ka* and the local *gwoka*.

Local clubs devoted to *gwoka* for listening and *zouk* for dancing draw adventurous music-lovers, but the major hotels put on tamer folklore shows, which include the usual Caribbean mix of steel drums and calypso with variations on an indigenous theme. Discos and nightclubs are found at major tourist areas such as Gosier and St. François.

DOMINICA

Although it is the largest and most mountainous of the English-speaking islands, **Dominica** feels small, because it has only 82,000 inhabitants, little development, an effusive display of natural beauty and a friendly atmosphere. Christopher Columbus reached Dominica a few days before he made his way to Guadeloupe. It was Sunday (November 3, 1493), so he called the island that in Latin.

The Spanish, as was so often the case, showed little interest in the island, and by the 17th century it was in British hands. The French, however, were not immune to its economic charms, namely good soil and climate, and started establishing their own plantations. Tension led to push, push led to shove, and soon the two colonial powers were bickering and skirmishing over a piece of real estate that didn't belong to them in the first place. The native Caribs soon nicknamed their island "Land of Many Battles."

The Treaty of Aix-la-Chapelle signed between the two countries in 1748, left the Caribs the land, but the French still coveted their little *Dominique*. After winning the Seven Years War against

France, the British took control of the island, but still had to be wary of their Gallic neighbors whose presence was felt from Martinique and Guadeloupe. The French were ultimately thrown out in 1805, and they burned down their capital Roseau on departing.

In 1939, Dominica was shifted from the Leeward to the Windward Island Federation and given more attention by the British government after much neglect. In 1978, it gained its independence while remaining in the Commonwealth. Mary Eugenia Charles acted as Prime Minister from 1980 to 1995, the first woman in the Americas to hold such a high political position.

Carnival begins two weeks before Ash Wednesday. Afro-Caribbean elements are obvious, but the French tradition is strong. France is also linguistically present in the local patois, even though. English is the official language.

Roseau and Back

Roseau, the capital and largest town on Dominica, located a mile from the nearest deepwater harbor, is a pleasant little town caught in a time warp. It was rebuilt on a grid pattern after the 1805 fire, and still has a very colonial look. The **Old Market Plaza** is now a pedestrian zone. Its rows of wooden houses add to the quaint flair of the town, while the Saturday market itself is held at the north end of **Bay Street** at the mouth of the **Roseau River**. **Tropicrafts** is a tiny manufacturer founded by Belgian missionaries after World War Two. Their specialties are basketworks, grass mats, handbags and dolls. Roseau also has other handicraft centers selling fine local work.

The **Botanical Gardens** located to the east of town, have recovered from Hurricane David and once again display local flora and imported goods in full glory.

Other nice towns to visit are **Soufrière** and **Scott's Head** to the south; **Canefield**, **Massacre** and **Portsmouth** on the west coast; and **Rosalie**, **Castle Bruce** and **Marigot** on the east coast. The **Transinsular Road**, the main route running through Marigot and **Roger**, connects the east and west coasts. Near **Pont Cassé**, right at the center of the island, are several intersections. The coastal road has beautiful views, but drivers should pay attention.

Dominica's most beautiful beaches are remote and solitary. **Prince Rupert Bay** is a long, golden beach on the northwestern coast. **Pointe Baptiste**, **Calibishie** and **Hampstead** are pure white sand beaches, while to the north of Marigot, the beaches are covered with black sand.

Dominica's rocky, rugged coastline has already been discovered by scuba divers. The **Dominica Undersea National Park** was created a few years ago around **Douglas Bay** near Portsmouth.

Rain Forest and Volcanoes

Dominica is one of the last pristine islands, a land of volcanic origin with fog-enshrouded mountains of mysterious and enchanting beauty, primeval forests, swiftly flowing rivers that cascade down from dizzying heights, bizarrely shaped cliffs rising from the sea, and a peerless assortment of plants, animals, birds and insects.

The rain forest, which grows between 1000 and 2500 ft above sea level (300 and 760 m), is a luscious, fertile ecosystem, where plants grow to unbelievable sizes. Farther up, the misty forests tend to have a dense low growth.

More than 135 bird species have yet been identified on Dominica. The *sisserou* (or imperial parrot) and its relative, the *jaquot* (or red-necked parrot), are indigenous to the island and currently on the endangered species list. Forest thrush, blue-headed hummingbirds, as well as purple-throated caribs and Antillean crested hummingbirds can also be seen.

DOMINICA

DOMINICA

In addition to the usual cast of Caribbean fauna, Dominica is home to such species as the generically namede *crapaud* (an indigenous frog), *tête-chien* (boa constrictor) and a rare iguana. More benignly, hawksbill, leatherback and green turtles nest in coastal sands.

Much of the southeastern part of the island has been incorporated into the **Morne Trois Pitons National Park**. Hiking here is very good, but you should never go without a gude, as a large part of the park has not been explored yet.. The **Middleham Trails** lace through the rain forests of the park's northwestern sector, and other trails lead to the volcanic high country.

East of Roseau is a small path leading through the Roseau River Valley to **Trafalgar Falls**, a chain of hot and cold water falls that now and then dry up owing to activity from the hydroelectric plant upstream. Natural phenomena up here are legion and all inter-related. To the northwest comes **Ti Trou Gorge**, a gorge where warm water from **Boiling Lake** flows to meet a cold stream before pouring into **Freshwater Lake**.

Boiling Lake, the second-largest such natural wonder on earth (only New Zealand has a bigger one, and Hévìz in Hungary is only warm by comparison), is a six-mile (9 km) guided hike from Laudat. It has a diameter of 300 feet (100 m). The lake lies in **Desolation Valley**, thus named because sulfuric emissions have killed the surrounding forest.

In the center of this volcanic island is the **Northern Forest Reserve**, where Dominica's highest point, **Morne Diablotin**, rises 4747 feet (1447 m) above sea level. It may be climbed with a guide.

On the northwestern tip of the island, is **Cabrits National Park**, two dry woodland hills separated by a marsh. **Fort Shirley**, an 18th-century fort and museum, is situated on a small peninsula jutting out just north of Portsmouth.

Finally, there is the stark and battered east coast, where about 2000 Caribs still reside in the **Carib Indian Reservation** It is in fact the Caribbean's last enclave of the pure descendants of pre-Columbian peoples still ruled by a tribal chief. **Salybia** is the jumping-off point for a tour into this 4500-acre-reserve inhabited by about 2000 Caribs.

Cuisine

The cuisine is less international than on other islands, and local specialities are particular to just this island. *Crapaud*, a mountain toad, is a local delicacy sometimes nicknamed "mountain chicken." *Tee-ree-ree* are delightfully named, powerfully seasoned fishcakes. Freshwater crayfish and stuffed land crabs, the local version of *crabe farci*, are delicious. Tropical fruits and vegetables abound, and they are always fresh.

Above: The beaches on Dominica are for the most part black sand ones.

GUIDEPOST GUADELOUPE / DOMINICA

GUADELOUPE
(Area code 590)
Access and Local Transportation

American Airlines and Air France serve Guadeloupe via San Juan. Air Guadeloupe flies between Guadeloupe and the Îles-des-Saintes and Marie-Galante. Caribes Air Tourisme flies to the Îles-des-Saintes. The outer islands may also be reached by boat from Pointe-à-Pitre and Trois Rivières (for Terre-de-Haut) and Grand-Bourg (for Marie-Galante). Buses, taxis and rental cars are available in Guadeloupe, Marie-Galante; mini-buses provide transport on Terre-de-Haut.

Accommodations

GUADELOUPE: *EXPENSIVE:* **Arawak**, Gosier, Tel: 842424. Lush beachfront setting. Pool, tennis (including nights), water sports. **Auberge de la Vieille Tour**, Montauban, Gosier, Tel: 842323. Located on a bluff overlooking the resort, this inn is built around an old sugar mill. Beach, pool, tennis, water sports. **Club Med Caravelle**, Ste. Anne, Tel: 882100. Attractive complex with full Club Med program. **Méridien**, B.P. 37, St. François, Tel: 885100, Fax: 884071. Top French chain's 271-room outpost in a developing resort area. Three restaurants, pool, tennis, water sports, full activities program.
MODERATE: **Bois-Joli**, Anse à Cointe, Terre-de-Haut, Îles-des-Saintes, Tel: 995038. Quiet hilltop inn with water views, nearby beach. **La Bougainvillée**, 9 rue Frebault, Pointe-à-Pitre, Tel: 901414. Best in-town hotel, top-rated restaurant. **Salako**, B.P. 97190, Gosier, Tel: 842222. Comfortable hotel. *La Caribe* disco attracts lively nightcrawlers. Many sports.
BUDGET: **Les Flamboyants**, Gosier, Tel: 841411. 14 lovely rooms in an old colonial house. **Salut**, St. Louis, Marie-Galante, Tel: 970267. Tiny guest house in a miniature town.

Restaurants

GUADELOUPE: **L'Amour en Fleurs**, Ste. Anne, Grande-Terre. **Auberge de la Vieille Tour**, Gosier. **La Balata**, Gosier. **La Belle Créole**, Murat, Marie-Galante. **Café de la Marine**, Terre-de-Haut, Îles-des-Saintes. **La Canne à Sucre**, rue Henri VI, Pointe-à-Pitre. **Chez Violetta La Créole**, Gosier. **Le Foyal**, Anse Mir, Terre-de-Haut, Îles-des-Saintes. **Le Karacoli**, Deshaies, Basse-Terre. **Le Neptune**, Grand-Bourg, Marie-Galante. **Les Oiseaux**, St. François, Grande-Terre. **Le Relais des Îles**, Pompierre Beach Rd., Terre-de-Haut, Îles-des-Saintes. **Tatie Zezzette**, Capesterre, Marie-Galante.

Festivals

Guadeloupe *Carnival* celebrations begin the first Sunday in January and culminate in three major parades in Pointe-à-Pitre. The Sunday before Lent brings the selection of the Carnival Queen and a children's parade. For five days all business stops. Floats, costumed red devils and street dancing take place on Tuesday, *Mardi Gras*. On Ash Wednesday, "King Carnival" is burned on the funeral pyre, a parade and a night-time torchlight procession ushers in *Vaval*. Guadeloupe celebrates through Ash Wednesday, and grants itself a wild mid-Lent respite with *Mi-Carême*.
During the mid-August *Fête des Cuisinières*, costumed women carry baskets trimmed with kitchen utensils and over-flowing with island specialties to the Cathedral.
The *Creole Music Festival* takes place in Pointe-à-Pitre in early November. The traditional *Young Saints' Day* (December 28) is celebrated with a children's parade and charming costumes.
Terre-de-Haut in the Îles-des-Saintes is the site of the two-day-long *Fêtes des Saintes held* in mid-August, commemorating the first British expedition in 1666.

DOMINICA
(Area code: 809)
Accommodations

MODERATE: **Castaways Beach Hotel**, Box 5, Roseau, Tel: 809-44-96244/5. Hospitable beach hotel, 11 miles from Roseau. Water sports, tennis, beach barbecues, Creole cuisine.
BUDGET: **Anchorage Hotel**, Box 34, Roseau, Tel: 809-44-82638/9. Casual 32-room hotel half a mile from the capital. Coastal views, pool, water sports, restaurant.

Restaurants

Cartwheel Café, Bay Street, Roseau. **Guiyave**, 15 Cork Street, Roseau. **Orchard**, Great George & King George V Streets, Roseau. **Papillotte's Wilderness Retreat**, near Trafalgar Falls. **La Robe Créole**, Victoria St., Roseau.

Formalities and currency

Passports are required of all visitors to Guadeloupe or Dominica.
Guadeloupe uses the French Franc ($ 1 = appr. 5.3 FF), but US and Canadian dollars are widely accepted.
Dominica uses the Eastern Caribbean Dollar (EC$), currently at $ 2,68 per dollar).

Tourist Information

Office Départemental du Tourisme, 5, Place de la Banque, 97110 Pointe-à-Pitre, Guadeloupe, Tel: 820930.
Dominica Division of Tourism, P.O. Box 293, Roseau, Tel: 448-2045, Fax: 448-5840.

MARTINIQUE

THE BEAUTIFUL TRIO

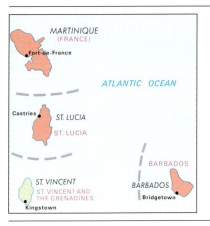

MARTINIQUE
BARBADOS
ST. LUCIA

The beautiful trio of islands located in the southeastern Caribbean is rich in constrasts. Martinique is very French, tropical and basically sprawling. Barbados is British, dry and rather small, and St. Lucia has a more Caribbean cultural mix, and is more tuned into tourism than the other two.

MARTINIQUE

Columbus discovered the island of Martinique in 1493, but first set foot on it on another trip in 1502. Already during his first trip he named it *Martinica* for St. Martin.

The French settled it 133 years later, battling the Caribs and importing slaves to work the sugar plantations. Louis XIV officially annexed the island in 1674. A British interim in 1762 ended a year later at the close of the Seven Years War between Britain and France, when the French traded off their possessions in Canada for their prosperous islands in the West Indies.

In that same year 1763, the island's most famous daughter, Marie-Josèphe Tascher de la Pagerie, was born. She

Preceding pages: Everywhere on the islands one can find traces of Christian mission (here in St. Pierre / Martinique).

went on to marry first the viscount of Beauharnais, who was executed in 1794, and then general – later emperor of France – Napoléon Bonaparte. The French Revolution stirred up the island prompting the British to invade again, but the Congress of Vienna in 1815 restored the status quo ante. Slavery was abolished in 1848. In 1946, Martinique was officially made a French overseas Department and a region in 1974.

In 1902, after days of rumbling, Montagne Pelée erupted, destroying the capital St. Pierre, killing 30,000 people, sparing only one, a prisoner in the local jail. The capital was then subsequently moved to Fort-Royal, which was renamed **Fort-de-France**.

A Lively Town

The history of this vivacious town and harbor stretches all the way back to the 17th century, but its breakthrough only came in this century. Nowadays, Fort-de-France has 120,000 inhabitants. Its narrow streets, lacey balconies and **La Savanne**, a shady 12-acre park beside a yacht-filled harbor, comprise one of the most picturesque towns in the Caribbean, certainly the loveliest of any of the larger islands. Hotels, restaurants, cafés and boutiques line the edges of Place de la

Savane, and on a spit of land to the south stands **Fort Louis**, a still-functioning military base dating from colonial times. It overlooks the entire harbor complex. To the west of the parc is the **Musée Départemental de la Martinique**, a museum with a distinct focus on pre-Columbian artifacts.

To the north is the **Bibliothèque Schoelcher**, a Byzantine-style library built by Henri Pick for the World Fair in Paris in 1889. It was dismantled and shipped to martinique. Pick, who was involved in designing the Eiffel Tower for the Eiffel Company, was also responsible for the **Cathédrale St. Louis**, a solid piece of work that replaced several predecessors all destroyed by natural disasters. The streets around the Cathédral are dotted with colorful shops among which one even finds a number of branches of major French department stores.

Above: A floating bar, special incentives for a swim in the crystal-clear waters. Right: Turn-of-the-century architecture.

To the northwest is a picturesque **fruit and vegetable market**, and on the **Rivière Madame** a lively fishmarket is held every day, where the catch of the previous night is put on appetizing display.

The great cultural event of the city is the **Festival Culturel** in July, which attracts great names from the artistic world of art, music, theater and dance.

Isle of Flowers

The Caribs called Martinique *Madinina* ("Isle of Flowers"), and indeed it is still lush and flowery. The **Jardin de Balata**, to the north of Fort-de-France, is the best known botanical garden here and a favorite with visitors who especially like tropical plants. Nearby is **Sacré-Coeur de Balata** (1928), a downscaled replica of the great white church overlooking Paris.

A trip around the 427-square-mile (1106 sq. km) island reveals its diverse nature, which is interspersed with enchanting fishing villages. Close to the capital, on the western coast, is the Baroque **Church of Case-Pilote**, a beautiful man-made work of architectural art. The **Centre d'Art Musée Paul Gauguin**, at **Anse Turin**, north of **Le Carbet**, where Columbus landed, recalls the five months the artist spent there in 1887, and exhibits works of his and of local artists.

In the vicinity are the ruins of **St. Pierre**, another must on the life list of any Martinique guest. The **Musée Volcanologique** has a very impressive display of various items unearthed after Pelée's eruption in 1906. **Cyparis Express** offers daily town tours that include a visit to the cell where the lone survivor was imprisoned.

From St. Pierre, a road leads into the island and along the east coast. Between **Le Morne Rouge** and **Ajoupa-Bouillon**, another road forks off taking you toward **Montagne Pelée** (4583 feet/1397 m), whose crater can be climbed. A hiking path leads from Ajoupa-Bouillon to the **Gorges de la Falaise**, a stretch of dramatic cascades that into a river and provide for delightful swimming.

The **Route de la Trace**, whose highest point is a stretch along the **Pitons du Carbet** volcanic group (3924 feet/1196 m) begins near **Deux-Choux**. This road, which heads for Balata and Fort-de-France, is lined on both sides by thick tropical vegetation. It is very serpentine in part, and drivers unfamiliar with it and the tropical driving style of others should take care. Deux-Choux offers an excursion eastwards and to the **Caravelle Peninsula**, where the ruins of the former mansion **Château Dubuc** stand in the middle of a nature protection area.

To the south of Fort-de-France bay is the pretty village of **Les Trois-Ilets**, where, as most believe, the Empress Joséphine was born. That hallowed site is today a museum (**de la Pagerie**). Another museum is the **Musée des Coquillages** in nearby **Anse-á-l'Ane,** which exhibits shells and handicrafts made of shells.

Close to Trois-Îlets, numerous beaches have spawned a major hotel strip. Hotel beaches permit topless bathing and frequently charge non-guests for cabanas, towels or lockers.

A ferry across the **Baie des Flamands** brings crowds from Fort-de-France to the beautiful white sands around **Point de Bout**. **Grande Anse** near **Les Anses d'Arlets** is a spectacular and very populous stretch of sand. **Anse Mitan**, by comparison, is quieter and **Anse Diamant** around the next point is a two-and-a-half-mile sweep. **Ste. Anne**, on the southwest coast, is dominated by the Club Med. On the southern tip of Martinique, **Grande Anse de Salines**, with the beaches of **Dunkerque**, **Baham** and **Anse Trabaud**, combine scenery, sun, sand and solitude.

Evenings, the resorts also have something on tap, be that the casino at the Hoetel Méridien in Trois-Îlets, or the numerous jazz clubs, piano bars and discothèques. Eatin out, too, is a special event. The classic French cuisine, French

nouvelle, traditional Creole fare and the latest *nouvelle* Creole coexist in delicious harmony.

Sports

An 18-hole golf course at Trois-Îlets enhances this place's popularity with vacationers. Tennis courts are found at the large hotels, and the Squash Hotel near Fort-de-France specializes in its namesake sport. Horseback riding is surely among the best in the Caribbean, and bicycle tours are another fabulous way to see the island.

Hiking on Montagne Pelée and elsewhere on this mountainous island is a treat for hardy adventurers. Watersports such as sailing, windsurfing, scuba diving or else deep-sea fishing are readily available. Spectator sports include some rather exotic varieties, namely: snake-, mongoose- and cockfighting.

Above: Los Barbados, the bearded ones, referred first to this fig genus.

BARBADOS

A tall bobby, sporting the typical helmet, directs traffic across a roundabout as vehicles drive around on the left side of the road. Lord Nelson's statue is the centerpiece of **Trafalgar Square**. Ladies sit in the shade, sipping tea in the afternoon. An athlete wields a cricket bat. Polo ponies thunder across a green playing field. A golfer is poised to tee off. And yet, this is not the British Isles, but the eastern Caribbean island of **Barbados**. Located 100 miles (160 km) east of the Antilles chain, Barbados is out of the Caribbean mainstream and therefore has had little trouble in preserving the character that has earned it the nickname of "Little England."

Barbados was – rather unusual for an island of the Caribbean – not discovered by Columbus. The fierce Caribs, who had earlier displaced the peaceable Arawaks, left Barbados sometime in the 16th century, and the island was later occupied by a handful of Amerindians when Portuguese stopped by en route to Brazil. They named this most windward of the Windward Islands *Los Barbados* (the Bearded), supposedly after the bearded fig trees growing there.

When Captain John Powell claimed Barbados for King James I in 1625, it was uninhabited. 80 settlers arrived two years later. Parliament first convened here in 1639. A great number of the small farmers left the island in the 1650s, when big plantations were introduced and slaves were imported. Barbados became one of England's most prosperous colonies in the following centuries. Full independence was achieved in 1966.

Bridgetown

Bridgetown is located on the southwestern corner of Barbados. It was founded in 1628, and nowadays has a population numbering 102.000. Its pleas-

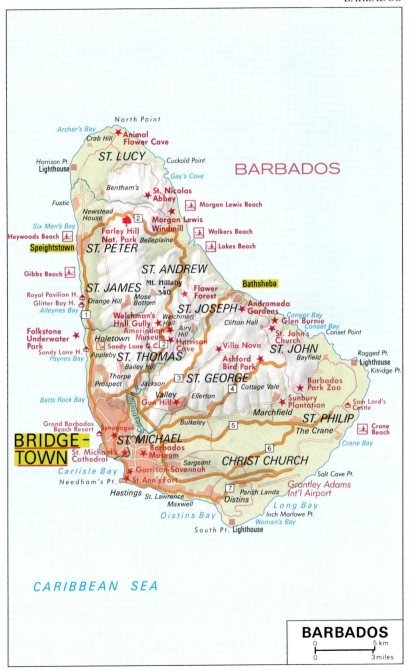

BARBADOS

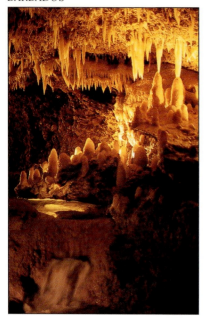

ant harbor, at the estuary of Constitution River, is called the **Careenage**. North of the Chamberlain Bridge over the harbor basin is **Trafalgar Square**, where Admiral Nelson has been standing in effigy since 1815. St. Michael's Row, which branches off to the east, takes you to **St. Michael's Cathedral** (17th-18th century).

Broad Street, which is always crowded, plunges into the consumer side of town. The colorful **vegetable and fish markets**, well worth visiting, are in the southwestern part of Bridgetown around St. Mary's Church (18th century), whose park marks the end of Broad Street.

North of town is the **synagogue** built in the 1660s by Jews who fled Recife, Brazil, making it one of the oldest extant in the Western Hemisphere. And the only time George Washington ever left North America, he slept in Barbados, in a house

Above: Spelunker's delights inside Harrison's Cave on Barbados. Right: Scenes from a back street.

on **Bay Street** (south of Chamberlain Bridge) now marked with a plaque.

On the eastern outskirts lies the former defensive complex of St. Ann's Fort, and close by the **Garrison Savannah**, with a horsetrack and the **Barbados Museum**, a complete collection documenting local culture and natural history tucked away in a former military building from the 19th century.

Exploring Little England

All roads lead to Bridgetown. The island is divided into eleven parishes, named after saints. Highway 1 follows the palm-lined western shore for about 7 miles (10 km), passing beautiful bays and recommendable hotels. In **Speightstown**, the former sugar harbor of the island, you can undertake two trips: to the north to the **Animal Flower Cave**, a sea cavern carved out of the coral limestone of the steep cliffs; or to the northeast, to the 19th-century **Farley Hill Manor** in the middle of a national park by the same name. **St. Nicholas Abbey** is quite close, one of the oldest manors on Barbados, dating back to the 17th century.

Highway 2 is the way to **Harrison's Cave**, a spelunker's paradise, in fact an entire system of caves with underground streams, lakes, stalagtites and stalagmites, and even a waterfall. **The Amerindian Museum** is a little way to the north, a documentation center for indigenous culture; and nearby too is **Welshman Hall Gully**, a rocky valley with tropical growth, and limestone and coral caves acessed by hiking paths.

Highway 3 crosses the island from Bridgetown to **Bathsheba** in the **Scotland District**. This is the east coast, marked by mellifluous hills and a shoreline pounded by the open sea. On the way there is **Gun Hill**, a 670-foot (210 m) elevation that offers by fare the most beautiful views of the island. A little further to the northeast is the **Villa Nova**, a

19th-century manor. Not far either is **Turner's Hall Woods**, a small reservation where you will find apes and other animals that are not native to Barbados. Close to Bathsheba is **Andromeda Gardens**, a botanical garden located before the dramatic background of the Atlantic coast, where luscious tropical vegetation has been tamed by English horticultural art. Finally, to the southeast is the 18th-century **St-John's Church**, which should not be missed.

As with its companions. Highway 7 passes by a number of pretty bays along the south coast and accesses the **Barbados Park Zoo**. On the other side of **Grantley International Airport** lies **Crane Bay**, site of an erstwhile pirate's castle and today a luxury hotel appropriately named **Sam Lord's Castle**. The insidious reefs along **Ragged Point** provided pirate Lord with plentiful bounty. The old estate of **Sunbury Plantation** which is also nearby, has been turned into a museum with some very fine exhibits on the colonial period.

Sports

Tennis, cricket, polo, squash, riding or else a variety of water sports – Barbados offers them all. The 18-hole **Sandy Lane Golf Course** is the site of the Barbados Amateur Open Golf Tournament on the third week in October. The island also has another three nine-hole courses.

Bicycling is becoming a very popular sport on Barbados. But the real challenge for the athletic types is *Run Barbados*, which takes place during the firstweekend in December. It has a marathon run and a 6-mile (10 km) run for men and women.

Dinner and Thereafter

Barbados may display the most British lifestyle this side of Land's End, but food, like the accent, has a distinctive Caribbean lilt. Bajan delicacies include flying fish, lobster, shrimp, dorado, red snapper, king fish, crane chubb and sea eggs (urchin roe). Other specialties, some of East Indian origins, include *cou-cou*

Above: The joy at leaving school for the day seems to be indeed international.

(cornmeal and okra), *jug-jug* (Guinea corn and peas), pepperpot (spicy meat stew), *roti* (curried meats wrapped in a pancake) and *conkies* (spiced cornmeal, coconut, some raisins, pumpkin, and sweet potatoes steamed in a banana leaf). Bajan rums are among the world's best.

As for post-prandial activities, there is a busy, sophisticated late-night scene. Popular clubs include **After Dark**, **Pepperpot**, **The Warehouse** and **The Boatyard**, all in Bridgetown. Sleek revues and nightclub entertainment are featured at larger hotels, and there are party cruises on two ships sailing out of The Careenage. For island authenticity, one might try one of the small establishments that offer Bajan music and dancing.

ST. LUCIA

First the Arawaks and later the Caribs laid early claim to this mountainous oval, which they called *Iguanalao* (place of the *iguana*). There are still disputes over the European discovery of this scenic island, the second largest of the Windwards, which is located south of Martinique and north of St. Vincent and The Grenadines. Some believe that Columbus reached it in 1502, while others think that Juan de la Cosa, Columbus's navigator, had sighted it nearly three years earlier.

But history is clear about the first British mariners to tread upon this luxuriant and scenically compelling island, and what happened to them. An English party sailing en route to Guyana was unfortunately blown off course, landed near where Vieux Fort is located today in 1605 and was promptly attacked by a group of Caribs. Only 19 of them survived and finally managed to escape from the island in canoes.

The first successful colony, however, was a French settlement established at Soufrière in 1651. Caribs battled Europeans and Europeans battled each other for dominance of this island in a manner seldom paralleled in the history of the Caribbean. St. Lucia changed hands between the English and the French 14 times within about 150 years, until the island eventually became an English plantation colony in 1824. A small number of the Caribs' descendants, though, were ultimately transplanted by the British to the reservation on nearby Dominica, but nevertheless still a handful of black Caribs remain on St. Lucia.

In 1979, the little island achieved independence while remaining within the safe framework of the big British Commonwealth. Today, the island is striving for economic vitality and extensive modernization. Tourism is seen as crucial to the St. Lucian economy by the government. In addition to sugar, coconut, coffee, citrus and sea-island cotton plantations, coal mines have been in operation since 1883, a rare natural resource in the Caribbean. The most important fruit export is

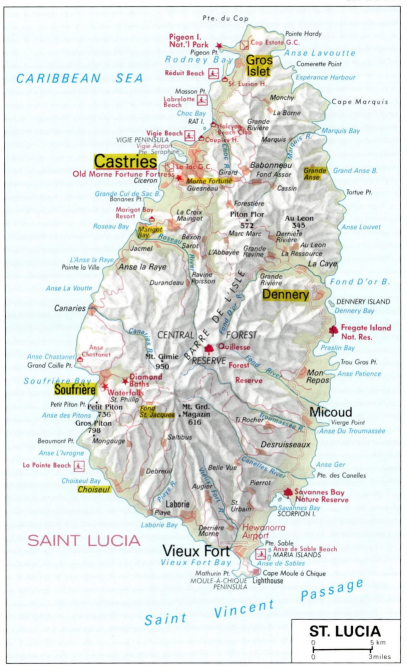

ST. LUCIA

bananas, an industry tourists can view for themselves at three plantations. Textiles, toys and sports articles are also being considered in the islands diversification programs. Lately, too, a tanker terminal was built.

Tourism over the past few years has grown into the most significant economic sector, according to the government. The island does, after all, offer every possible amenity, notably aquatic sports, sailing, surfing, waterskiing, scuba diving, snorkeling and deep-sea fishing. The drier folk can find pleasure in golf, tennis, riding and squash. Six charter companies have yachts for rent. Part of the tourism effort has resulted in a parallel project to upgrade the major roads, which are as scenic as any in the islands. There are fabulous coastal drives on both sides of the southern two-thirds of St. Lucia as well

Above: Modern technology has not improved on the old-style fishing boats. Right: The mighty Pitons, hallmark of St. Lucia and the entire Caribbean.

as a trans-island route running between the capital of Castries on the northwest coast and **Dennery** on the east-central portion. Roads also lead up the west coast to **Pointe du Cap** and to various upland attractions in the center of the island.

Luxurious hotels, condo developments and villa communities have transformed this island from a somehow sleepy place into a very busy one. Of course, the tourist boom has had two sides.

The growing number and size of hotels, the increasingly aggressive promotion of tourism such as establishing ties with international travel agencies, and the expansion of cruise-ship capacity bringing in up to 40,000 additional transient visitors, have all put a severe strain on the originally the islanders. , but its negative effects indeed are quickly felt by those who prefer a landlubber's view of the Caribbean.

Castries and Environs

Built around a deep harbor with the soaring mountains as an impressive backdrop, the city of **Castries** is ideally situated. It burned several times, the last major fire having devastated the city in 1948. Castries is therefore a modern city with no less than 50.000 inhabitants.

The **Harbor** is at the center of Castries and has always been the economic heart of the country. Nearby is the new tender jetty, Spanish-style duty-free facility with 23 shops and restaurants at **Pointe Séraphine**, which was tailor-made for the cruise crowd. The **Market** near the harbor does have a lot more color. On weekends it's a good place to find handicrafts. Woodcarving is a popular local craft. Good examples may be found at **Noah's Arkade** in Castries, **Endovic's** at Morne Fortune, **Choiseul Wood Carvers** on the south end of the island and the **Artist's Workshop** in **La Cléry.** Prety souvenirs and batiks for wall coverings or clothes can be bought at **Cari-

ST. LUCIA

belle Batik, Tapion Craft and Erma of St. Lucia.

Back to sightseeing, however. The old Morne Fortune fortress perched at the southern end of town affords a scenic view of Castries and its harbor. The little fortress museum shows pre-Columbian artifacts.

To the north of Castries lies one of the great witnesses to St. Lucia's turbulent military history, the British Naval Station at Pigeon Point. Pigeon Point, once an island, is now a 40-acre historic national park, open-air museum and beach, connected to mainland St. Lucia by a man-made causeway. The ruins of Rodney's massive fortress and an attractive beach (for swimming and picnicking) are the major sites here.

On the way to Pigeon Point is the populare Vigie Peninsula, which served as a both French and British outpost during the 18th century. The genius loci has long since taken off to other climes: Nowadays the peninsula is known as a popular spot to bathe.

In fact, the western coast of St. Lucia around Casries has quite a few nice beaches for swimming, notably the remote and solitary Labrelotte Bay. The newest yacht harbor is Rodney Bay, with 140 berths.

Picturesque Marigot Bay, lying to the south of Castries, is the harbor where *Doctor Doolittle* was filmed and where sailors now gather. A ferry ride to Doolittle's restaurant is an enchanting excursion.

Natural Wonders

Among St. Lucia's special natural features are a number of conical mountains. The highest is the Morne Gimie, standing at 3117 feet (950 m). But the island's true hallmark is the Pitons – Grand Piton at 2618 feet (798 m) and Petit Piton at 2415 feet (736 m) – twin peaks soaring into the clouds.

Near Soufrière is what is billed as the world's only drive-in volcano. Indeed, you can drive right up to the eerie moon-

scape produced by Soufrière's boiling pools, bubbling mud and steaming *soufrières*, the vents for which several Caribbean volcanos are named. It will interest the technically-minded to know that St. Lucia has tapped into the volcano to produce electricity from geothermal sources; and walking about the volcano, one can spot the installations.

The **Diamond Falls** and the **Mineral Baths** that can be admired or enjoyed nearby, are also part of Nature's special gifts on St. Lucia. The waters here reputedly even have healing powers.

A heritage and restoration program has been announced to preserve and enhance the old village of **Soufrière**, the site of the first French settlement on the island and its oldest capital as well.

Most sightseers just pass through this old town en route to St. Lucia's natural wonders, but the old section of town is currently being restored. The **Soufrière Heritage Center** and the **Historical Architectural Walk** have been established to restore the old churches, the typical gingerbread houses and other historic treasures, and a new market for arts, crafts and food now takes place daily at a permanent site.

A newly-built jetty and marine boardwalk are designed to make Soufrière more accessible as an alternative port of entry. The sand on the beach of Soufrière is also special in that it is light gray in color.

Off to the southeast lies the **National Rain Forest** in the viciniy of **Fond St. Jacques**. A tropical rain forest with exotic plants and splendid flowers still thrives in this natural preserve with a surface area of 30 square miles (77 sq. km).

The **Moule-à-Chique Peninsula**, with a lighthouse forms the southern end of the island and affords excellent views of St. Lucia and the ocean. On a clear day you can see beyond the off-shore reefs all the way to St. Vincent.

Above: Another chance for celebration during the Festival of the Rose. Right: Gearing up for a beauty contest.

Those attracted to nature and ecology will have to pay a visit to **Maria Island**, where a rare species of lizard is found and where frigate birds and other sea birds nest.

Another fine place for birdwatching is the area around Grande Anse bay on the east coast on the level of Castries. Leatherback turtles nest on St. Lucia, and excursions to watch them can always be set up through the St. Lucia Naturalists' Society.

The coasts, especially the less densely populated eastern ones, have many picturesque fishing villages which also beckon the island guest. Brightly painted wood fishing dories, which are still built and decorated in the traditional way, and fish nets hanging out to dry, both provide a colorful motif for photographers.

St. Lucia is also a fine place for hikers. Old footpaths connect most of the villages with one another, and the National Rain Forest mentioned above is crisscrossed with hiking trails of varying degrees of difficulty.

Even mountain climbers will find something to do on the two Pitons. A climb lasts about 2 hours, but you will have to find a guide. Finally, there is always the possibility of exploring the island on horseback.

Food, Festivals and Fun

French culture is part and parcel of St. Lucia's society, and not only in the dialect and place names, buit also in the cooking. French, British and East Indian influences blend freely into local Creole cuisine.

St. Lucia's specialties include pumpkin soup, pumpkin souffle, an unusual *calaloo* (spinach, dumplings and salted beef), *poule dudon* (sweet and very spicy chicken), breadfruit roasted over coals in a special clay pot and *tablette* (coconut candy). There is fresh seafood in various Creole and continental incarnations, such

as fried flying fish, snapper, kingfish and *lambi* (conch).

St. Lucia's telltale indication of Franco-British influence is in the festival calendar, which respects both *le jour de l'an*, an old two-day French celebration of the New Year, and Queen Elizabeth's birthday in June. St. Lucia's own national holiday in mid-December, is also a major celebration. A local peculiarity, too, are the many small feastdays celebrated throughout the island during the year.

Dancing is something that no one will have to miss in St. Lucia. Bars and hotels in the tourist areas, or even little rum dives around the island have some space to shake a leg. A special attraction is the *jump up* street festival that takes place in Gros Islets each Friday night with dancing to calypso, reggae, zoul, soca and American pop music, fueled by beer and rum. Tourists are welcome to the grand party. Besides quite enough to drink, there are a plethora of little food stands and snack places that will take care of the mightiest hunger.

MARTINIQUE / BARBADOS ST. LUCIA
(Area codes: Martinique 596, Barbados 1246, St. Lucia 1756)

Accommodations
MARTINIQUE: *EXPENSIVE:* **Hotel Bakoua**, Pointe du Bout 97229, Tel: 660202. Grande dame of island resorts, reopened after a multi-million-dollar renovation. Sporty beachfront for the daytime, sheer elegance in the evenings.
Hotel Frantour, Anse-à-l'Ane 97229, Tel: 83167. Newly renovated and expanded beachfront luxury resort. Extra welcoming to those with families. **Hotel le Méridien**, Pointe du Bout 97229, Tel: 660000. Modern 300-room behemoth with all luxury and convenience. Also bungalows.
MODERATE: **Impératrice**, La Savanne, Fort-de-France 97200, Tel: 630682. In-town hotel with good location and lively bar that draws in the young crowd. **PLM Azur Carayou**, Pointe du Bout 97229, Tel: 660404. Grade-A neighborhood and beachfront location at mid-price.
BUDGET: **Auberge de la Montagne Pelée**, Morne Rouge 97260, Tel: 523209. Small 12-unit inn, ideal for upcountry hikers.

BARBADOS: *EXPENSIVE:* **Glitter Bay**, Tel: 422-4111, Fax: 422-1367, and **Royal Pavilion**, Tel: 422-4444, Fax: 4220118. Exquisitely decorated sister resorts under joint management, but each with their different styles, both luxurious, opulently equipped hotels. **Sandy Lane**, St. James, Tel: 809-422-1311. Luxury resort with the best golf to be had on Barbados plus other amenities.
MODERATE: **Grand Barbados Beach Resort**, Aquatic Gap, Tel: 426-4000, Fax: 429-2400. Well-appointed 133-room hotel, bordering on the deluxe. Convenient to Bridgetown. **Sam Lord's Castle**, St. Philip, Tel: 423-7350, Fax: 423-5918. The largest island hotel. Lavishly equipped busy resort in the American style.
BUDGET: **The Nook**, Rockley, Tel: 809-429-6570. Budget two-bedroom apartments with air conditioning and maid service. Swimming pool.

ST. LUCIA: *LUXURY:* **Anse Chastanet**, Soufrière, Tel: 459-7000, quiet, special aquatic sports and tennis courts. **Rendezvous**, Malaga Beach, Tel: 452-4211, Fax: 452-7419.. All-inclusive hotel (all meals, airport transfers, sports, etc.) steeped in an atmosphere of studied romance.
Sandals St. Lucia, La Toc, Tel: 452-3081/9, Fax: 452-1012. Luxurious hotel with all amenities, including swimming, tennis and golf. **St. Lucian**, Réduit Beach, Tel: 452-8351, Fax: 452-8331, elegant complex by the seaside.
MODERATE: **Sandals Halcyon**, Choc Beach, Tel: 452-5331. Good value tropical resort with full water sports facilities, only for couples. **Marigot Bay Resort**, Marigot Bay, Tel: 451-4357, Fax: 451-4353. Studios and cottages of various sizes placed in delightful settings. Pool and watersports.
BUDGET: **Tropical Haven**, La Toc, Tel: 809-452-3505. Seven-room guesthouse, good restaurant. Vacation apartments and houses, contact: Antilles Voyages Atmosphère, 2, rue de Moulins, F-75001 Paris, Tel: (0033)-1-44778611, Fax: (0033)-1-49260363.

Restaurants
MARTINIQUE: **La Biguine**, rue de la Folie, Fort-de-France. Downstairs grill and upstairs fine dining in charming old Creole house. **La Fontane**, Route de Balata, Fort-de-France. Elegant hillside restaurant with upscale Creole cuisine. **La Grand' Voile**, Pointe Simon, Fort-de-France. Stylish upstairs restaurant near yacht club. **Le Mareyeur**, Pointe des Nègres. Creole family fare with weekend entertainment.

BARBADOS: **Bagatelle**, St. Thomas, Gourmet restaurant. **Brown Sugar**, St. Michael, Creole cuisine. **Koko's**, Prospect, St. James, view on the sea, new-Barbadian cooking. **Pisces**, Christ Church, by the seaside, fish specialties.

ST. LUCIA: **Coco's**, Gros Islet. Seafood restaurant run appropriately by a fisherman. **Eagles Inn**, Rodney Bay. Moderately priced Creole fare in garden setting. **The Green Parrot**, Columbus Square, Castries. Elegant restaurant specializing in fine Caribbean fare. Entertainment with audience participation on Saturday. **Hummingbird**, Soufrière. Relstaurant with a quiet, relaxing atmosphere, serving St. Lucian delicacies from English, East Indian and West Indian roots. **Dasheene**, Crede cooking tucked away up in the Pitons.

Access and Local Transportation
MARTINIQUE: International carriers and AOM, CORSAIR and AIR LIBERTÉ serve the Fort-de-France airport. Inter-island flights are via Air Martinique, Air Guadeloupe and LIAT.
L' Express des Iles runs a catamaran ferry service linking Martinique with Grenada, St. Barts, St. Lucia, Guadeloupe, Dominica and St. Vincent.
BARBADOS: American Airlines, BWIA and Pan Am fly to Barbados from the USA. LIAT has inter-island services. A departure tax of 20 BDS$ is levied.
ST. LUCIA: Air Canada, American Airlines, British Airways and BWIA are the international carriers serving St. Lucia. LIAT, Air Martinique and Helena Air and Caribbean Express (see Martinique above) link in with other islands.

GUIDEPOST MARTINIQUE / BARBADOS / ST. LUCIA

The departure tax is 20 EC$ if flying to another Caribbean island and 27 EC$ to a non-Caribbean destination. On all three islands, buses, private taxis, shared taxis, ferries and rental cars provide local transportation.

The taxis of the Barbados Transport Board, Tel: 436-6820, also offer tours (including guide service) either for a fixed hourly sum or for an agreed price.

Formalities and Currency

Proof of citizenship is required, along with on-going or return ticket. A passport at least six months old works best.

Martinique's legal tender is the French Franc, but US and Canadian dollars are widely accepted

Barbados' currency is the Barbados Dollar, 1 US$ is equal to 2 BDS$.

St. Lucia uses the Eastern Caribbean Dollar, currently 2.68 EC$ to 1 US$.

Festivals

MARTINIQUE: Holidays are New Year's Day, *La Fête des Rois* (Epiphany, celebrated with dancing and a cake called *galette des rois*), *Carnivale* (five days before Lent, with red devil costume parade on Shrove Tuesday the highlight), *Mi-Carême* (mid-Lent holiday with one-day reprise of carnival festivities), Easter Monday, Labor Day (May 1), Slavery Abolition Day (May 22), Ascension Thursday, Pentecost Monday, Bastille Day (July 14), Assumption Day (August 15), All Saints Day (November 1), Armistice Day (November 11), Christmas Eve and Day and New Year's Eve. Top local festivals include the *Festival of Fort-de France* (18-day art festival in July) and the *Fête Nautique du Robert* (Atlantic seaside festival on the Sundays of September).

BARBADOS: Important celebrations are the Christian holidays, New Year's Day, Errol Brown Day, January 21, (honoring Barbados's first prime minister), *Holetown Festival* (late February, English-style festival commemorating the first settlement), *Oistin's Fish Festival* (mid-April, nautical themes dominate commemoration of the signing of the Charter of Barbados), May Day, Whit Monday, *Crop Over Festival* (seven-week summer festival celebrating sugar cane harvest, ending on *Kadooment Day*), Barbados Best on Stage (July and August performing arts), United Nations Day (October 1), *Grand Bathsheba Festival* (early November, music festival), *Independence Day* (November 30), and *Mount Gay Christmas Regatta* (late December yachting event).

ST. LUCIA: Holidays and festivals are New Year's (January 1-2, a fiesta at Castries' Vigie Sports Field), Independence Day (February 22, includes parade and galas), Carnival (Monday and Tuesday before Lent), Good Friday, Easter Sunday and Monday, May Day, Whit Sunday (early June), *Corpus Christi* (mid-June), St. Peter's Day (June 29, fishermen's festival with decorated boats), Emancipation Day (August 6), *Fête de la Rose* (August 30, Feast of St. Rose de Lima, celebrated with a spectacular flower festival), Thanksgiving Day (beginning of October), *Fête de la Ste. Marguerite* (October 17, flower festival), All Saints and All Souls Day (November 1-2), St. Cecilia's Day (November 22, religious festival with music), St. Lucia's Day (December 13, national holiday commemorating Columbus' discovery of the island), Christmas Day and Boxing Day (December 26).

Museums / Art Galleries

MARTINIQUE: In Fort-de-France, the top museum is the **Musée Départmental de la Martinique**, St. Pierre, (archeology). Elsewhere are the **Musée de la Pagerie** (Empress Josephine's birthplace at Trois-Îlets) and the **Centre d'Art Musée Paul Gauguin** (Fort-de-France) and **Musée Volcanologique** (Anse Turin). Other small museums document the history of transportation, slave history and shells.

BARBADOS: The **Garrison Historical Area** is the highlight of Bridgetown's historic Garrison Savannah. Several historic plantations, some operating as house museums, are open. An **Amerindian Museum** is in St. Thomas parish.

ST. LUCIA: The museum at **Old Morne Fortune Fortress** overlooking Castries features pre-Columbian artifacts. The **Soufrière Heritage Center** documents the colonial period.

Shopping

All three islands are known both for excellent local crafts. In addition, Fort-de-France offers small branches of famous Paris shops, while St. Lucia is actively seeking the duty-free trade. Shops are concentrated in the Pointe Séraphine jetty terminal, which has a special mall for this purpose.

Tourist Information

MARTINIQUE: **Office Départemental du Tourisme de la Martinique**, Rue Ernest Deproges, 97200 Port-de-France, Tel: 637960.

French West Indies Tourist Office, 610 Fifth Avenue, New York, NY 10020, Tel: 1-212/757-1125.

BARBADOS: **Barbados Tourism Authority**, P.O. Box 242, Harbour Road, Bridgetown, Tel: 427-2623, Fax: 426-4080.

ST. LUCIA: **St. Lucia Tourist Board**, Pointe Séraphine, Castries, St. Lucia, Tel: 452-4094.

ST. VINCENT

ST. VINCENT

NUTMEG AND VANILLA

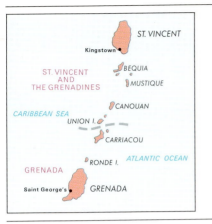

ST. VINCENT
GRENADA
THE GRENADINES

The Grenadines, with Grenada on one end and **St. Vincent** on the other, are the southernmost of the Windward Islands. In between is a chain of eight large and some 120 small islands, the tiniest of which hardly appear on a map. Only Trinidad & Tobago, which are geographically closer to South America than to the Caribbean archipelago, lie farther to the south. Grenada and St. Vincent & Grenadines, two independent mini-states, are members of the Commonwealth, and the queen is still their highest official.

ST. VINCENT

Although St. Vincent was discovered by Christopher Columbus on January 22 (St. Vincent's Day), during his third voyage in 1498, the island long remained under the control of a warlike band of Caribs, who successfully resisted all efforts at white colonization. It later passed back and forth between the English and the French.

In 1675, a slave ship sank close by, and the Africans who managed to swim ashore joined up with the Caribs. Out of their union with island women the so-called Black Caribs emerged, fierce enemies of the colonial powers throughout the Carib Wars of the 18th century. It was not until 1795 that the Black Caribs were finally defeated. Most were exiled first to the island of Baliceaux and later to Roatan, off the coast of Honduras, but a small group of their descendants still lives in the village of Sandy Bay.

The ultimate victory over the Black Caribs in 1804 meant that the British finally were the undisputed rulers of the island. In 1871, it was integrated into the Windward Islands as a Crown colony. Colonial status tapered off in 1969 when St. Vincent became an associate Commonwealth state and ended with independence in 1979, with the island nation remaining in the British Commonwealth. St. Vincent governs most of the nearby Grenadines, including Young Island, Bequia, Mustique, Canouan, Tobago Cays, Mayreu, Union Island, Palm Island and Petit St. Vincent.

St. Vincent has struggled with nature as well as with man-made disasters. For instance, the island's major volcano, Soufrière, erupted in 1812, 1902, 1971 and 1979. The 1902 eruption was the worst, killing 2000 Vincentians. A massive tidal wave in 1896 and major hurricanes in 1898 and 1980 also took their toll both in human lives and in economic terms.

Preceding pages: The marketplace in St. George's, Grenada, is always lively. Left: Dealing in nutmeg, an island specialty.

ST. VINCENT

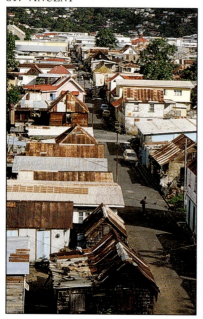

Above: Kingstown's corrugated iron roofs rust quickly in the warm and damp air.

St. Vincent has been called one of the most British isles of the West Indies, yet the fabric of its society is also woven of African, Portuguese, East Indian and modern pan-Caribbean threads. Most hotels and restaurants are clustered in Kingstown and in the bays to the east. Accordingly, that is the touristic center of the island.

Capital Kingstown

St. Vincent is shaped like an oval with a slightly flattened southwestern coast where **Kingstown**, the pleasant capital, is located. The hills form a verdant backdrop, and the harbor is busy with traffic in inter-island ferries, pleasure boats and small cruise ships. Unusual arcades give this tropical downtown an interesting olfashioned ambience quite different from many places in the Caribbean. Kingstown looks much as it did in the 18th and 19th centuries, thanks to a good number of older extant buildings. Its old-fashioned market still takes place Saturday mornings on **Bay Street**.

Three churches are the leading landmarks, the Anglican **St. George's Cathedral**, the **Methodist Church** and **St. Mary's Catholic Church**, the latter an eclectic complex originally completed in 1823 and renovated in the 1900s. Its rather fanciful style is obviously drawn from several architectural inspirations, none of them indigenous.

Fort Charlotte, built in 1806, towers 600 feet (200 m) above Kingstown and offers spectacular vistas of the town and the Grenadines. In the old officers quarters is an exhibition of paintings depicting the history of the Black Caribs.

St. Vincent had its **Botanical Gardens** long before it had this powerful fort. The oldest in the Western Hemisphere, they were begun in 1765 to grow medicinal plants for this remote island colony. The gardens also contain an aviary for rare parrots and the **National Museum**, with a small collection of Carib artifacts, some dating back over 6000 years.

The **St. Vincent Craftsmen Centre**, located in the western part of town, a cooperative, has an excellent selection of handicrafts, such as wood carvings, straw and batik wares, ceramics and jewelry. Many of St. Vincent's most ambitious painters display their new works in the **Bounty Café** in Kingstown. But much of the best art appears in the form of cheap and striking miniatures, namely stamps for which the island nation is well known to collectors.

The Emerald Island

Driving around this volcanic island reveals the source of the nickname "Emerald Island." Its coast is strewn with pretty little villages, where fishing and boat building are still the major enterprises. One particularly rewarding tour is

ST. VINCENT / GRENADINES

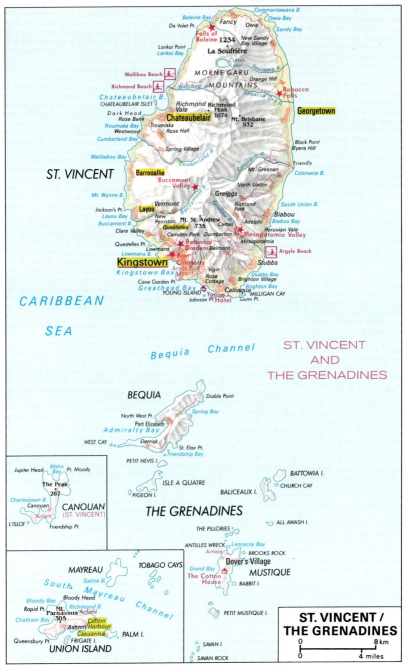

ST. VINCENT

along what is called **Queen's Drive** (which begins at Arnos Vale Airport atop Dorsetshire Hill) and **Leeward Highway** as it is later called (along the western coast).

Although St. Vincent does not have the crescent shaped bays so common to the Caribbean, it does have leeward and windward coastlines and, typically, the best beaches are on the leeward (western) side. Tucked away near such quaint villages as **Questelles**, **Layou**, **Barrouaille** and Chateaubelair along St. Vincent's beautiful west coast are pleasant black sand beaches. All of the island's numerous beaches are public. **Layou**, to the northwest of Kingstown, is especially worth visiting for its exemplary display of pre-Columbian **petroglyphs** (rock carvings). They have been estimated as dating to the 6th century AD. A triangular face was carved into the so-called

Above: In the Grenadines, often the whole village helps bring in the catch. Right: The perfect way to take some refreshments.

Carib Rock. And near Barouallie there is another "Carib Rock" with a face, this one surrounded by a shining halo.

The **Buccament Valley**, to the east of Layou, is a lush rain forest that ranks as the best of several bird-watching areas and is under consideration as the site of a new 600-acre parrot sanctuary. St. Vincent is trying to protect such rare species as the St. Vincent parrot (still endangered), along with the whistling warbler, black hawk, cocoa thrush, crested hummingbird, green tanager and green heron.

The **Falls of Baleine**, a magnificient cascade plunging own 60 feet (20 m) into a rock-rimmed fresh-water pool is on the northern coast. It can be accessed by foot or in a boat from Chateaubelair or Richmond Beach.

Some may choose to take a closer look at **Soufrière**, the still active volcano which dominates St. Vincent. A guide is required for this day hike from the east side of the base to the 4048-foot-high (1234 m) crater. The hike begins in the valley of the **Rabacca Dry River** near

ST. VINCENT

Georgetown and goes nearly three hard miles up to the lip of the crater. The option is returning via a 12-mile (18 km) trail down to Chateaubelair on the western coast.

Agriculture is still important on this touristic island. **Mesopotamia Valley**, to the northeast of Kingstown, is known for its breadfruit, coconuts, arrowroot, cotton, bananas and other tropical fruits. Those with an interest in such matters, can visit an arrowroot processing mill in **Colonarie** and a 3200-acre coconut plantation at Rabacca Dry River, one of the largest in the world.

The Sportive Life

There are, of course, the usual Caribbean sports to be practiced on St. Vincent and off. Fishermen go after ballyhoo, mahi, bonito, kingfish, mackerel and red snapper. Nearby, sailors and windsurfers ply the local waters. Scuba divers plunge into reefs which are up to 90 feet below the surface, to walls, coral formations and even a couple of wrecks.. Horseback riding on endless black sand beaches, hiking to Soufrière's crater, cycling and tennis are also available. The island's nine-hole golf course at the **Aquaduct Golf Course** is presently being expanded to 18 holes.

GRENADA

The "southern anchor" of the paradisical Grenadines is one of the most idyllic of all Carribean islands. Gorgeous Grenada (pronounced "gre-nay-dah") combines the intimacy of a small island (133 square miles/345 sq. km)) with the vibrancy of a larger one.The long pier at the port of St. George, the **Carenage**, can accommodate cruise ships and its **Point Salines International Airport**, which was begun by Cuban workers (once charged with being bloodthirsty *guerilleros* by the Reagan administration) and finished with U.S. aid, can handle big jets.

The Caribs occupied this island, which they called *Camerhonge*, when Chris-

GRENADA

topher Columbus stopped by on his third voyage in 1498. He called the island *Concepción*. The French took over and called it *Grenade*, and the British then simply changed the final "e" to an "a." In 1783, it became a British colony and was noted for its cinnamon, nutmeg, mace and other rare spices. In fact, it is still frequently referred to as the "Spice Island." In 1795, an unsuccessful slave revolt was duly recorded, but emancipation did not occur until 1834. Crown colony status was achieved in 1877, and full independence in 1974. Grenada and its neighbor islands of **Carriacou** and **Petit Martinique** now form a nation with an elected government and Commonwealth affiliation.

A coup in 1979 gave it a left-wing, Cuba-friendly governmentIt was in turn replaced by a conservative administration ushered in by the U.S. after a startling invasion in 1983.

Above: Maurice Bishop, the murdered Prime Minister, lives on in his people's memory.

A Tour of Spice Island

Grenada is mountainous, lovely and lush, and its capital **St. George's** is supposed to be one of the most picturesque and pleasant towns in the Caribbean, a symphony of mewses and narrow streets lined with pastel-colored houses ducking under red-tile roofs. Strolling along the **Carenage** harbor bay, you come to **Fort George**, which is solidly placed upon a spit of land. Besides the sense of history imbuing the place, this old bastion provides one of the finest views of the harbor and city. The nearby **National Museum** displays a great number of artifacts from Africa and from Arawak, Carib and colonial days.

The **markets** are to the north of St. George's along one of the main shopping strips. The **Yellow Poui Art Gallery**, **Glencraft** and the **National Institute of Handicrafts** show works of the best local painters, woodcarvers and artisans. Popular handicrafts include textiles, straw and shell creations. Especially interesting is the straw work using wild pine leaves from the town of **Marquis**, which is located on the eastern shore.

Grenada's carnival takes place the second week in August and features calypso, steel bands, dancing and various parades. The main pageant day is Monday, with a couple of festivities at **Queen's Park** in St. George's. *Jab jab molassi* involves smearing oneself and anyone else within reach with black grease to represent the devil.

Sightseeing out of town consists of a trip to solitary bays, fertile valleys, hills where the air is somewhat cooler, and by the island's highest mountain, **St. Catherine**, standing at 2755 feet (840 m). The government is in the process of expanding its system of parks and wildlife sanctuaries, and the reforestation programs to repair hurricane damage are among the most ambitious in the Caribbean.

GRENADA

GRENADA

Close to St. George's, at the **Bay Gardens**, are three easy-to-visit acres of botanical interest. The **Grand Étang** includes a national park known as the **Grand Étang Forest Reserve** and is famous for its exuberant flora and fauna. Monas monkeys and mongoose, both imported from Africa three centuries ago, can be seen there. **Mount Qua Qua** rises up above the northern shore of the lake, which lies at 1690 feet (515 m). At 2303 feet (702 m), this mountain is just three feet lower than **Mount Sinai** that marks the southern end of the tropical rain forest.

45 species of butterflies are found fluttering about at **La Sagesse Nature Center**, and **Levera Beach** up in the north is home to 86 species of tropical birds. **Concord Falls** are lovely to view and fun to splash under. **Carib's Leap** is the sight at **Sauteurs**. This name, meaning "jumpers" in French, recalls the cliff from which the last Caribs jumped to their deaths to escape subjugation by the French.

Another particularly interesting place to visit is the town of **Gouyave**, fragrant with nutmeg, where you can see how different sorts of spices are grown and processed. The farm **Dougaldston Estate** is one place that can be visited.

Beaches

Of Grenada's altogether 45 beaches, **Grande Anse Bay** on the arid coast to the south of St. George's is truly outstanding. There is a hotel strip, but it is relatively unobtrusive, since no building may be higher than a coconut palm. Beach facilities are also available to non-guests for a fee, and when a big cruise ship is in port, hordes of passengers do just that. Nearby **Musquetta Beach** and **Horseshoe Bay** are less crowded, while **Levera Beach** on the northwestern tip is downright isolated.

Above: The sea and inland water pools leave the swimmer nothing more to be desired. Right: Carnival in Grenada.

Sports

Grenada bills itself as the "gateway to the Grenadines," and as such, it is a great way station for sailors. Regattas take place here several times a year. Yachts for charter are available, with or without crew. For good diving and snorkeling try, for example, **Molinère Reef**, **Boss Reef** or **Spice Island.**

There is a nine-hole golf course at the **Grenada Golf & Country Club**, and there is always good hiking at Grand Étang National Park.

Grenada's Specialities

Both Caribbean culture and local food specialties can be enjoyed by visiting the bustling markets in St. George's or **Grenville**, the latter of which is known as Grenada's breadbasket. Even if not out to buy anything, these spots are terrific just to watch everyday life in progress. Take-home spices are packed to go at the **Marketing Board** in St. George's.

Grenadans say they grow 28 varieties of fruit, catch 22 kinds of fish and harvest a dozen spices. This forms the basis of the cuisine of this tiny island.

Fish stew, *lambi* (conch), curried chicken, *totou* (armadillo) and barbecued goat and are some of the tastiest specialties available. *Oil Down,* an intriguingly named dish, is made of breadfruit and salt pork steamed in fresh coconut milk. Locals also like to remind curious visitors that Captain Bligh not ony introduced the breadfruit tree to neighboring St. Vincent, but he also left one on Grenada.

The island's rum is indeed famous, and Grenadans even go as far as taking credit for the word *grog*. One theory states that it is the acronym for *Georgius Rex Old Grenada,* which was stamped on kegs of rum shipped back to England, while another claims, more simply, that it stands for *Grand Rum of Grenada*. There are other fine drinks to taste, however, and ones that will not affect your concentration. *Sea moss milk*, for example, is made of vanilla, an algae and milk.

THE GRENADINES

Dealing with Caribbean island descriptively is a constant struggle to find superlatives. But if there is any place on earth that currently merits the description of "tropical paradise," it is this chain of idyllic islands in the St. Vincent-Grenada orbit that embody what so many visitors expect from the Caribbean – tranquil settings, crystal-clear waters, warm sand, silently swaying palm trees, informally elegant resorts and casual guesthouses, some refined and tasteful entertainment and friendly, welcoming people. **The Grenadines** doubtlessly display all of these qualities. Some of the 100-odd islands are dominated by a single resort. Others have a few unpretentious guesthouses. Still others have virtually no tourist facilities and perhaps not any human habitation at all.

Above: Honorable distinctions... Right: In the Grenadines, people and wares are carried to shore in rather precarious vessels.

The Grenadines are no secret to real connoisseurs of the Lesser Antilles, who have languished on the islands, sailed the blue waters that surround them, dived the beautiful reefs that abound in them, and have generally been entranced by their matchless ambience.

What makes them individually and collectively so special is that they are tiny, and even those "invaded" by resort development are truly unspoiled. This is the island group that has made a fine art of the dedicated resort island – a previously uninhabited island now given over to a luxurious, tranquil, service-oriented resort. Nowhere else has this concept been so refined.

The Grenadines, along with the two larger islands that enfold them like parentheses, are also surrounded by some of the world's best sailing waters. This is the ideal place to attempt one's first bareboat charter, for the waters are always clear, the boat traffic is largely pleasure craft (and small fishing boats and ferries whose skippers are accustomed to novice sailors), and one is never out of sight of land. Other water sports, including sunfish sailing, fishing, snorkeling, diving, swimming and windsurfing, are also of the best and are important options in the leading resorts. The beachcombing is exemplary as well.

The Grenadines will always remain quiet oases with few visitors, because, with few exceptions, they are tedious to get to (except for those with small private planes). It is necessary to fly from the mainland to a large jet-port, then perhaps hop to St. Vincent and finally travel, usually by sea, to the island of choice. It is worth every minute because the Grenadines are truly spectacular.

Bequia

Nine miles (15 km) south of St. Vincent is **Bequia** it's (pronounced "beh-kwee"), which at seven square miles ranks among

the largest of the Grenadines. It is also the most enchanting. **Port Elizabeth** is the tiny main town. Sailors from all over the world have dropped anchor in **Admiralty Bay**, its sheltered harbor, and perched on barstools made of whalebone to swap tales with each other. The barstools were come by honorably, since Bequia's sea-faring sons have built whaling boats and gone to sea in them for years. Hence the **Whaling & Sailing Museum,** excellent, nigh-deserted beaches, small hotels and guesthouses and a rare sense of privacy characterize this blessed island.

Bequia is perhaps the most highly publicized of the Grenadines, for it was one of the first to be discovered by people wishing to trade the turmoil of Europe and North America for the quiet lifestyle of the Caribbean.

An expatriate community (including a number of elegant, modern cave-dwellers), cosy little bed and breakfasts, way-stations for sailors, early dive and snorkel centers and quaint inns have all gotten their share of publicity, but, fortunately, Bequia has never been overrun and remains as picturesque and perfect as one may expect.

Canouan

If Caribbean fame rested solely on beach quality, the name of this tiny island 25 miles (40 km) south of St. Vincent would be on everyone's lips. Powdery sand, reef-sheltered coves, fine boat anchorages and just two hotels, including the beautiful Beach Hotel, comprise the attractions of this most serene little island.

Carriacou

Even amid the very informal and quiet Grenadines, **Carriacou** stands out like a palm tree on a beach. It consists of a tranquil crescent-shaped island of breeze-swept hills and sandy beaches. At 13 square miles, this is the largest of the Grenadines, yet **Hillsborough**, the capital, has fewer than 600 residents, plus a

market, a few government buildings and the **Carriacou Historical Society**, a nice little museum of Amerindian and European objects. Although it was once noted for its cotton plantations, this island, located 16 miles (26 km) from Grenada, has turned to seafaring.

The village of **Windward** on the east (naturally the windward) coast is populated by Scottish descendants who still build sturdy wooden island schooners in a traditional manner.

Harvey Vale is a small village located on the western coast. In the vicinity is **Tyrell Bay** an almost picture-perfect natural harbor. Needless to say, this is public knowledge, and the bay is now the site of one of the Caribbean's most important and popular regattas, which takes place in August.

Above: Luxuriant vegetation thanks to the trade winds that sometimes bring rain. Right: Home, sweet home, the friendly smile of the Grenadines.

Mayreau

This tiny, nearly deserted island, which is situated about 25 miles south of the island of St. Vincent is already slated for luxury resort development. The **Tobago Cays** (7 miles/ 11 km northward) are part of **Mayreau**.

Mustique

Princess Margaret has vacationed on this secluded island of **Mustique** for years, whereas Princess Diana and her little princes have done so more recently. Situated some 18 miles south of St. Vincent, it is at once the best known and perhaps most exclusive of the Grenadines. Half of this studiously un-commercialized little island remains privately owned and dotted with *lifestyles* of the Rich & Famous-type villas which draw international celebrities and aristocrats.

Perched atop a 500-foot hill, **The Cotton House** is the island's one resort hotel, and its spectacular views, genuine seclu-

GRENADINES

sion and casual, tropical elegance are a match for any of the many private mansions. Pristine and lovely are probably the most accurate descriptions of this rather sporty, yet very opulent resort, which is geared for people who can afford to go anywhere but chose not to.

Palm Island

8000 coconut palms or so, one is told, line the pure white beaches of this 110-acre gem, which barely rises from the surface of the sparkling blue sea. The beach at **Casuarina** on the west coast is one of the best and most secluded in the Caribbean. This island (also known as Prune Island) has now been turned into a luxurious resort with 22 private villas.

Petit Martinique

A scenic 745-foot (227 m) volcano dominates tiny **Petit Martinique**. The 500 residents, many of whom remain sailors and boat-builders, are largely descended from French settlers. There are no accommodations at all on the island, but it is a nice day trip from Grenada.

Petit St. Vincent

This 113-acre island was perhaps the model for Palm Island. Its exquisite informality, outstanding sporty atmosphere and the fine service appeal to picky guests, who are joined by yachtsmen who drop anchor and frequently stop by for a rum punch in the airy bar.

Union Island

Located about 40 miles from St. Vincent, **Union Island**, with its idyllic landscape composed of dramatic ridges and surprisingly lofty mountains, has more than once been called the Tahiti of the Caribbean. It could well be that. What adds to the magic is that the highest peak was appropriately named **Mt. Parnassus**. **Clifton Harbour** is the main town and another excellent yacht anchorage.

GUIDEPOST ST. VINCENT / GRENADA / GRENADINES

ST. VINCENT / GRENADA / THE GRENADINES
(Area code: 1809)

Access and Local Transportation
Grenada's **Point Salines International Airport** is served by BWIA International and Pan Am from New York and Miami, by American Airlines from San Juan, by Air Canada from Toronto and by British Airways from London. LIAT serves St. Vincent via Barbados. LIAT, Mustique Airways and Air Martinique offer various intra-island services.

Daily ferry service from Kingstown and St. George's reaches all of the inhabited islands. Taxis are available on most islands, and rental cars (drive on the left) can be hired on larger ones. An international driver's license is required, or a temporary local one for 8 US$ can be issued at the time you rent a car.

The *Osprey Express*, a speed boat, runs to Grenada and Carriacou in 90 minutes, twice a day (exc. Wednesdays). Departure 9 a.m. and 5:30 p.m. from Grenada, and 6 a.m. and 3:30 p.m. from Carriacou. Fare is US$ 28.

Currency and Formalities
The Eastern Caribbean Dollar is the currency of St. Vincent, Grenada and the Grenadines. At this writing, 2.30 EC$ equal 1 US$. For entry into St. Vincent and the Grenadines, you will need a passport and ongoing tickets, departure tax is 20 EC$.

Festivals
On **St. Vincent**, *Carnival* takes place the last week of June and first week of July. Nicknamed *Vincy Mas*, this 10-day festival of calypso, street dancing, steel bands and colourful costume parades was moved in 1977 to avoid conflicting with the traditional pre-Lenten timetable of similar events in Trinidad and elsewhere.

Grenada's *Carnival*, for similar reasons, is now celebrated in mid-August. Nearby Carriacou's smaller carnival on Shrove Tuesday, traditional *Mardi Gras* time, is highlighted by costumed pierrots who recite Shakespeare.

In late June, *Fisherman's Birthday* in Gouyave, Grenada, is a blessing of the fishing fleet, culminating in a street fair. The annual *Carriacou Regatta* in mid-August includes various yacht and boat races, plus Big Drum dancing. Union Island's *Big Drum Festival* is held in May to mark the end of the dry season.

Holidays are New Year's Day, *St. Vincent and the Grenadines Discovery Day* (January 22), *Grenada Independence Day* (February 7), Good Friday, Easter Sunday, Easter Monday, Labour Day (May 1), Whit Monday, Emancipation Day (or August Monday, St. Vincent, first Monday in August), Thanksgiving Day (Grenada, October 25), *St. Vincent Independence Day* (October 27), Christmas Day and Boxing Day (December 26).

Museums / Art Galleries
Local archeology and history museums include the **National Museum** in the **Botanic Gardens** in Kingstown, St. Vincent; the **National Museum** in St. Georges, Grenada, and the **Carriacou Historical Society** in Hillsborough.

Shopping
Handicraft shops and sportswear boutiques (in the bigger towns and flossier hotels) comprise the main shopping options. Chains such as Stecher's and Y. Lima have outposts on the larger islands for cameras, watches, jewelry, perfume and the like. Grenada and the Grenadines also have good marine-supply and dive shops.

Tourist Information
St. Vincent & The Grenadines Dept. of Tourism, Egmont St., P.O. Box 834, Kingstown, St. Vincent, Tel: 457-1502.
St. Vincent & The Grenadines Tourist Board, 801 Second Ave., 21st Floor, New York, NY 10017, Tel: 1-212/687-4981.
Grenada Department of Tourism, The Carenage, St. George's, Grenada, Tel: 440-2279/2001.

ST. VINCENT

Accommodations
LUXURY: **Young Island**, P.O. Box 211, Young Island, Tel: 458-4826. Exclusive island resort 200 yards off-shore with cottages and suites. Two 44-foot sailboats for guests' use. **Grand View Beach Hotel**, P.O. Box 173, St. Vincent, Tel: 458-4811. An old atmospheric plantation house with pool, a trail to the beach, tennis and squash, restaurant.
MODERATE: **Cobblestone Inn**, P.O. Box 867, Kingstown, St. Vincent, Tel: 456-1937. A historic sugar warehouse has been converted into a charming in-town inn. Great cocktail lounge. **Mariner's Inn**, P.O. Box 868, St. Vincent. Informal old West Indian house on Villa Beach, with antique furnishings. Boat bar is liked by sailors. A Friday night jump-up and barbeque is popular with locals as well as tourists. **Sunset Shores**, P.O. Box 849, St. Vincent, Tel: 458-4411/2. Beachfront hotel with 20 rooms, private patios, pool bar, and a good restaurant.
BUDGET: **Haddon Hotel**, P.O. Box 133, St. Vincent, Tel: 456-1897. Simple rooms in small lodge with hillside location. Tennis courts. **Umbrella Beach Hotel**, P.O. Box 530, St. Vincent, Tel: 458-

GUIDEPOST ST. VINCENT / GRENADA / GRENADINES

4651. Nine well-located rooms with kitchenettes offering excellent value on Villa Beach.

Restaurants

ST. VINCENT: **Basil's Bar & Restaurant**, Cobblestone Inn, Bay St., St. Vincent (also on Mustique), Tel: 457-2713. **The Bounty Café**, Halifax St., Kingstown. **The Dolphin Restaurant and Bar**, Villa Beach, Tel: 457-4337. **Juliette's**, Middle Street, Kingstown. **Restaurant à la Mer**, Indian Bay Beach Hotel, Tel: 458-4001.

GRENADA

Accommodations

LUXURY: **Calabash Hotel**, P.O. Box 382, St. George's, Tel: 444-4334. Award-winning luxury hotel with 28 suites (12 more under construction) on eight beachfront acres on Prickly Bay. Fine food and service, pool. **Cinnamon Hill and Beach Club**, P.O. Box 292, St. George's, Tel: 444-4301/02. Spanish-style condo-hotel with spacious luxury units, private terraces, poolside restaurant. **Ramada Renaissance Resort**, P.O. Box 441, St. George's, Tel: 444-4371. Luxury chain hotel on Grande Anse Beach with 184 deluxe rooms, private balconies and all amenities. Dining options from poolside snack bar to elegant restaurant. Large cocktail lounge. Children under 18 free in parents' room. **Secret Harbour**, P.O. Box 11, St. George's, Tel: 444-4548. A resort best known for its yacht charter operations, carries on here with yachts available by the hour or day, as well as packages offering several nights on land. Pool, tennis, beach, bar, restaurant and sailboats. **Spice Island Inn**, P.O. Box 6, St. George's, Tel: 444-4258. Sporty beachfront suites with private pool, spa or whirlpool. Excellent cuisine. Relaxed atmosphere.
MODERATE: **Blue Horizons Cottage Hotel**, P.O. Box 41, St. George's, Tel: 444-4316. Informal, yet luxurious suites with kitchenettes. Poolwith bar, spa, lounge, spacious grounds at Grande Anse Beach.
BUDGET: **Homestead Guesthouse**, Gouyave, St. John's, Tel: 444-8526. Tiny budget guest-house. **No Problem Apartments**, P.O. Box 280, St. George's, Tel: 444-4634. Newly expanded complex offering 20 well-equipped units with maid service. Free coffee bar, rental bicycles, transportation to Grande Anse Beach. Pool with bar. **Roydon's Guest House**, Grande Anse, St. George's, Tel: 444-4476.

Restaurants

GRENADA: **La Belle Créole**, Blue Horizons Hotel, Grande Anse. **Delicious Landing**, The Carenage, St. George's. **Mama's**, Lagoon Rd., St. George's. **Nutmeg**, The Carenage, St. George's. **Red Crab**, Lance aux Épines Beach. **Rudolf's**, The Carenage, St. George's.

THE GRENADINES

Accommodations

EXPENSIVE: **Canouan Beach Hotel**, Canouan, The Grenadines, Tel: 458-8888. 43-room beachfront resort with great views, restaurant, bar, private catamaran for diving and other sports, private airstrip. **Cotton House Hotel**, Mustique, The Grenadines, Tel: 458-4621. World-class luxury hotel with extraordinary food, service. Rooms are in cottages around a historic plantation house. Sports. **Palm Island Beach Club**, The Grenadines, St. Vincent, Tel: 458-8824. Private island with 20 stone cottages provide solitude. The resort has excellent sports and fitness programs and a casually elegant atmosphere. **Petit St. Vincent**, Petit St. Vincent, The Grenadines, Tel: 458-8801. Idyllic hideaway on a gorgeous private island with secluded cottages, excellent service, all water sports. **Salt Whistle Bay Club**. This is the only hotel on Mayreau, offering quiet stone cottages hidden by Caribbean greenery alongside the fine beach. Fourteen units are available, bar, restaurant, watersports. **Sunny Caribee Plantation**, 12FX Belmont Box 16, Admiralty Bay, Bequia, St. Vincent, Tel: 458-3425. Lushly landscaped tropical gardens with 25 luxury units. Tops for scuba diving.
MODERATE: **Frangipani**, Bequia, St. Vincent, Tel: 458-3255. Classic Grenadine guesthouse with six spare rooms in the main house, plus better appointed units nearby. **Silver Beach Resort**, Carriacou, The Grenadines, Tel: 443-7373. Informal, yet comfortable beachfront resort with 18-room hotel suites with kitchenettes. Pool, diving, windsurfing, fishing. **Spring on Bequia**, Bequia, St. Vincent, Tel: 458-3414. 10-room resort on Spring Bay on the Atlantic. Seclusion, fine food, gardens and pool.
BUDGET: **Firefly House**, Box 349, Mustique, The Grenadines, Tel: 458-4621. Small private villas overlooking Britannia Bay, operating as a B&B. **Prospect Lodge**, Carriacou, The Grenadines, Tel: 443-7380. Two informal, cosy cottages. **Keegan's Guest House**, Bequia, St. Vincent, Tel: 458-3254. Seven rooms on Lower Bay, with dining room serving affordable local cuisine.

Restaurants

THE GRENADINES: **Anchorage Yacht Club**, Union Island, Tel: 458-8221. **Basil's Bar & Restaurant**, Mustique, Tel: 456-3350. **The Old Fort**, Mt. Pleasant, Bequia. **Peter's Place**, Carriacou.

TRINIDAD AND TOBAGO

CALYPSO, CARNIVAL, WHITE SAND

TRINIDAD
TOBAGO
ISLA DE MARGARITA

TRINIDAD

Near South America, just about eight miles from the coast of Venezuela, are **Trinidad & Tobago**, two islands that comprise the Caribbean's southernmost nation. They are as different and as complementary as peanut butter and jelly. Trinidad is large and has a multi-cultural, urban and industrialized society. Tobago is small, quiet, rural and oriented to the sea. It is one of the many islands that claim to have been Robinson Crusoe's. Visitors to Trinidad go for business, a glimpse of a unique ethnic blend or for carnival. The latter is still wildly imaginative with elaborate costumes, music and general merriment. People come to Tobago for sun and sand, and to sip rum punches in a tranquil atmosphere. Since the two islands are linked by frequent air shuttles, it is easy to combine them into a two-for-one experience.

Columbus discovered these islands in 1498 and named the larger one Trinidad, either to honor the Holy Trinity, or because he saw three hills from his ship. He landed near present-day **Moruga**, a town

Preceding pages: Fishermen still work with traditional means, but pollution of the seas is a threat to their existence. Left: Trinidad, synonymous with an exotic and shrill carnival.

on the southern coast. There were seven native tribes on the island at that time, some related to South American Indians and some to Caribs. In 1530, the Spanish built José de Oruna, now St. Joseph, as a jumping-off point for the gold-seekers heading to the South American continent to find *El Dorado*. Sir Walter Raleigh passed through in 1595, looted the colony, and used the opportunity to caulk his ship with asphalt from Pitch Lake.

The Spanish rebuilt the place, but when smallpox decimated the inhabitants (especially the Indian population), they built a town elsewhere along the coast. It was named Port of Spain. Slaves were imported from Africa to work plantations, a process which began in the 1600s and reached its zenith in the following century. Over time, French – particularly those fleeing the Revolution – Dutch and Latvian settlers came when land grants were issued to non-Spanish Catholics.

Throughout their turbulent early history, the islands were the object of contention between Spain, Britain, France and the Netherlands. Sir Ralph Abercromby ultimately claimed Trinidad for England in 1797 while the French were too occupied with their Revolution.

Tobago's name is believed to be a corruption of the word "tobacco," which the Amerindians grew there. In 1764, James,

TRINIDAD AND TOBAGO

Duke of Courland (an island in the Baltic Sea), was issued a land grant for the island and settled it with fellow Courlanders. Tobago was conquered by the Dutch, occupied by the French, ceded to England under the Treaty of Amiens in 1802, returned to the French fold and, finally, recaptured by England and merged with the colony of Trinidad in 1889.

Slavery was abolished in 1834, and to fill the labor shortage, immigrants were recruited from the United States, the Canary Islands, England, Scotland, Ireland, Germany, Switzerland, Bengal (Bangladesh today), Syria, Lebanon and China. There was even a wave of free African immigrants to the recently emancipated colony. The phrase, "If you don't have five bloods, you're not Trinidadian," stems from this multiethnic history.

Trinidad & Tobago became an independent nation within the British Commonwealth in 1962 and, while remaining in England's coat tails, became a parliamentary republic with an elected president in 1976. By then it had become relatively prosperous by Caribbean standards, with tobacco, sugar and cocoa as the agricultural staples and natural resources such as pitch asphalt, gypsum, coal (anthracite and lignite), sand, gravel, iron ore and, most important, oil and natural gas. In fact, petroleum products dominate the economy, and there are oil refineries at Point-à-Pierre and Point Fortin. Iron and steel are important economic factors as well. Tourism, surprisingly enough for a Cribbean nation, is seen as an additional rather than vital source of income.

Many bird-watchers are attracted to the coast of Trinidad. Trinidad & Tobago have 400 bird species, more than any other Caribbean island. Many birds, are South American rather than Caribbean. Little Tobago has 13 varieties not found on Trinidad. In an effort to protect the habitats of the species found there, national parks, reserves and various other conservation areas have been designated.

TRINIDAD

The wild poinsettia (Chaconia) is the national flower, and other flowering trees and blossoms abound.

Port of Spain

Port of Spain, the capital and largest town of Trinidad (with a population numbering about 150,000), is situated on the **Gulf of Paria**, on a leeward peninsula in the northwestern corner of Trinidad. **San Andres Fort** was built in 1785 to guard the harbor. Today it harbors offices for the local government.

The ideal place to begin a little trip around the city mixing sightseeing with shopping is on **Frederick Street**, one of the main commercial strips. It is an ideal place to get into the local mood, as locals also exercise their consumer rights here. In spite of several malls – including the massive **Gulf City** in San Fernando –

Above: Red House, the seat of parliament in Port of Spain. Right: This cactus is called Turk's Cap for its funny shape.

Frederick Street remains the traditional place to do one's shopping on the island. The most interesting finds are sari silks, East Indian jewelry, records and tapes; and wood carvings. Local crafts may be purchased for instance at the Footprint Art Craft Shop, the Handcraft Center, the Mount St. Benedict Abbey Gift Shop or else the Trinidad & Tobago Blind Welfare Association Shop.

Frederick Street begins at the harbor, near Fort San Andres and South Quay. Independence Square, an equally daunting shopping mile, boasts among others the Neogothic structure of the **Cathedral of the Immaculate Conception**, completed in the year 1832. And busy **Queen Street** has its own religious monument on its eastern end, the **Jama Masjid**, the beautiful Friday Mosque of Trinidad overlooked by a gentle minaret. Only a few meters further to the north is another verdant nook in Port of Spain, **Woodford Square**, where the Neogothic **Cathedral of the Holy Trinity** was erected for the benefit of the Anglican Church in 1823.

TRINIDAD

The **Red House**, a kind of Renaissance palace built in 1907 and serving today as the seat of parliament, stands on the western edge of the square. Frederick Street, however, proceeds on its northward path to the **National Museum**, which presents relics and artifacts from the artistic, historic, archeological and geological heritage of the island. If carnival is not on, this might be the only occasion to examine some carnival costumes.

The museum is only a few steps away from Port of Spain's great center for rest and relaxation, the lavish, 200-acre green belt of **Queen's Park Savannah**, a sporty place with many playing fields and a mid-park race course with non-stop action taking place within its generous three-mile circumference. This piece of greenery in the midst of the city lies to the north of the harbor. Near the Savannah are the **Botanic Gardens**, begun in 1818 and now known for tropical and subtropical plant species from South America and Southeast Asia, and the **Emperor Zoo**, with quite a number of animals native to Trinidad. This town, with its harbor, hills, green spaces and a center composed of old churches, historic mansions and mid-rise office buildings, somehow calls to mind an image of a tropical Boston.

Excursions can be made to the cool hills above the city, where visitors enjoy a view of Port of Spain from choice spots, the most accessible of which is the look-out on **Lady Chancellor Road**, at some 600 feet above sea level. The mountain ranges of Venezuela are visible from here on clear days. Another great spot is **Fort George**, that has kept an eye on Trinidad since 1804.

The shrine called **Our Lady of Laventille** has a tower which also affords a grand view. However, it is quite a walk up from the main road. From here one can make a detour to the **Blue Basin Falls** on the **Diego Martin Valley.** A steep path from the upper falls leads down to a clear pool in which one can cool off.

Traveling Trinidad

The tropical lushness of the **Northern Range** is easily accessible from the capital. In **St. Joseph**, or San José as it was called, the original capital situated due east of Port of Spain, one can take a look at **Jinnah Masjid Mosque**, a classical Arabic structure named after Muhammad Ali Jinnah, an Indian Moslem leader who founded the state of Pakistan. Perched on a hill above it, is the tranquil recluse of **Mount St. Benedict Monastery**.

To explore upcountry Trinidad, one should continue eastward to the **Lopinot Historical Complex**. This former estate, once known as *La Reconnaissance,* was belonged to Charles Joseph, Comte de Lopinot, a French officer who fled the revolution. There is a **museum** on the grounds. Caurita Plantation in the vicinity has been turned into a 400-acre wildlife sanctuary. Tours are with guide only.

Near **Arima**, a road forks off to the north to the **Asa Wright Nature Center**,

located in the **Spring Hills Estate**. Overnight accommodations are available here. It is the world's only breeding colony of guacharo, the nocturnal oilbird, in **Dunston Cave**. About 70 species thrive in **Aripo Range**, including the yellow-legged thrush, which lives at altitudes above 2000 feet (600 m).

The way to the north coast of Trinidad is over **Blanchisseuse** on **Paria Bay** where you find the pretty **Paria Falls**. Farther along the north coast are **Maracas Bay**, **Tyrico Bay** and **Las Cuevas Beach**. Some of the best surfing can be done along the northern shore.

The way back to Port of Spain is through charming, fertile valleys. One of the oldest golf clubs on Trinidad, the St. Andrew's Golf Club, moved from Queen's Park Savannah to its current 18-hole location in **Moka**, which lies in the northern **Maraval Valley**.

Above: Pitch Lake, a natural source of asphalt. Right: Today the oil drums cost more than the oil they once carried.

The 15,000-acre **Caroni Bird Sanctuary** is the prime destination for daytrippers heading for the southern part of the island. It is home to plovers, egrets, herons and the scarlet ibis. Boat tours wind through this brackish mangrove swamp.

Chaguanas, the next larger town on the way, is where Vidiadhar S. Naipaul spent his youth. Naipaul, born in 1932, is above all noted for his novels in which he often returns to his Caribbean roots. Many of the island's East Indians live south of Port of Spain: Hindu flags flutter from bamboo poles as a tribute to some family event, rice paddies are cultivated by men in dhotis, a herd of water buffalo ambles in the shimmering heat.

A more distant, yet absolutely vital sanctuary is the **Wild Fowl Trust** near **San Fernando**, on the island's southwestern peninsula, an area threatened by industrial development and oil refining. Nearby is **Pitch Lake**, a 100-acre, 130-foot-deep repository of hot black tar, which provides Trinidad with its asphalt industry. Legend says that Pitch Lake

was created when an entire Chaima Indian village disappeared into the ground as punishment for eating sacred hummingbirds that embodied ancestral souls. Scientists talk more prosaically about volcanic heat acting on a pool of crude oil.

Matura and **Manzamilla Bays** are the two best beaches on the east coast, which faces the Atlantic, and a little further south is **Mayaro Bay**. The coastal road traverses **Nariva Swamp** at one point, which is also rich in bird life.

Gastronomic Specialties

What Trinidad lacks in beaches it makes up for in food. This is where its multi-ethnic background presents itself at its very best. Dishes include suckling pig, pepper pot and pigeon pea soup. *Calaloo*, a stew-like soup, is made of a leafy green called *dasheen*, fat pork, salt beef, a pig's tail, onions, chives, crabs, okra, coconut milk and garlic. It is not a light concoction, but it is one of the best indigenous dishes. *Pastelles* (minced meat and corn flour wrapped in banana leaves) are vestiges of Spanish colonial days. Black pudding and *souse* have French roots. *Roti* (a thin pancake with a seasoned dark meat, chicken or fish filling), *pilau* (spicy rice and meat) and *saheena* (deep-fried patties of split peas, spinach and *dasheen*, often served with a mango chutney) reveal East Indian origins. Crab dishes are among the tastiest seafood selections and *matete*, stuffed crab, is one of the best. One might also try tiny fresh-water oysters that grow around mangrove roots and *cassadou*, a local fish usually served stuffed.

Fried shark is another specialty, and one will also find good Chinese and Indonesian fare. Adventurous gourmets can sample *tatoo* (fried iguana), *manicou* (opossum stew), *quenk* (wild pig), *lappe* (rabbit), *buljol* (salted catfish) or cold *souse*, in which parts of the pig most people will not touch are made more palatable by a generous infusion of onion, lime, cucumber and a outrageously spicy pepper sauce.

Rum specialties, often flavored with local Angostura bitters, are the mixed drinks of choice. A ginger beer called *mauby* is popular. Fruit juices or coconut milk help to quench one's tropical thirst.

Calypso and Carnival

Trinidad's major contributions to Caribbean culture are calypso music and steel drums. Calypso is a distinctive music in an rousing 2/4 and 4/4 rhythm, with roots, like so much in Trinidad, traced to Africa, France and Spain. Percussion instruments made of household pots and pans replaced African shango drums, which, during slavery, were outlawed by plantation owners. With the advent of the oil industry, musicians fashioned oil drums, small tanks and other metal containers into steel drums or *pans*. Bands are composed of ping pongs, piano pans, second pans and tenor kittles.

Above and right: In many of the rural areas of Tobago, time seems to have stood still.

For dancing and music, many places favored by locals in Port of Spain are louder, wilder, more authentic and, perhaps, somewhat disquieting for some tourists.Limbo shows, cabaret performances and folk shows feature stylized versions of these lyrical forms of musical expression. The most important theater is **Queen's Hall** in Port of Spain, and the **South National Theatre for the Performing Arts**, in San Fernando, puts on folk performances.

The year's undisputed highpoint is Carnival, a three-day bacchanalia of many colors and costumes held just before Lent. Judges award prizes to the best "bands" for their costumes and show. The most elaborate costumes in the Mardi Gras parade, held anually the Monday and Tuesday before Lent, can be ten- or 12-foot high contraptions of frames, fabrics, feathers and other ornamentations, based on a central theme. The main characters and musicians usually ride on a flatbed truck, while their fellow band members walk alongside.

The parade can last five or six hours. While Carnival itself was imported to Trinidad by the French, the music and costumes were clearly improved on by the Africans.

TOBAGO

20 miles (36 km) and lightyears away from bustling Trinidad is tranquil Tobago, an island of soothing trade winds, fine-sand beaches, golf greens and resorts. Once dotted with large sugar plantations, Tobago is now primarily a touristic island. The main town, **Scarborough**, has a pastoral English name, but is actually a dusty little place. Its main attractions are **King George Fort** (1770), the **House of Assembly** (1925) and the **Botanical Gardens**.

Fort James (1768) overlooking Great Courland Bay, **Fort Granby** guarding Barbados Bay and **Richmond Great House**, an old manor which has been turned into a hotel, are remnants of Tobago's history. **Grafton Estate**, on **Great Courland**, was a privately run bird sanctuary. The patroness died, and therefore feeding is no longer regular, but the corico, blue mot-mots, tanagers and woodpeckers still thrive there.

Tobago's landscape is a rare combination of rolling hills and forests fringed by sandy beaches. The **Forest Reserve**, a long central highland strip, is especially interesting for birdwatchers. Hikers in the upper regions should beware of snakes.

Little Tobago, also called Bird of Paradise Island, is a tiny island off the northeast coast, near Speyside. As the only place in the Northern Hemisphere where one can see the bird of paradise, indigenous to New Guinea and imported early in the 20th century, Little Tobago is another mecca for birdwatchers, who camp there in order to observe the bird in the early morning hours.

The most famous, popular and attractive beaches are located at and near **Pigeon Point**, Tobago's western tip where resort hotels are concentrated. The main

ISLA DE MARGARITA

beach, which gets crowded at peak times, has lockers, a bar, sports equipment rentals and other facilities. **Grafton Beach** and **Man O' War Beach** are often less crowded. Since it is so tiny, Scarborough itself has a better beach than most other island cities.

Buccoo Reef, at Tobago's southwestern end, is an underwater garden. It was long considered to be one of the Caribbean's best for diving, snorkeling and glass-bottom boating. Until the passage of the Marine Preservation Act protecting the reef from souvenir-seeking divers and anchor-dragging boats, it was also one of the Caribbean's most endangered wonders. Experts say the law is loosely enforced, but the reef appears to be stabilized, and marine life is regenerating.

The bestseason for deep-sea fishing is February and March, especially for wahoo, mullet and marlins. Visitors more attached to land will find enough to do at and around the **Mount Irvine Bay Hotel**, which is known as top turf for golfers and has excellent facilities for tennis players.

ISLA DE MARGARITA

This 373-square-mile (1150 sq. km) island traces its history to pre-Columbian pearl gatherers and was one of the few which the Spaniards actively colonized. It is therefore a Caribbean resort destination that marches to a distinctly Latin rhythm – with good reason, for it is politically part of Venezuela and, until recently, was primarily a local resort area.

La Asunción, the island's diminutive capital, is buried in the interior. The real hub of the tourist industry, however, is **Porlamar,** an emergent port town whose traditional colonial style is giving way to modern tourist trends. Ever since it was granted free-port status it has become a major shopping center, particularly for neighboring Venezuelans. **Pampatar** and **Santa Ana** are better bets for getting a sense of the old island flavor.

The coast of the eastern island is lined with hotels in every category, but there are also white sand beaches, coral reefs and remote bays.

TRINIDAD AND TOBAGO
(Area code: 1868)

Accommodations
TRINIDAD: *LUXURY:* **Asa Wright Lodge**, P.O. Box 10, Port of Spain, Tel/Fax: 667-4655. 20-room lodge, more expensive than luxurious, at the nature preserve. **Holiday Inn**, P.O. Box 1017, Port of Spain, Tel: 625-3361, Fax: 625-4531. City location, children free in parents' room. **Trinidad Hilton**, St. Ann's Rd./Lady Young, Port of Spain, Tel: 624-3211, Fax: 624-4485. Luxurious 412-room hotel over-looking Savannah, city and harbor; children free.
MODERATE: **Alicia's House**, 7 Coblentz Gardens, Port of Spain, Tel: 623-2802, Fax: 623-8560. 17 rooms, pool, tropical gardens, restaurant. **Blanchisseuse Beach Resort**, Marianne, Blanchisseuse, Tel: 628-3731, Fax: 627-0856. 6 rooms under German management. **Mount Plaisir**, Grande Rivière, 7 rooms, right on the beach. **Hotel Normandie**, P.O. Box 851, Port of Spain, Tel/Fax: 624-1181. Comfortable rooms, with pool, shops and restaurant on site. Favored by business guests; children free. **Kapok Hotel**, 16-18 Cotton Hill, St. Clair, Tel: 622-6441, Fax: 622-9677. Better rooms at higher rates, but all guests enjoy pool, views, comfort, good French and Polynesian restaurants.
BUDGET: **Naden's Court**, 32 St. Augustine Circular Road, St. Augustine, Tel: 645-2937. Friendly budget guesthouse; rooms/private or shared baths.
TOBAGO: *EXPENSIVE:* **Arnos Vale Hotel**, P.O. Box 208, Scarborough, Tel: 639-2881/2. Traditional, popular north coast hotel. Swimming pool, tennis, pleasant garden, excellent views and lovely atmosphere. **Grafton Beach Resort**, Grafton, Tel: 6390191. One of Tobago's largest resorts, with pool, beach, lovely views, many amenities. **Mt. Irvine Bay Hotel**, P.O. Box 222, Mt. Irvine, Tel: 639--8871/3. Relaxing classic, with fine pool, dining, golf, tennis, beach. Excellent service.
MODERATE: **Crown Point Beach Hotel**, P.O. Box 223, Scarborough, Tel: 639-8781/3. Cabins and condos, all with kitchen facilities. Pool and tennis. Located on Store Bay. **Kariwak Village**, P.O. Box 27, Scarborough, Tel: 639-8545. Cottages with kitchens. A definite family favorite. Pool, good restaurant. **Man O'War Bay Cottages**, Charlotteville, Tel: 660-4327. Tranquility on the north coast.
INEXPENSIVE: **Della Mira Guesthouse**, Bacolet, Tel: 639-2531. Bargain B&B with pool. **Store Bay Holiday Resort**, Store Bay Rd., Scarborough, Tel: 639-8810. Excellent value.

Restaurants in Port of Spain
La Boucan, Trinidad Hilton, Lady Young Road. **Il Giardino**, 6 Nook Ave., St. Ann's. **Hott Shoppe** for **Hot Roti**, Mucuparo St. **Rafter's**, 6 Warner St. **Tiki Village**, Kapok Hotel, Forest Lane, St. Ann's.

Access and Local Transportation
Piarco International Airport, 16 miles southeast of Port of Spain, is served by the BWIA, the national carrier, Air Canada, American Airlines and British Airways. ALM, LIAT and Cubana link Trinidad with other Caribbean destinations, and Aeropostale has flights to mainland Venezuela and Isla de Margarita. Trinidad levies a 50 TT$ departure tax and 18 TT$ security charge. BWIA and LIAT make frequent hops between Trinidad and Tobago.

Formalities and Currency
Valid passport. The Trinidad & Tobago Dollar (TT$) is fixed to the US$ at 2.40 TT$ to 1 US$.

Festivals
On Trinidad, Port of Spain's *Carnival* picks up steam for several weeks in January and February, peaking with parades and parties the Monday and Tuesday preceding Ash Wednesday. These two days are public holidays, as are New Year's Day, Ash Wednesday, Good Friday, Easter Monday, Whit Sunday, *Eid ul-Fitr* (marking the end of Ramadan), *Corpus Christi*, Labor Day (June 19), *Emancipation Day* (first Monday in August), *Independence Day* (August 31), *Republic Day* (September 24), *Divali*, Christmas Day and Boxing Day (December 26). *Hosein*, a solemn Moslem festival, is celebrated with processions where marchers bear wooden mosques. It takes place 10 days after the new moon in the month of *Moharram*, usually in September. *Divali*, the Hindu festival of lights honoring the goddess *Lakshmi*, takes place in October or November. Tobago celebrates Easter with crab, goat and donkey races on Sunday and Monday and puts on a two-week *Heritage Festival* in July.

Museums / Art Galleries
The **National Museum** in Port of Spain is the islands' largest and most comprehensive showcase for art, culture and history. Small local-interest museums are found at the **Lopinot Historical Complex**, the **Arima Museum** with its Amerindian exhibits, **Pitch Lake** with artifacts disgorged during asphalt mining and at the **Mt. Irvine Bay Hotel** on Tobago. Port of Spain's leading galleries are Art Creators & Supplies, The Art Gallery, Kacal's Artist in Wood and Moart Gallery. There is a small gallery in Fort King George in Scarborough.

Tourist Information
Tourism Information Trinidad, 10-14 Philips St., Port of Spain, Tel: 623-1932/4, Fax: 623-3848. **Tobago Tourism Info**, Crown Point Airport, Tel: 639-0509, Fax: 639-2125/4643, Fax: 639-3566; or NJB Mall in Scarborough, Tel: 639-2125/4636, Fax: 639-3566.

THE ABC ISLANDS

THE DUTCH ABC

ARUBA
BONAIRE
CURAÇAO

Probably only the Dutch, with their gift for rescuing what appear to be the most unpromising lands, could have seen the possibilities in the three sister isles of Aruba, Bonaire and Curaçao – sunny, desert islands off the coast of Venezuela.

The Spanish considered them worthless and never bothered to colonize them particularly seriously. Seen from the air it appears the Spanish were right. They are arid, brownish lands covered with scrub brushwood and cactus – not at all like the Caribbean beloved of travel brochures. A glance at the surrounding waters, however, tells another story. The sea here is incredibly clear and its colors are unique, even for the Caribbean.

Generally, the climate is dry and perpetually sunny. Temperatures range from 80° to 85° F (about 26° to 31° C). The temperature variance between winter and summer is only four degrees. Annual rainfall is 20 inches. The islands lie twelve degrees north of the equator, which contributes to their balmy climate. They are completely outside the hurricane belt, and the ferocious storms so feared by other peoples of the Caribbean are almost unheard of here.

Preceding pages: The ABC-Islands are a veritable paradise for divers. Left: New houses are designed in the old style.

Along with truly pleasant weather, the people on these so-called "ABC islands" offer a warm *bonbini*, meaning welcome in the native *Papiamento,* to all visitors. Almost everyone on the islands is fluent in four languages – English, Dutch, Spanish and Papiamento, an exotic, musical language which combines Spanish, Portuguese, African and Dutch words. It originated as the jargon of the slave-dealers of Curaçao.

In plantation days the Dutch supplied the whole of South America with slaves. They also made money on the medicinal aloe cactus that grows on the island. In the 19th century they scratched around and found some gold and harvested salt from ponds to sell on the world market. When oil was found in Venezuela, they went on to build huge refineries.

Aruba has had *Status Aparte* since 1986, and is therefore an autonomous member of the Kingdom of Holland. Bonaire and Curaçao, on the other hand are still very much bound up politically to the other islands of the Dutch Antilles, Saba, Sint Eustatius and Sint Maarten.

ARUBA

Not only is Aruba first alphabetically, but also the most developed in terms of tourism and the most independent, even

ARUBA

though it is the smallest in size. In 1986, under an agreement with the Netherlands, Aruba separated from the other islands that make up the Netherlands Antilles, although it still remains within the realm of the kingdom.

First inhabited by the Arawak Indians, the island was claimed for Spain in 1499 by Alonso de Ojeda. Today, even though the people of the island represent some 40 different nationalities, Indian ancestry is still evident. The last Indian in Aruba is said to have died in 1862, a recent date in comparison to the rest of the Caribbean.

In 1643, the Dutch took over the neglected territory with only little opposition from the Spanish. Peter Stuyvesant was appointed governor of the Netherlands Antilles that same year, and stayed for altogether four years before moving on to what is now New York.

Possibly the most significant year in Aruba's history was 1928, the year that

Right: Fresh fruit and vegetables can be found every day in the harbor of Oranjestad.

Lago Oil and Transport Company arrived. Lago, soon to become a subsidiary of *Standard Oil*, came to Aruba seeking a good seaport and a stable government for an oil refinery to process petroleum from Venezuela. The plant grew to be the world's largest, producing 440,000 barrels of oil a day and employing more than 8000 people. The refinery actually shut down in 1985, but reopened later on a much smaller scale. Since then Arubans have succeeded in preventing a severe economic crisis by making tourism step by step the dominant industry.

The combination of Dutch influence and hard-working people has produced a land well-tuned to tourists's needs. The standard of living is one of the highest in the West Indies and American lifestyles are more evident here than on all the neighboring isles. Basic facilities such as schools, water distillation plants, airport and hospital are first-rate. Residents are proud of their land and enjoy showing it to visitors. The crime rate is low and visitors are not bothered by the persistent

ARUBA

hagglers who have become so common on some other Caribbean islands. Tourists flock here for the miles of white beaches which seem to be made from spun sugar, and day after day of cloudless skies and constant cooling trade winds. Also, they enjoy the lively hotels, restaurants and casinos where standards of food and service are uniformly high.

Oranjestad

Oranjestad, the bustling capital with a population of about 20,000, still divulges the hall marks of the old colonial days. Its main avenue, **Nassaustraat**, is lined with banks, offices and stores offering duty-free bargains from all over the world. Although the selection is wider in Curaçao, shopping in Oranjestad is popular and pleasant.

The **Schooner Market** (a fleet of small fishing boats and island schooners moored in the harbor) is a popular floating market. Every morning, fresh fish and produce are sold directly from the boats. Venezuelan boats filled with fresh fruit and vegetables that do not grow in the arid land of Aruba, also offer their bounty along the wharf. The harbor of Aruba at Oranjestad is a permanent fixture in the itinerary of the larger cruise boats, thanks to its first-rate facilities.

Touring the Island

Outside of town in the *cunucu*, or country-side, the landscape is dominated by cactuses and the windblown divi-divi tree, the symbol of the island. Formidable fences made of cacti are designed to keep goats out of islanders' gardens. The coast on the leeward side is smooth and serene, but on the windward side, in comparison, the scenery is rugged and even wild. The pounding surf sends high walls of spray over the huge jagged rocks which form the coastline. It is accordingly desolate and windswept, and the powerful ocean

has completely undercut the cliffs at **Andicouri Bay** to form a natural bridge. Also interesting are the rock formations of **Boca-Mahos Bay**.

Along the northeast coast, near **Bashiribana**, are abandoned **Gold Mines** and the ruins of a **Pirate's Castle** that dates to 1499.

The sea along the southwestern coast is stunningly aquamarine; the beaches are pure white. Palm trees surround the pools and little grass-thatched cabanas line the shore. The island's casinos open before lunch and its discos close not before sunrise. Nightlife is lively and usually centers around the casinos, although particularly many smaller hotels without casinos offer nightly musical entertainment with some dancing.

The wind never really seems to stop in Aruba, which keeps humidity down and blows mosquitoes and other insects away. Daytime activities on Aruba center mainly around the beach and sea. Sailing as a matter of course is very popular and diving has just recently been gaining a

following, as has been dune gliding. A top spot for dive and snorkel trips is the wreck of the *Antilla*. This German freighter lies in about 55 feet (17 m) of water and its mast is just visible from shore. When World War II broke out, the *Antilla* was docked in Aruba, a Dutch port. Having no guns to protect his ship, the German captain decided to scuttle it.

Hooiberg, or **Mt. Haystack**, near Sta. Cruz in the very center of the island, is Aruba's most prominent peak. Several hundred carved steps lead up to its 541-foot-high (152 m) summit from which one can see Venezuela on a clear day.

Another wonderful view is from **Miralamar Pass** a few miles to the southeast, and from the **Jamanota**, the island's highest elevation (616 feet/188 m).

Not too far away are caves where Carib or Arawak Indians left ancient markings. At **Fontein Cave** there are several drawings and symbols etched in red pigment, that suggest a remarkably sophisticated artist. The symbols are thought to be very ancient.

Northeast of Hooiberg, house-sized stacks of diorite boulders continue to puzzle geologists and impress visitors.

BONAIRE

The island of Bonaire is the second largest of the ABC islands but it is definitely the smallest in terms of population. With merely about 10,000 inhabitants living on 112 square miles (288 sq. km), it even is one of the most sparsely settled Caribbean isles. After Bonaire had become Dutch, the *Dutch West India Company* soon started to develop the island's economy particularly with saltmining and farming.

British and French privateers operated on Bonaire between 1800 and 1816, and the British briefly occupied the island during the Napoleonic Wars and leased it, including its 300 slaves, to a merchant

Above: This divi-divi tree has resisted many a storm. Right: The natural bridge at Andicouri Bay (Aruba), dug by the Ocean.

BONAIRE

in New York for about $2400 annually. By 1816 the Dutch had returned to power and set up a system of government plantations for local crops, cattle and salt. Since salt production was so labor intensive, a large number of slaves were imported from Africa. The slave huts at the southern tip of the island served as shelter for the people working in the salt pans. When Dutch slavery was abolished in 1863 the industries quite suddenly could not be sustained. The island was divided up into parcels and the lots sold. Nowadays the *Antilles International Salt Company* produces salt in lagoons.

The first tourist hotel opened in 1951, but only in the past 20 years has the island boomed as recreational divers discovered the beauty of the Bonaire coral reef and came to appreciate the consistent weather and sea conditions.

Nature Park Island

Bonaire is 24 miles (79 km) long and no more than seven (11 km) wide at the broadest point, making it ideal for a day tours. There are actually two islands, Bonaire and uninhabited, 1,500-acre **Klein** (*little* in Dutch) **Bonaire**.

Kralendijk, the small, colorful capital, has changed little in the past 20 years. There are casinos here, but they are small and certainly low-key in comparison with neighboring Aruba. The houses are in colonial style, the harbor is a pleasant place to walk, and no one should miss the little **Island Museum**.

Probably the best night shows around take place under the sea. During the day, with natural light, one dives in a kind of blue-tinged twilight. At night, however, with a camera's flash or underwater light, the true colors of the reef come alive. Lobsters scurry across the bottom and silently swaying corals open their polyps for feeding. Some fish do sleep, allowing one to get very close to study them. Bonaire is not just surrounded by coral reefs, it *is* a coral reef itself, providing some of the most accessible and varied diving in the entire Caribbean.

BONAIRE

Despite its modest size, Bonaire is a giant in the park and preservation sector. The entire island is a marine park, the first of its kind in the Caribbean and also one of the largest in the world. Funded by the *World Wildlife Fund* and managed by the Netherlands Antilles National Parks Foundation, which is known locally as STINAPA, the whole project is dedicated to conserving and enhancing the fragile marine eco-system. More than a decade ago spearfishing was outlawed, as was the removal of shells, corals and sea fans, dead or alive for that matter. Anchoring a boat outside Kralendijk is illegal as anchors smash delicate corals. Dive sites are rigged with mooring buoys and some of them are periodically removed to give the reef respite from the divers.

Since reefs are everywhere, divers or snorkelers just have to walk into the water and look down. Visibility is in the 60- to 90-foot range and water temperature varies between 78 and 80 degrees F. More than 80 named dive sites lie along the leeward shore of Bonaire and around Klein Bonaire. Dive boats make two and sometimes three trips a day for those who wish to venture further offshore or off Klein Bonaire. Reefs abound with seafans, gorgonians and tube sponges. Black corals, crinoids, plate corals and vase sponges provide colorful habitats for a variety of marine life. Tiny seahorses, christmas tree worms, and hermit crabs provide motifs for the macro-photographer. Marine life includes queen and French angelfish, tilefish, trunkfish, parrotfish, butterfly fish, triggerfish, pufferfish, squirrelfish, Spanish hogfish and groupers. Stingrays and moray eels are common on most reefs. Wreck diving enthusiasts should enjoy the *Hilma Hooker*, which was intentionally sunk as a dive attraction in 1984 and now sits on her starboard side in 90 feet of water.

Daytime dives take you down into a bluish twilight, whilst at night, using a flash or an underwater projector will re-

veal the full glory of the reef's colors. Lobsters crawl across the ocean floor, corals open up their polyps to catch their prey, some fish sleep, and can be examined at incredibly close range.

But parks here are not just limited to the shoreline. The northern quarter of the island is occupied by the 13,500-acre **Washington/Slagbaai National Park**, which is open daily from 8:00 a.m. to 5:00 p.m. The 22-mile (35 km) route laid out through the park is marked by yellow arrows. Roads are rugged and one will have to drive slowly – all the better to see and appreciate the birds, such as flamingoes, as well as the beauty of the landscape. Cactuses, lizards and iguanas (some four- foot long) dominate the fauna and flora. The park also has beaches. **Boca Slagbaai** has restored buildings from a period 120 years ago when the area was a plantation producing charcoal, salt and aloe. Long ago wild goats were slaughtered here for shipment to Curaçao, hence the name, meaning "slaughter bay."

At the southern tip of the island lies the Flamingo Bird Sanctuary around the spot where the Antilles International Salt Company runs its business. When saltmaking was resumed near pekelmeer a little while ago, the company was careful not to ruin the habitat of the Flamingos. These tall, elegant birds get frightened of airplanes and the like, and in their panic can break their wings or legas. The Aruba government, private citizens and the salt company have cooperated in preserving the local colony, which is estimated at 4000 nests.

CURAÇAO

This island is the largest and most populated of the three isles, and it is also the most Dutch in appearance and character. When the Europeans showed up in 1499, it was inhabited by the Caiquetios, a seafaring tribe from the Arawak group

Above: Machines do the work once performed by slaves in the salines of Bonaire.

of Venezuela. The Caiquetios established the basic trade link which still exists with Venezuela, 35 miles away. They also gave the island its name, although there are tales claiming it is a corruption of the Portuguese *coraçao*, meaning "heart."

When the Dutch claimed Curaçao in 1634, they realized that the natural harbor was an ideal location for privateering. It became the main Dutch base for trading with the rest of the Caribbean and South America. By 1643 there were enough inhabitants to warrant the appointment of a governor. The Dutch dispatched Peter Stuyvesant, to the island. He tried to increase Dutch holdings by leading an expedition to Sint Maarten, which was then held by Spain. The Spanish fired a shot which tore off his right leg. He had it replaced with a wooden one, laced with silver, which gave rise to his nickname: "Old Silver Nails." The leg was buried in either Sint Maarten or Curaçao, and Stuyvesant was later reassigned as governor of what is now New York.

The Dutch held off British and French colonial greed, and by 1815 could claim the island entirely for themselves. The land itself is not fertile, but the harbor of Willemstad became a boon, especially with the opening of the Panama Canal in 1914. It's the fifth largest in the world today.

Oil refining after World War Two further increased its economic significance.. Nowadays refineries and phosphate mining are the two most important industries on Curaçao after tourism.

From its earliest days Curaçao has had a reputation for accepting visitors, an obvious fact when looking at its multiethnic social make-up. The island has welcomed Catholics, Jews, Protestants, Moslems, famous people such as Simon Bolivar, who hid out here twice during his campaigns for the liberation of South America from the Spanish yoke, as well as the tourists who come for the sun, shopping and casinos.

Willemstad

It was during this initial development that the capital town of **Willemstad** took on the storybook air that characterizes it today. Although it is not quite adequate to say that Willemstad looks like a typical Dutch town, the Dutch did bring their architecture to the tropics and adapted it to local conditions. Streets were carefully laid out with neat, solidly constructed houses. A colonial governor was reported to have complained that the glaring tropical sunlight reflecting on the whitewashed houses gave him a severe headache. So the obliging citizens are said to have painted their houses in every conceivable hue to try to ease his pain. Whether this tale is true or not, Willemstad remains uniquely colorful. The early houses have been transformed into bustling shops, but the original architecture and the pastel hues remain, giving the capital a distinctive skyline.

The best way to experience Willemstad is on a walking tour. There is a good one on Wednesdays and Thursdays at 5:45 p.m., which goes through the downtown area and the old town with its wonderful old buildings in pinks, yellows and blues, and with typical Amsterdam-style gables and façade decorations.

A good way to round off this visit of the old town is dinner at the **Java Indonesian restaurant** right on the water, where the palate is treated to special flavors: The *rijstafel* is one of many courses to be sampled at an Indonesian festival meal.

The capital is clearly divided into two sections by the **St. Anna Baai**, the access channel to the safe natural harbor, the so-called **Schottegat** – the **Punda**, where the shops and the old town are located, and the **Otrabunda**, or the "other side."

The pontoon bridge over the channel was originally completed in 1888 and dedicated as the **Emmabrug** (Queen Emma Bridge). The bridge swings open

more than 30 times a day to admit the ocean-going ships that use the harbor canal. In such cases, free ferry service keeps traffic moving from one side of town to the other. Also, close to the habor is the imposing **Julianabrug** (Queen Juliana Bridge) built in 1974, which arches high over the harbor carrying vehicle traffic on four lanes. Two powerful forts stand sentinel over the entrance of the harbor: **Fort Amsterdam** in the southwest of Punda, and **Fort Nassau**, in the mouth of St. Anna Baai in the Schottegat.

A few minutes walk from the Emmabrug, in an inlet off St. Anna Baai, is a **floating market**. Many Venezualans park their boats and schooners there and sell tropical fruit and vegetables, dried meat, fish, cloths and beer. The new market, established in the covered market building, is open every Saturday at 6:00 a.m., and offers Curaçao's own products.

Above: The old part of Willemstad is known as Punda is an architectural gem. Right: St. Marta Baai in Curaçao.

Curaçao has some of the best shopping in the Caribbean. Treasures and trinkets are offered in a five-block area in central Willemstad. Its main shopping strip – offering all kinds of articles – is on and around the **Bredestraat**, which is the extension of the Queen Emma Bridge leading into the old town. Elegant and expensive stores selling jewelry, porcelain, watches and other precious and costly objects have opened here. The firm **Spritzer & Fuhrman** has a branch here, of course: Its history began in Willemstad. In 1927, the two Austrians Karl Fuhrman and Wolf Spritzer opened a watch repair shop, and soon after added a retail collection of gold and jewelry. Today the company has 30 branch stores spread out through the Caribbean – six alone in Willemstad – specializing in watches, glassware, porcelain and expensive jewelry.

The **Mikve Israel-Emanuel Synagogue** on Columbusstraat, off the Bredestraat at **Wilhelmina Park**, was dedicated in 1732. Supposedly it is the oldest such temple in continuous use in the Western Hemisphere. There is a central courtyard and the interior of the building is carpeted with a layer of white sand, symbolic of the Jews' 40-year journey through the desert to the Promised Land. Four 24-candle chandeliers, three of which are more than 250 years old, hang from the genuine mahogany ceiling.

Next door is the little **Jewish Museum**, housed in a 200-year-old building that used to be a rabbi's house. A 300-year-old *mikvah*, a communal bath used for ritual purifications, was discovered in the courtyard.

The main square in Otrabanda is Brionplein, which opens up at the foot of the Queen Emma Bridge. It was named for Curaçao's favorite son and its best-known war hero, Pedro Luis Brion. He is credited with preventing several British invasion attempts, although they did finally capture the island in 1800. He forced the British withdrawal three years later, however, and in 1814 he became admiral of the fleet of Colombia under Simon Bolivar and fought for the independence of Colombia and Venezuela.

Another rewarding place to visit on the "other side" of Willemstad is the **Curaçao Museum** standing a little way to the west. It has a documentation on the history of the island.

Excursions on the Island

Curaçao is 37 miles (60 km) long and no more than 7 miles (11 km) wide. It is covered with a savannah, cactus, bushes and the typically wind-bent divi-divi tree. This island's beaches do not measure up in size with Aruba but there are fine ones at **Westpunt Baai** up north.

Out of town, Curaçao's newest tourist attraction is indeed one of the best **sea aquariums** to be found anywhere. Set majestically on a point of land overlooking the sea, the aquarium recreates reefs that surround the island with a multitude

of reef fish, eels, sharks, lobster and other denizens of the deep. A restaurant, a bar and a hotel have opened alongside the aquarium. This is the best introduction to **Curaçao Undersea Park**, which extends from the eastern tip of the island to the Princess Beach Hotel. The submarine Seaworld Explorer sails through the underwater park daily at 11:30 a.m. and 3:30 p.m. The entire area under protection stretches along the southwestern coast. It is supervised by Tom Van't Hof, who also set up Bonaire's sea park. There is a total of 16 sites, including a shipwreck, which have been charted. An underwater nature path with information has also been arranged below the surface.

Nature lovers will particularly enjoy **Sint Christoffelberg National Park,** with Mount Christoffel (1230 feet/375 m) at its center, located in the north of the island. It boasts a wide variety of plants, trees and wildlife such as iguanas, rabbits, deer and birds. There are also **caves** with Indian petroglyphs and unusual rock formations, but they are hard to get to.

ABC ISLANDS
(Area codes: Aruba 2978, Bonaire 5997, Curaçao 5999)

Accommodations

ARUBA: *LUXURY:* **Americana Aruba Beach Resort & Casino**, on the beach, Tel: 64500, Fax: 63191, bar, casino, pool, tennis courts, shopping galery, Las Vegas show. **Radisson Aruba Caribbean Resort & Casino**, on the beach, Tel: 63555, Fax: 63260, about 400 rooms, bar, fitness center, tennis. **Aruba Palm Beach Resort & Casino**, Tel: 63900, Fax: 961941, about 200 rooms, large beach, pool, aquatic sports. **Best Western Bucuti Beach Resort**, Tel: 31100, Fax: 25272, one of the favorite hotels, both central and on the seaside. **Divi-Divi Aruba Beach Resort**, Tel: 23300, Fax: 34002, two pools, tennis, complete aquatic sports package, casino. **Tamarijn Aruba Beach Resort**, Tel: 24150, Fax: 34002, at the seaside, pool, tennis (among other sports), shops, and casino in the Alhambra Bar.

MODERATE: **Holiday Inn Aruba Beach Resort**, 602 rooms, giant pool, fitness centr, tennis, restaurants and casino. **Talk of the Town Resort Hotel**, Tel: 23380, fax: 33208, 63 rooms, a well-known restaurant, a pool and beach across the road. **Manchebo Beach Resort Hotel**, same owners as Talk of the Town. Guests have exchange privileges.

BONAIRE: *MODERATE TO BUDGET:* **Captain Don's Habitat**, Tel: 8290, Fax: 8240, presided over by diving pioneer and conservationist Don Stewart. Once a spartan dive community, it offers a diversity of accommodation including two-bedroom cottages, hotel rooms, and luxury villas, as well as a restaurant, bar and well-run dive operation. **Divi Flamingo Beach**, Tel: 8285, Fax: 8283, hotel and dive operation is wheel-chair accessible with pools, bar, casino and restaurants overlooking the sea. **Sonesta Beach Bonaire** is one of Bonaire's newest, overlooking the marina or the beach, a pool, water sports facilities, restaurants, a bar and a conference room. **Sand Dollar Condominium and Beach Club**, Tel: 8738, Fax: 8760, has studio apartments and one-, two- and three-bedroom apartments. The complex has a shopping center, pool, tennis courts, restaurant and bar, casino, marina and dive shop. **Sunset Beach Hotel**, Tel: 8448, Fax: 8470, is on the island's nicest beach, offering restaurants, shops, pool, tennis, dive shop, bars. **Sorobon Beach**, Tel: 8080, Fax: 5680, is a naturalist's resort where clothes are optional. There are 16 cottages with kitchenettes, dining room and bar and a pleasant beach. **Carib Inn**, Tel: 8819, Fax: 5295, is a small, 12-room diver's inn operated by American Bruce Bowker. Pool and a well-run dive operation.

CURAÇAO: *LUXURY TO MODERATE:* **Curaçao Caribbean Hotel & Casino** with beach, tennis, sweeping view of Piscadera Bay, several restaurants and casino. **Golden Tulip Las Palmas Hotel and Vacation Village**, also on Piscadera Bay, small beach, a casino, tennis, restaurants. **Hotel Curaçao Plaza and Casino** stands guard over the Punda side of the St. Anna Baai in Willemstad and is nestled in the ramparts of an 18th century fort. Pool, a rooftop dining room atop the 15-story tower which offers spectacular sunset views over Willemstad, two other restaurants, bars and a popular casino.

Holiday Beach Hotel & Casino, 5 miles (8 km) from Willemstad, Pater Euwensweg, has 200 rooms, a beach, pool, tennis, restaurants and the largest casino on the island. **Princess Beach Hotel** features all watersports with a golf course nearby, 202 rooms, tennis courts, restaurants and a casino. **Avila Beach Hotel** in Willemstad, Penstraat, is a beautifully restored 200-year-old mansion with 45 rooms and two suites on its own beach, an open-air restaurant and bar. **Golden Tulip Coral Cliff Resort & Casino**, Santa Marta Baai, on the bay by the same name, is a group of bungalows on the edge of the sea. The 35 apartments have kitchenettes and there is a restaurant, tennis court, beach, watersports and shuttle to town.

Restaurants

ARUBA: There are few Aruban native dishes although Indonesian dishes offer an exotic alternative, along with Argentinean, Mexican, German, Italian, French and New York-style *deli* fare. Major credit cards are generally accepted.

Bon Apetit is a rustic place within walking distance of many Palm Beach hotels. **Buccaneer** is a popular eatery which specializes in seafood. **De Olde Molen** is an old windmill originally built in Holland in 1804, which was dismantled, shipped to Aruba and reassembled in 1960. **Dragon-Phoenix** serves mostly Cantonese food. **Papiamento** is an antique house in town which offers continental menus in an elegant setting.

BONAIRE: Restaurants are few but serve delicious fresh seafood.

Le Chic overlooks Kralendijk Harbor and the pier, a French restaurant which specializes in fresh seafood. **Chibi-Chibi** at the Divi Flamingo Beach Hotel is attractively perched on piers overlooking the sea. Schools of tropical fish entertain the diners. **The Beefeater** is one of the island's oldest restaurants. Englishman Richard Dove created this handsome restaurant in an old town house. Steaks and seafood. **Zeezicht** means "sea view" and is the best place in town to watch the sunset over the water and

enjoy seafood and Chinese dishes. **China Garden** is housed in a restored mansion. Servings are large and prices low. **Den Laman Aquarium Bar and Restaurant** next to the Sunset Beach Hotel specializes in seafood.
CURAÇAO: Seafood, Indonesian and Dutch specialties are favorites.
Fort Nassau is built in the ruins of a fort dating from 1792. From the terrace there is a panoramic view of the sea, the harbor and Willemstad. **Bistro Le Clochard**, Riffort, on the Otrabunda side of the pontoon bridge, has been fitted into the ramparts of Fort Rif at the gateway to the harbor. **Le Récif**, under the arches of Fort Rif near the pontoon bridge serves Caribbean seafood. **Belle Terrace** is in a 200-year-old mansion on the beach in Willemstad, Scandinavian and local dishes. **The Catch of the Day** has a special three-course menu each night. **Bistro Larousse** was built in 1742, open for dinner only. **Rodeo Ranch Saloon & Steakhouse**, steaks, roast beef, seafood. **Fort Waakzaamheid Tavern**, Domi Mt., in Otrabanda, was the fort that Captain Bligh captured in 1804. **Playa Forti**, Westplunt, is built on the foundation of a fort dating from Bonaparte's days. The sea views are spectacular.

Access and Local Transportation

Aruba American, Continental, and Antillean Airlines provide service from the USA. In addition, there are charter flights from various cities in the USA and Canada. Air Aruba and ALM provide connecting service between Aruba, Bonaire and Curaçao. It is possible to include visits to Curaçao and/or Bonaire for the same fare from the States.
ARUBA: Cruise ships call year-round in Aruba. Taxis are not metered, so establish the fare before getting into the cab. Airport buses serve all hotels but require prepaid travel coupons issued by travel agents. Public buses offer regular service between hotels on Eagle Beach and Palm Beach and town. There are a variety bus, taxi and sea tours operated by DePalm Tours, Pelican Tours and Bruno Tours. Lee Air and Oduber Aviation operate charter flights with guided day tours to Bonaire and Curaçao.
BONAIRE: Bonaire ALM has some direct flights from Miami and New York. Many visitors travel first to Aruba or Curaçao and connect with ALM or Air Aruba to Bonaire. The departure tax is 10 US$. Taxis are un-metered, but government established rates are posted in hotels and at the airport. There are no public buses. Roads are narrow but good and cars rent for 25 – 50 US$ a day. Happy Chappy Rentals offers cycles and mopeds for 15 – 25 US$ a day. Bonaire Sightseeing, Flamingo Tours and Archie Tours offer bus tours or the north and south ends of the island. There are several afternoon or sunset cruises as well as water taxis to uninhabited Klein Bonaire.

CURAÇAO: American, Eastern, and ALM fly from the USA. Air Jamaica, KLM, BWIA, Avianca, VIASA and Pan AM also provide service from other islands and South America. There are weekly charters from the USA and Canada in winter. Cruise ships call year-round in Willemstad. Hotels outside town usually provide free shuttle bus service to town. Taxis are not metered, but there is an official tariff sheet. Taber, Daltino and ABC Tours offer sightseeing tours. ALM and Oduber offer tours to Bonaire or Aruba. The departure tax is between US$ 10 and 20. Helicopter tours: Pelican Air, Tel: 462-8155, Fax: 462-8182.

Customs and Entry Formalities

For American and Canadian citizen proof of citizenship and an ongoing or return ticket are the only requirements for all three islands. For citizens of other countries a passport is required.

Currency

The currency in Aruba is the Aruba Florin, which is divided into 100 cents. The current exchange rate is 1 US$ to 1.79 AFL. The currency of Bonaire and Curaçao is the Netherlands Antilles Florin (NAFl). The rate is same as the Aruba Florin. US dollars are accepted everywhere. Credit cards and traveler's checks are widely accepted.

Festivals and Special Events

ARUBA: *Carnival* celebrations offer the biggest events of the year and begin in mid-January, climaxing with *Grand Parade and Jump-up* on the Sunday before Ash Wednesday. The election of various carnival queens, music contests and smaller steel-band parades go on for weeks before. Aruba now claims to be the world's third-largest celebrator of Carnival after New Orleans and Rio de Janeiro.
BONAIRE: They celebrate *Carnival* here in February with dancing and parades. An *Annual International Sailing Regatta* is held in October. In honor of the *Queen's Birthday*, on April 30, the lieutenant governor hosts a cocktail reception at his home and everyone is invited.
CURAÇAO: Curaçao celebrates *Carnival* in a big way with music, parades and dancing. Willemstad hosts a monthly *Bon Topa Street Fair*, which is a good excuse to go to town for a party.

Tourist Information

ARUBA: Aruba Tourist Bureau, L.G. Smith Blvd., 172 Oranjestad, Tel: 23777. **BONAIRE: Tourist Board**, Breedestraat, Kralendijk, Tel: 8322 or 8649. **CURAÇAO: Curaçao Tourist Office**, Waterfront Plaza, Willemstad, Tel: 461-6000, Fax: 461-2305, and at the airport.

SAILING

As little as 30 years ago, the realization of the dream of sailing the waters of the Lesser Antilles was reserved for the few who owned their own boats or could afford to charter a private yacht. Quite a few sophisticated charter operations have since developed and are steadily expanding throughout these islands. This development, however, has had a negative as well as a positive effect. The exclusivity of sailing has now been removed and a foreign element – that of sheer luxury – has been injected. The greatest change, however, can be observed in the attitude of the island people themselves. It is understandably difficult for somebody trying to get by in a subsistence economy not to envy affluent outsiders who sail in on their expensive yachts. Never mind that an extended cruise vacation may be the only hard-earned escape of the year for some working people. That point may be lost on many islanders.

In the whole Caribbean, a rough rule of thumb would have it that the less an island depends on tourism, then the "nicer" it tends to be. Skippers may have to pay a few EC dollars to a local to have their dinghy watched or to tie up to a coconut tree. Yet the aggressiveness or surliness that can mark a visitor's stay at the more developed islands are usually offset on the "nice" islands by as much friendliness and generosity as one could hope to find. This said, there is no finer way to see the islands than under sail.

For the experienced sailor, bareboat chartering may be most appealing. After a proficiency check, the chartering party is checked out on the boat and steered towards a cruising area, then made entirely responsible for the boat until its return. State-of-the-art boats, designed for tropical charters, in the 30- to 50-foot range, come with water, fuel, ice, dinghy, fully equipped galley, sheets and towels – a tidy package at one price that competes favorably with other, land-based vacations. Provisioning plans are available. Partial provisioning, which allows for dinners out and options to stock up in the native market on local fruit and vegetables seems best. Provisioning completely is very time-consuming.

For the less than expert sailor or for the novice, crewed charters or learn-to-cruise options are a good option. In this case one must add charges of $75-$100 per day for the experienced captain who will handle the boat and guide one safely in recommending the best choice of course and anchorage as well.

A number of charter operators have added sailing schools to their program with the possible ultimate goal of certification for worldwide charter. The **Moorings and Offshore Sailing School** in Tortola, BVI; **CSY's Sail N'Learn Program**, also in Tortola; **CYOA** and the **International School of Sailing** in St. Thomas, USVI; and finally **Trade Wind Yachts' Sea School** in St. Lucia are examples for this growing trend.

Virgin Islands

Most popular and best for the novice and still inexperienced sailor, or anybody with trepidations about seasickness, are the Virgin Islands (except St. Croix!). Covering only 30 square miles of blue water, with few navigational hazards to worry about, and surrounded by green mountainous islands, they are perfect for a week-long cruise. Incessant tradewinds blow at a steady 15 to 25 knots, although without those long Atlantic swells that can make inter-island travel farther south distinctly uncomfortable for the land-lubber. Most of the time one can find bliss in protected waters, sailing the Virgin way, under jib alone.

Preceding pages and right: Sailing either on a yacht or in a boat is one of the main activities in the Lesser Antilles.

SAILING AND CRUISING

Leeward and Windward Islands

Steering southeast from the Virgin Islands one gets to the most northerly of the Leeward Islands. St. Martin/Sint Maarten is a base for exploring St. Barts, Anguilla, St. Kitts, Nevis and Saba. Trade winds blow strong. For here one sails on the open ocean with long swells that come direct from Africa. St. Lucia's central position makes it the appropriate base to explore the French West Indies and the Grenadines. From St. Vincent, Union Island and Grenada are spaced perfectly apart, never more than a day's sail away. Trades are strong, but there are superb anchorages in the lee of the islands, still uncrowded and relatively undiscovered. Several charter companies offer one-way charters to avoid back tracking and long beats to windward.

Windjammer Cruises

Besides sailing yachts and cruise ships there is yet another group of vessels sailing the Lesser Antilles: windjammers all, some more traditional than others. The 137-foot top-sail Schooner *Roseway*, for instance, spent 32 years as a pilot boat in Boston, and now sails the Virgin Islands in the winter. 34 passengers may share the sailing, navigating, deck-swabbing and galley work in a relaxed, informal atmosphere. Engines are extant but used merely for docking or for tight moves. Geared to a livelier lifestyle are Windjammer Barefoot Cruises. Grand old sailing vessels like the *Flying Cloud*, *Yankee Clipper*, *Fantome* and *Mandalay*, carry 80 to 100 passengers. The local yellow pages or else most travel agents will list addresses for yacht charters.

Charters

Recommendable firms are:
BRITISH VIRGIN ISLANDS: **Bitter End Yacht Club**, charter company: Virgin Gorda; **Sunsail**, charter company: Tortola; **Offshore Sail and Motor Yachts**, charter company: Tortola.

SAILING AND CRUISING

US-VIRGIN ISLANDS: **Caribbean Yacht Owners Association/ International School of Sailing**, Yacht Haven Marina, charter company St. Thomas. **Charteryacht League**, Homeport, St. Thomas.

WINDWARD/LEEWARD ISLANDS: **CSY 5402**, charter company: St. Vincent. Soleil et Voile, c/o Le Boat, Inc., charterharbors: Guadeloupe, Martinique and St. Martin. Sunsail, Charterbasis: St. Lucia. The Moorings, Charter harbors: St. Martin, Guadeloupe, St. Lucia, Grenada. Trade Wind Yachts / Sea School, chartercompany: St. Lucia.

Cruises

St. Thomas, Tortola, Martinique, St. Lucia, St. Martin, Antigua, Barbados, Guadeloupe, Grenada, Curaçao, Aruba, Trinidad, and a few others are on every cruise lines' Eastern Caribbean itinerary. A cruise allows a fleeting glimpse of the islands, the ship itself becoming the destination. Ports lend exotic diversion for those intent on shopping, diving and land activities. The ship is a full service resort in itself; forays are a possibility but not a necessity. The number of ships plying the eastern Caribbean can be quite bewildering. Probably the best way to set about chosing is to be clear about one's likes, dislikes and expectations.

If exploration or maybe a certain sense of adventure are the criteria, there are particularly the small vessels of **Special Expeditions**. Their 80-passenger ship, explores the Orinoco, lower Caribbean, and Panama Canal. American Canadian Caribbean Line and Clipper Cruise Line cruise the Virgin Islands in the winter and spring. 70 up to 100 passengers are the norm, most of them well-traveled and older, but with a zest to learn about and experience the natural beauty of the area. American-Canadian **Caribbean Lines** is informal, basic and inexpensive, with as

Above: Taking it easy, as long as the crew knows what it is doing. Right: Cruises are the place to turn into a deck chair potato.

SAILING AND CRUISING

fiercely loyal a following as the more up-scale **Clipper Cruise Lines**.

While choices for this type of cruise are limited, but growing, there are quite a many other ships to chose from. Ships fly flags of convenience and carry international crew, though most operate under American, Norwegian, British, Italian or Greek seafaring traditions, which set the tone and ambience.

Doubtlessly at the top in terms of price, service and exclusivity is **Cunard's** 4250-ton, 116-passenger *Sea Goddess* line, which sails St. Thomas, St. Martin, St. Barts and Antigua in winter. Formal and exclusive, with all outside suites rather than ordinary cabins, a retractable watersports platform for swimming, waterskiing, windsurfing, a branch of California's Golden Door Spa, special interest cruises for art and wine lovers, an all-inclusive fare and no tipping, it more resembles an affluent and expensive private club.

Cunard's British touch is also evident on the 589-passenger *Sagafjord* and 736-passenger *Vistafjord*, both of which hold ultra-deluxe ratings. These ships offer luxury cruising with gourmet meals, fitness program and supper club type entertainment in the Eastern Caribbean, starting off from Fort Lauderdale. The *Cunard Countess* and *Cunard Princess* are informal, relaxed, and reasonably priced, and sail out of San Juan to the lower Caribbean year round.

Royal Viking's cruise ships, mid-sized 28,000-ton, 710-passenger liners, are similar in ambience to Cunard's *Vistafjord*. They offer single seating, guest lectures, sedate entertainment and theme cruises from Fort Lauderdale to Barbados.

Norwegian Cruise Lines ships, including its famous flagship *Norway*, the former *SS France*, are under the same ownership as the Royal Viking Line, and sail to the eastern Caribbean from Miami and San Juan. The *Norway* carries 1800 passengers. Other ships are mid-sized and obviously geared towards the popular market. Sports programs and Broadway-style shows are a tradition on board.

SAILING AND CRUISING

Holland America Lines, now a subsidiary of *Carnival*, has maintained its elegant charm, reflected in the art and antiques aboard mid-sized ships like the *Noordam* and *Westerdam*, which carry 1100 passengers from Fort Lauderdale to the Eastern and Southern Caribbean.

Carnival Cruise Lines is the company that changed the image of cruising. Young, brash, sassy, and with continuous entertainment and action such as beer-drinking contests and skeet shooting, these are the fun ships. The *Holiday*, *Jubilee* and *Celebration* carry more than 1000 passengers each and ply the Caribbean year round out of Miami and San Juan at affordable prices.

Costa Cruises sails out of Fort Lauderdale and San Juan. Comparable in price to Carnival and Norwegian Cruise Line ships, but with a friendly and exuberant Italian flair. Chandris Fantasy Cruises aim at the budget passenger, sailing year round out of San Juan, while the Chandris Celebrity ships presumably appeal to more affluent passengers and sail from Fort Lauderdale and San Juan.

Princess Cruises provided the original *Love Boat* of TV fame. Snorkeling and scuba programs, as well as various theme cruises characterize their affordable ten- or seven-day cruises out of San Juan or Fort Lauderdale.

Royal Caribbean Cruise Lines built the first mega-ships for 2600 passengers, the *Sovereign of the Seas* and the *Monarch of the Seas*, the latter being the largest cruise ship in the world.

Windstar Sail Cruises offer a brand-new generation of ships: computer-controlled sails help propel the upscale 180-passenger vessels. All outside cabins, *nouvelle cuisine*, scuba diving, windsurfing, waterskiing and deep-sea fishing off Antigua, St. Thomas or Barbados, are all part of the programm.

Epirotiki Lines' 12,500-ton, 525-passenger *World Renaissance* sails between

Above: Shows at the midnight hour on the S. S. Norway. Right and far right: Solitary entertainment on board.

SAILING AND CRUISING

Trinidad and Martinique in the winter, with lecturers on board, Greek ambience, and all at affordable prices.

Like the Windstar vessels, *Club Med I* is a new generation sailing vessel with computer-driven sails. With a capacity for 320 passengers, it is the largest sailing vessel afloat and offers a modified Club Med concept, with sailings from Martinique to the Tobago Cays and Grenada, or the Virgin Islands in the north.

Before shipping off, it is worthwhile to consider points of departure. Embarkation in Fort Lauderdale or Miami means more days at sea, fewer ports; San Juan means a maximum number of ports.

Price is also a consideration. In each category there are variations, depending on cabins and the time of year traveled. Everybody prefers an outdoor cabin, but savings can be substantial on an inside one for those who do not require a window. Holiday times are most expensive, popular with families, while summer sailings are preferred by the budget traveler.

Booking far in advance can easily save money, and so can booking just prior to departure when cabins are still unsold. Cruises are labeled all-inclusive and that is indeed true if you do not drink any alcohol or take shore excursions. Only a few lines include tips. Sea Goddess and Holland America Lines are exceptions. Suggestions, which can feel like orders, as to the "proper" tip are given frequently and average about $8-12 per cruise day, divided between waiter, bus boy and cabin steward. Port charges are usually part of the final bill presented to the passenger just prior to sailing.

First-time cruisers are often adversely surprised by the cost of the shore excursions. Study the brochure carefully and ask your travel agent for details! City tours on these small islands and shopping are better accomplished on your own. With guide book in hand and an inquisitive mind, the traveler has a chance to take pleasure in discovering the islands at a comfortable pace, and then retreat to the comforts of cruise ship and cabin while heading off to the next port of call.

DIVING, HIKING AND CAMPING

Some Caribbean islands are volcanic, others are coralline, still others are tiny outcroppings that appear merely on maritime charts. Around each are undersea rock formations, brilliant marine life and shipwrecks that await exploration by scuba divers and snorkelers. Marine ecology is increasing awareness of the fragility of the environment beneath the sea. And to protect delicate coral and else assure the continuation of other species, underwater parks are proliferating.

If the Caribbean were drained, it would appear sas a very huge crater whose most prominent feature was a curving mountain range. Even with the water in place, many mountains thrust from sea level to the clouds. Hiking the region's major mountains is a real adventure, but even a meander on a low-lying country lane or a beachcombing stroll gives a pedestrian's eye view of the island of choice.

Camping is forbidden on most beaches and totally prohibited on some islands, but where it is possible, roughing it offers another great Caribbean experience because the sounds, the smells and the feel of the tropics surround one like a cocoon.

Snorkeling and Scuba Diving

To get a proper glimpse of the magical world underwater, you need just a well-fitting face mask, snorkel, fins and minimal swimming skills, for indeed wonderful sights are found in shallow waters all over the Caribbean. Most resorts will lend or rent equipment and can point out good snorkeling right off-shore.

Exploring the marine environment and even scouting out a wreck takes more equipment and more skill. Equipment can be your own, rented or a combination, including snorkeling gear plus a wet

Right: Rock climbers and other acrobats can try their skills on any number of steep cliffs.

suit, tank for compressed air, regulator, weight belt and buoyancy control device. Those items, plus a certificate from PADI, NAUI or another organization, constitute a passport to a magical world underwater. Listed below are the best diving sites:

ANGUILLA: **Prickly Pear Island, Prickly Pear Cays** and **Sandy Island** are shallow enough for novice divers and night dives. **Sandy Deep** is a spectacular wall dive, whereas **Paintcan Reef** and **Authors Deep** are absolute deep dives. *ANTIGUA*: Much of the diving is done at scenic but shallow barrier reefs, including **Sandy Island Reef, Horseshoe Reef, Barracuda Alley** and **Little Bird Island**. **Shirley Heights** and **Sunken Rock** are deeper than 110 feet. *ARUBA*: Snorkeling and scuba diving are held in equal favor, but merely divers can explore two wrecks, the freighter *Antilla* and the tanker *Pederales*. Reef depths are about 14 feet (4 m). *BARBADOS*: This is one of the top islands for diving, because there are 70 wrecks in the immediate vicinity. Snorkeling is good. *BARBUDA*: Wrecks and reefs, none of the them overrun, lure divers and snorkelers. *BONAIRE*: Clear water, fabulous coral reefs and more than 1000 marine species make Bonaire by far the best of the ABC islands for undersea adventurers, and one of the best in the world. *DOMINICA*: The west coast between **Castle Comfort** and **Scott's Head** offers the most promising spots, and wreck diving is possible off **The Cabrits**, where a new marine park has been established in **Tacouri Bay**. *GRENADA* and the *GRENADINES*: The **New Guinea Reef** is comprised of three types of black coral. **Bequia**, which is a Mecca for both divers and snorkelers, has a wall on the leeward side which is an undersea sanctuary. **Carriacou, Mustique,** the **Tobago Cays** and **Palm Island** are best for novices and snorkelers. *GUADELOUPE*: **Pigeon Point,** off the west coast, is one of the world's best dive sites, and, thanks largely to the efforts of

Jacques-Yves Cousteau, the waters have been declared an underwater natural park. The marine life is rich, and several dive operators specialize in the area. **Maledenure** is the starting-off point. The **Petit Cul-de-Sac Marin Baie** offers half-a-dozen good places, while **Terre-de-Haute** boasts 20 sites. *MARTINIQUE*: A dozen ships sank in **St. Pierre**'s harbor, making it a prime wreck-diving spot. The leading boat dive sites are **Îlet Ramier**, **Cap Salomon** and **Les Anses d'Arlets**, while **Carbet** has good shore dives. **Rocher du Diamand**, known as the Caribbean Gibraltar, offers both wreck diving and plentiful coral and marine life. Snorkeling is good in **Les Anses d'Arlets** and **Ste. Anne**. *SABA*: This volcanic island provides some of the Caribbean's most dramatic underwater scenery. Submarine mountains, lava flows, overhangs, walls and cliffs compete for divers' attention with coral reefs, pinnacles, elkhorn forests and stands of brilliant tube sponges. Tarpon, barracuda, porpoises and sea turtles are common. Humpback whales migrate past from February through April. A marine park was created around Saba in 1987 with permanent moorings for dive boats. *ST. BARTHÉLÉMY*: Decent diving is found near **Gustavia**. Snorkeling is good in many spots. *ST. KITTS*: Good snorkeling and diving are found around **Basseterre**. *ST. LUCIA*: **Anse Chastenat** boasts one of the top wall dives in the Caribbean, down to 200 feet. Reef dives and three wrecks are also close by. *ST. VINCENT*: The **St. Vincent Reefs** offer good diving from 50 to 90 feet. *SINT MAARTEN / ST. MARTIN*: Good snorkeling is available at **Dawn Beach** on the Dutch side. Snorkeling and scuba trips are arranged to various nearby sites. *TOBAGO*: Shallow **Buccoo Reef** offers easy snorkeling; scuba diving is done farther off-shore. *TRINIDAD*: **The Bocas** off the northwest peninsula are the only site here with at least mediocre diving, but the water is relatively cold and the currents strong. *VIRGIN ISLANDS*: These islands have everything: great coral reefs, abun-

HIKING

dant marine life, several shipwrecks and even a sunken plane to explore. Of the U.S. Virgin Islands, **St. Thomas** has after all acceptable diving, **St. Croix** has very good diving and **St. John**, half of which comprises a national park, has in fact great diving, plus an underwater snorkeling trail. **Buck Island** has two snorkeling trails and local guides are available. The small, predominantly uninhabited islands in the British Virgins offer many options. **West Dog** is a national park with permanent moorings. The wreck of the *Rhone* between **Peter Island** and **Salt Island** was used to film the undersea footage in *The Deep*, and other less famous wrecks are found around **Anegada**. There is excellent snorkeling off **Norman Island** and **Marina Cay**, as well as all around startling rock formations known as **The Baths** on **Virgin Gorda**, although the latter tend to get crowded.

Above: When diving beware of the occasional moray eel. Right: The aloe plant, an ancient source of medicine.

Hiking

One of the best ways to get to know the tropical flora and fauna of the Caribbean is on foot. Sturdy boots and rain gear are strongly recommended. Here are some options, with or without the services of a guide. *BARBADOS*: Moderate walking trails has the **St. Lucy Coast**, notably one along an old railroad track from **Bath** to **Bathsheba**. Escorted walks are sometimes organized by the National Trust and as well the Outdoor Club of Barbados. *BONAIRE*: Trails and unpaved roads wind through **Washington / Slagbaai National Park**, known for its 150 species of birds. *DOMINICA*: There are many hikes. The **Morne Trois Pitons National Park's Middleham Trails**, which are leading through the rain forest, are excellent, while the demanding hike to **Morne Diablotin** in the **Northern Forest Reserve** definitely requires the services of a guide. The **Cabrits National Park** has easy trails. *GRENADA*: A park system with several hiking trails is currently being developed. **GUADE-LOUPE:** The fabulous **Parc Naturel**, with miles of well-marked trails graded according to difficulty and interpretive facilities, makes this island a favorite with hikers. Trails range from easy walks through various eco-systems to long, rough treks. The park service provides a brochure titled "Walks and Hikes." *MARTINIQUE:* **Parc Naturel Régionale de la Martinique** guides lead hikers to different parts of the island. The most popular trails lead up to **Montagne Pelée**, a challenge best undertaken with a guide. **Grand Rivière**, **Le Pêcheur** and the **Gorges de la Falaise** offer moderate and easy trails. Trails through the **Presque' Ile de la Caravelle Nature Preserve** are also easy. *MONTSERRAT:* (Note: Soufrieère eruption in Aug 1997!) Two scenic spots, the **Great Alps Waterfall** and the summit of **Chances Peak**, are accessible by steep trails. Mellower trails wind through the **Foxes Bay Bird Sanctuary**. *SABA:* The conservation association is preserving and marking old donkey trails which cover a range of distance and steepness (toughest is Mt. **Scenery**). *SINT EUSTATIUS:* Several trails through the rain forest and dry uplands lead to and around **Quill Crater**. *ST. LUCIA:* Registered guides accompany hikers on long treks to the summit of the **Pitons**. The **Central Forest Reserve** also provides some taxing terrain, and therefore, a guide is mandatory. *ST. VINCENT:* Hiking **Soufrière** is the main option here. *TRINIDAD:* Trails are available in several of the island's nature reserves and national parks. *VIRGIN ISLANDS:* The **Virgin Islands National Park** in St. John is laced with trails, and rangers act as guides. **Gorda** and **Tortola** have hiking trails.

Camping

BONAIRE: Beach camping is permitted but there are no developed sites.

GUADELOUPE: Well developed sites, tent rentals are available at **Les Sables d'Or** on **Grande Anse Beach**, near **Deshaies**. RVs of various types may be rented as well. Camping is also permitted in the **Parc Naturel**. *MARTINIQUE:* Camping is permitted nearly everywhere, but one should check with local officials before selecting a specific spot. **Anse-á-l'Ane** near **Trois Ilets**, **Vauclin** on the southeast Atlantic coast, and **Ste. Anne**, **Diamant** and **Ste. Luce** on the south coast have some campgrounds with basic facilities. Small RVs can be rented from local firms. *ST. LUCIA:* Camping is permitted on most of the beaches. *VIRGIN ISLANDS:* **St. John's Cinnamon Bay Campground**, operated by the United States Park Service, is presumably one of the best in the Caribbean, with tent sites, splendid views and a great beach. Privately operated campgrounds are Maho Bay in St. John, Brewer's Bay on Tortola, Larry's Hideaway and Campsites on St. Thomas' Hull Bay and Tula's N&N on Jost Van Dyke.

TOURISM QUANDARY

THE TOURISM QUANDARY

Anyone who visited the Caribbean several decades ago will invariably be astounded at the changes. Indeed, there have been many. In those blissful days of the mid-1950s, when tourism began in earnest – stimulated by World War II returnees who had been lucky enough to be stationed in this paradise – the islands were a completely different place than they are today. Few people went there, they were isolated, inexpensive, quiet. Nowadays, tourists remembering isolated beaches with not so much as a cottage upon them return to discover vast multi-service resorts catering to thousands of people. It seems that every beach is being developed, every little pocket of quiet being discovered. Some say the Caribbean is not the Caribbean anymore, especially those who live there.

Above: Child's play today could become the fashion of tomorrow. Right: Just the place to spend a honeymoon.

If visitors come to feel proprietary about their favorite stretches of paradise, one can well imagine how those who have been raised here feel. Some visitors sense resentment on the part of the locals – a barely suppressed facial expression, an arch tone of voice, or more obvious mannerisms such as the hurling of a *voodoo* curse or picking one's pocket. Aggressive behavior, once quite fashionable, has been on decline in recent years, most likely due to the plain economic necessity of having to cater to the aliens. The same development that chews up those desolate spots provides an estimated 300,000 jobs for citizens who desperately need them. The only thing they resent, they will say, is when visitors misbehave. Invariably, some tourists do, many unintentionally. Islanders put up with persistent photographers, obnoxious drunks and cut-throat bargain-hunters who want to buy for less than cost.

An estimated $6 billion is generated by Caribbean tourism. Residents benefit in other ways from the patronage as well. Services are slowly being upgraded for all. Water, electricity, telephone lines – not many would argue against such improvements. Still, there is a negative side to all this development as even the most revenue-hungry government functionary would admit. The environment really suffers from increased population, garbage dumping, litter and pollution of the very waters that helped lure tourists in the first place. Sometimes the infrastructure cannot support the projects. If the sewers back up and the lights go out at the wrong time in the wrong place the most paradisiacal island of the Lesser Antilles could face a public relations nightmare. As one tourism official admits: "A small hotel can get away with charm if the lights go out. A large resort cannot."

In order to guarantee these services, hotels have to make enormous investments and usually they are not alone in pouring out cash. The government in

TOURISM QUANDARY

each island encumbers large sums for projects it may not be in a comfortable position to fund. There are also no guarantees that once completed, these projects will return their investments. If they do not, the islanders benefit from the aforementioned improvements, intended for the hotel guests and left over for the residents. But the budget gaps remain for the government, *ergo* the tax payer.

Other drawbacks arise from the influence of the visitors. Drug problems and crime are picking up in previously unaffected areas. One has to go all the way to little islands such as Saba to find places that are still crime-free. Apart from these drawbacks, though, is the one that most fear from development, the one that is most obvious to returning visitors. Overdevelopment eventually destroys a beautiful site. It is a lesson governments of certain islands, St. Martin clearly among them, should have learned already in the past. Hotel rooms on this side of the French/Dutch island have more than doubled in recent years and more are still being built. Most visitors there generally agree that whatever charm the island had was lost long ago. People come to see natural scenery, not cranes.

In some cases governments have been careful about their island's development. St. Barts has numerous hotels and a few more are planned, but they are kept small. By restricting the size of resorts, local powers demonstrate their recognition of the importance of protecting their island's environment. Some small islands, however, are well on their way to problems. Nevis, an island too small to even have an airstrip, is about to get a vast Four Seasons Resort. And other islands are also being populated by a Radisson or Ramada, even in out of the way places like the Turks and Caicos.

To lovers of the true, disappearing Caribbean, this is a rather discouraging note. But anyone who gets depressed can still wander out to Saba and Statia and stay in a tiny guest house with only a few people around. The true Caribbean does still exist in parts.

CARIBBEAN CUISINE

Market day on the islands: A gently jostling crowd moves past all the tidy bundles of cinnamon, the bowls of fresh nutmeg, the neat little stacks of tomato and breadfruit on burlap sacks, big bunches of *calaloo* greens and Scotch bonnet peppers, hands of bananas and plantains. Barrels of salt cod lead to the butcher section where a proudly displayed cow's head advertises the day's choice meat. By the water, fishermen and their wives proffer a bounty of flying fish, grouper, crabs and conch still in its shell. Brightly dressed women, fanning the humid air, bargain patiently for a good price on the soursop and the papaya.

The scene repeats itself every Saturday in Grenville in Grenada, be it by the waterfront of Point-à-Pitre in Guadeloupe, in the sleepy settlement of Plymouth in Montserrat, or in one of the many other eastern Caribbean island towns. High duties on imported goods found in the few supermarkets and the better quality of fresh ingredients insure that markets will survive. Even the chefs from the island restaurants, who undoubtedly have direct suppliers of crawfish (the spiny Caribbean lobster), as well as imported steaks, roasts and items for the tourist menu, will shop at the market for fresh food. Although one wonders why an indifferent continental cuisine is still served in many restaurants when there is a diverse local bounty to select from. Caribbean dishes, after years of snooty neglect, are finally reaching the visitors' table. Except for the French islands of Martinique, St. Barts, Guadeloupe and St. Martin, where the French culinary tradition has always vied with the imaginative Creole cuisine, and where natives and visitors alike frequent restaurants, the average islander does not eat out much. Life, for many residents of the Lesser Antilles, continues to be a matter of economics and tradition. While the young in the larger islands' tourist towns are inevitably getting an exposure to even the worst kind of americanized fast food, visitors are starting to discover the joys of native food other than the rum punches and conch fritters yet generally served in most resorts. Here and there, small three- and four-table restaurants have started to open up, serving the best traditional food the islands has to offer, as well as substances one may not want to try, like roasted iguana, an acquired taste born out of need and now questionable in terms of nature conservation.

The roster of food is varied: *Calaloo* soup and pepperpot, peas and rice; christophene, *cou cou* and fried flying fish. The Caribbean cuisine is rich indeed, a cauldron of ingredients reflecting the traditions and tastes of a polyglot people, enriching and adding to food supplies that exist in the region, adapting foods and spices from each other so that today one can speak of a Caribbean cuisine with local and regional variation. First on the scene were the Arawak and Caribs who lived very well of the sea and the land. They ate flying fish, grouper, snapper, turtle, shellfish and, of course, conch. In the Spanish-speaking islands, that large muscle of the queen conch shell is now known as *concha,* in the French Caribbean and some eastern Caribbean islands it is *lambi* and, everywhere else, *conch*. Conch soup or chowder, in fritters, 'cracked' (pounded to tenderize it) and deep fried, served with salad – its uses are legend throughout the Caribbean basin. The roe of sea urchins is still considered a delicacy, good when deviled in Barbados or served with eggs in Nevis. Cassava, the brown, sweet tuber, was known to the Arawaks, who pounded it into flour to make cassava bread or *cassareep,* a syrupy residue from boiling cassava with cloves and cinnamon,

Right: Restaurants and hotels often offer Lucullan feasts for their customers.

CUISINE

which later became the main ingredient of pepperpot, an Amerindian meat stew from Guyana, but known in various adaptations throughout the islands. Local lore has it that pepperpots were kept going through generations just by adding fresh meat and cassareep.

The demise of the Arawaks and the institution of the plantation economy meant the importation of African slaves into the islands. In the holds of slave ships came many of the staples of today's Caribbean cuisine: *yams,* peas, *okra* or else *ackee,* which would surely provide a way to supplement a scanty diet and to uphold cherished cultural traditions. Today, in Barbados, *cou cou,* a side dish of corn meal and okra, is eaten along with the famous fried flying fish.

Then rice was introduced by the Spanish. Nowadays, no Caribbean meal would be complete without peas and rice, the mainstay on many islands. Pigeon peas, *congo* or *gungo* peas, straight from Africa and not really peas but beans, red kidney beans and black beans complement the rice. *Calaloo,* with almost as many spellings as uses, is also served throughout all the islands. Trinidad and Guyana's stews include salt pork, the spinach-like *calaloo* or *dasheen* leaves, crab meat, okra and fresh fish, while in the other islands it is served almost always as a soup. Imaginative modern-day cooks use *calaloo* greens quite often in *quiches* and smooth, broth-like soups.

A side effect of the plantation economy was the introduction of salt meat and salt fish to supplement the vegetarian slave diet. Ingenious cooks developed some of the most popular island dishes with it. Salt cod fritters are sold on almost every island as finger food: *accras de morue* in Martinique, *bacalaitos* in Puerto Rico. In Jamaica they show up under the delightful name of *stamp and go.*

Until emancipation, the Caribbean was just one point in the infamous slave trade triangle. Molasses produced on the islands was sent to New England for distillation into rum and shipped to Africa in exchange for more slaves. Nowadays,

CUISINE

large-scale sugar production does not exist in the Lesser Antilles anymore. But enough is grown for almost each island to have distilleries. Light and aromatic in the French islands, dark, rich and sometimes pungent in the English-speaking ones, rum is the drink of the Caribbean – served as punch in resorts or carried home in refillable bottles from rum shops.

Angostura bitters from Trinidad, the orange flavored Curaçao liqueur and a number of non-alcoholic drinks such as *coco frio* and *maubi* continue to help quench island thirsts in the wake of the world-wide acceptance and distribution of Coca Cola and refined sugar products.

Abolition changed the islands' economy. Plantation owners attempted to retain it through the importation of Chinese and East Indian indentured servants, whose contribution to the Caribbean pot was enthusiastically adopted. As far

Above: Spices – a bargain. Right: Cockfighting, a spectator sport in which a lot of money changes hands.

north as the Virgin Islands, goat and conch curries stand out in an otherwise undistinguishable native cuisine. Mango chutneys, already beloved by the Britishers on the islands, are locally cooked. *Roti,* the flat East Indian bread, frequently stuffed with vegetarian or meat fillings, and *bakes,* the round fried cakes, are served warm with jam in the morning or as a lunch accompaniment.

Today, the popularity of these foods has spread beyond the large East Indian concentration on the southern island of Trinidad. Curried dishes also became widely popular, known as *kerry* in the Dutch or Papiamento speaking islands and *colombo* in French Creole cuisine. The East Indian melange of curries and spices just added another happy ingredient to a regional cuisine that was already enamored with spice. Allspice, called *pimento* on the islands, was known to the pre-Columbian Arawaks. Others like cinnamon, mace and nutmeg were introduced and took hold. Chili peppers, including the Scotch bonnet, hotter than hot, form the basis for the many popular pepper sauces and *salsas* that lend flavor to island meals. Islanders believe the hot, spicy food helps keep them cooler in the hot, humid tropics. *Coui, pickapeppa, sauce chien, sauce piquante* and *sofrito* are a sampling.

The cuisine of the West Indies would not be complete without the fruits considered exotic in more temperate climates. Columbus found pineapple and papaya, affectionately known as *paw paw* in English speaking islands. Mangoes, introduced from India, now are mighty trees which, together with the descendants of Captain Bligh's cargo of breadfruit, shade cottages and line roads, the fruit ready and free-for-the-picking by the casual passer-by. Coconuts and guavas, *soursop* and *sweetsop, carambola, mamey* and *otaheiti* apple, and island staples like bananas and mango are turned out in tarts, custards and ice cream.

GAMBLING

Everyone thinks of beaches, calypso and reggae, of sun and rum in the Caribbean, but several islands of the Lesser Antilles are almost equally popular for blackjack, craps and roulette.

Indeed, those enamored of the roll of the dice or the spin of the wheel may possibly miss the breezy tropical beaches and languor-producing sunshine entirely while spending their few wakeful island hours ensconced in mammoth or modest gambling casinos. The most glowing of these are the glitter palaces attached to equally ostentatious resort hotels, filled with green felt and gaudy neon – the hum of money changing hands punctuated by gasps, buzzers and bells, all holding out the promise of easy money.

In contrast to the often realized sunny tropical promise of the Caribbean islands of the Lesser Antilles, this other promise is only rarely fulfilled, but is one that nevertheless lures thousands, day after day, rain or shine.

Among the islands covered in this volume, casino gambling is found on Antigua, Guadeloupe, Martinique, the Netherlands Antilles, St. Kitts, St. Martin/Sint Maarten and St. Vincent. For those playing the horses, there are loosely scheduled and informal racing sessions held in Barbados, on the **Garrison Savannah**; in the British Virgins, in Tortola; at St. Croix's **Flambouyant Race Track**; or at the **Estate Nadir Track** in St. Thomas.

Most countries, however, do not at all allow their residents to gamble in their casinos, solely visitors, and fully solvent guests are frequently lavished with free drinks and other useful inducements such as free tickets to shows.

The legal gambling age in most countries is 18, although it is 21 on French islands, which also have the only casinos charging admission and requiring proof of age. The action does not usually go on round-the-clock, as in Las Vegas casinos, but closes down at 3 a.m. or later. The following is a list of casinos in the islands of the Lesser Antilles:

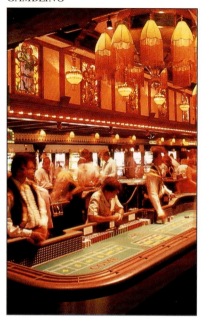

Above: Glittering hotel-casinos were imported from the United States. Right: Music is almost everywhere n the Caribbean air.

ANTIGUA: No free drinks for gamblers will be offered at five casinos: Flamingo Hotel & Casino, Halcyon Cove Beach Resort & Casino, St. James Club, the newest, King's Casino and the Ramada Renaissance Royal Antiguan Resort, featuring an expensively remodelled Las Vegas-style casino. Hours generally run from 9 p.m. to 5 a.m.

GUADELOUPE/MARTINIQUE: Admission for those over 21 years of age (photo-ID required), admission fee. No free drinks at all. Two casinos are located in Guadeloupe: Casino de St. François de la Marina and Casino de Gosier-les-Bains. Hours are 9 p.m. to 3 a.m., sometimes later. The single casino in Martinique is open from 9 p.m. to 3 a.m. and located at Méridien Trois Ilets.

NETHERLANDS ANTILLES: Casinos in Aruba, Bonaire and Curaçao range from more glamorous, conservative ones, rivaling Bahamian and Puerto Rican casinos for opulence and variety of ways to lose one's money, to smaller, friendlier places to drop one's cash at. All the casinos offer hospitable free drinks for players, and one, at the Aruba Concorde Hotel & Casino, stays open round-the-clock. Other casinos in Aruba include the Alhambra Casino, with a Moorish-fantasy theme, complete with 30 boutiques and a 24-hour deli, Americana Aruba Hotel & Casino, Aruba Palm Beach Hotel & Casino, Golden Tulip Aruba Caribbean Resort & Casino, Holiday Inn, Hyatt Regency Aruba, and Sonesta Hotel Beach Club & Casino. Hours generally run from 5 p.m. to 5 a.m., but some, such as the Holiday Inn or Sonesta's Crystal Casino are open longer hours. Bonaire's casino is located at the Divi Flamingo Beach Hotel & Casino. Hours are 4 p.m. to 4 a.m. Curaçao eventually offers gamblers opportunities to play from noon to 5 a.m. at the Curaçao Caribbean Hotel & Casino, Curaçao Plaza Hotel & Casino, Holiday Beach Hotel & Casino, Las Palmas Hotel, Princess Beach Hotel & Casino, or at the San Marco Hotel.

ST. KITTS: From 5 p.m. to 5 a.m. gamblers are exclusively found at the Royal St. Kitts Casino, the only casino on the entire island, which is part of the Jack Tar Village. Blackjack, craps, roulette, slots are the names of the games.

ST. MARTIN / SINT MAARTEN: Hotels and resorts on the French side of the island offer transportation for gamblers over 21 years of age to the Dutch side, where all the casinos are located: in Philipsburg, at Seaview Hotel & Casino, or at Casino Royale at Maho Beach, Divi Little Bay Beach Resort & Casino, Great Bay Beach Hotel, Maho Beach Hotel & Casino, Mullet Bay Hotel & Casino, Pelican Resort & Casino, Sint Maarten Beach Club & Casino or Treasure Island Hotel & Casino at Cupecoy. Hours are generally 7 p.m. to 4 a.m.

REGGAE / RASTAFARI / STEELBANDS

REGGAE, RASTAFARI AND STEELBANDS

Caribbean visitors usually expect the lilting sound from the steel drums, the almost hypnotic rhythms of reggae, and they are never disappointed. They can be heard everywhere. Generic performances cannot be avoided in tourist haunts. Not authentic, in reality. The real music of the Caribbean is much more local, varying between islands, and is more complex. Percussion and vocal styles that came from West Africa blend with harmonies and melodies derived from European and Indian music. New Orleans rhythm and blues, and soul and jazz also figure in here – the result of U.S. radio stations broadcasting this music to the islands. To most visitors, though, Caribbean music will always be steel bands and reggae. They have become such an integral part of the Caribbean experience that it is almost Pavlovian in scope. Listen to a few strains of any of that music and you will begin to feel warm breezes blowing, as well as the urge to stare at a beach and have a rum punch. Perhaps more so here than elsewhere, these lively sounds and haunting rhythms translate musically the feelings of the place.

Reggae is, of course, immediately associated with Jamaica, although nowadays it is played throughout the whole Caribbean. This music of the streets, with its sensuous rhythms and often angry, political lyrics came from the Rastafarian movement, and the movement of Marcus Garvey that predated it. Simply stated, those movements stress African roots, self-reliance and pride, but there is a special connection: Followers are regarded as children of the Negus, a title of Ethiopian kings descended from King Solomon and the Queen of Sheba. This gives their music a very special power.

Illustrative of that power is the career of the late Bob Marley, Jamaica's doubtlessly most famous ambassador of reggae. Both with the Wailers, one of reggae's founding groups, and on his own as an international solo artist, Marley was

revered on a level that could properly be described as religious. His political influence was such that he was invited to perform at the independence day celebrations in Zimbabwe in 1980 and was also awarded Jamaica's civilian award, the Order of Merit. When he died of brain cancer in 1981, at the age of 36, his full stature became definitely evident. He was given a state funeral with the prime minister and a great number of other government officials in attendance. The funeral procession extended 55 miles (90 km).

The current reggae scene, *A.M.* (standing for after Marley), is a splintered one. His widow Rita took over his studio and some of his predominance on the music charts. Four of his children formed a band called *The Melody Makers* that has had some modest success; son Ziggy Marley has done sporadically well. Other reggae stars have emerged or reappeared, such as *Toots and the Maytals*, early reggae stars who never made it as big as Marley, the *Mighty Diamonds* or *Third World*.

Some of the more successful practitioners of reggae have nothing to do with Jamaica, however. As often happens with anything innovative, outsiders soon come in and borrow. Virtually every Caribbean tourism enclave will offer at least one reggae band performance, or have reggae pouring through sound systems. Visitors to Anguilla may have merely the most vague perceptions about Rastafarianism, about the poverty boiling over in the Kingston streets that gave rise to this music, but everyone feels a seminal rumble when this music starts. Soon bodies involuntarily sway to the beat. Few people who hear it fail to be somehow taken by it. Though Jamaica remains the center of reggae, one can still catch a few good road shows in the Lesser Antilles.

The other pervasive sound of the islands, calypso, was born in Trinidad but it quickly spread to other islands – and

Above and right: Music is performed in many different ways and with a great variety of instruments in the Caribbean.

REGGAE / RASTAFARI / STEELBANDS

the world. Like reggae, it is an involving kind of music, one that soon forces the listener to become absorbed, banging out rhythms with his hands or on a table. And like all Caribbean music, it is a synthesis of many different cultures, a stew boiled down over generations that is perpetually changing. The origins of calypso are in dispute. Some argue that even the term *calypso* is not valid. They claim that the correct term is *kaiso*, a locally shouted *kudo* (like "Bravo!"), and today, that term is used along with calypso, just in case. But there are possible forerunners for the term *calypso*. The French had *carrousseau*, a drinking party. The Spanish had *caliso*, a topical song, and the Carib cultures had *carieto*, also a topical song. Finally, the Greek nymph Calypso was "She who conceals", a point that could apply to calypso songs with their hazy, double-entendre lyrics.

Tracing the tangled web that forms this music is not easy, but it undeniably starts with African rhythms. Slaves that French planters brought to the Lesser and Greater Antilles in the 1780s brought with them a tradition of improvised song that forms obviously the main ingredient of calypso. Several groups competed with each other to produce the most songs, led by singers with names like Elephant and Thunderer. Singers either inspired their groups to work harder or disparaged the efforts of their opponents. At night, after the day's work was finished, the leader of the most productive group celebrated his group's achievements and denounced the others in songs which gave rise to the tradition of the characteristical verbal dueling still audible in calypso today.

African roots are also evident in the fact that royalty never appears in public without its own praise-singers. This was a tradition continued in Trinidad, where a slave holder Pierre Bergorrat considered himself "royalty" and had his slaves sing his praises, while condemning his enemies in song duels. He named his favorite singer "Gros Jean, Master of Kaiso": the first calypso star. These verbal duels provided the basis for the music

REGGAE / RASTAFARI / STEELBANDS

accompanying the *kalenda*, an acrobatic dance with sticks popular among slaves, that is a very special form of martial arts. And the songs quickly became a major part of Trinidad's culture as that culture was just beginning to materialize. In 1838, the slaves were emancipated and their creativity burst forth. They appropriated the Europeans' carnival, turning a snobbish ball to a street party, propelled by African drumming. The outspoken songs they produced specifically for carnival soon became a popular institution.

Although free, the slaves had no land, so they flocked to cities for employment. At the same time, many residents of other islands, encouraged to immigrate by the Trinidad government, flocked to the same cities and competed for jobs. Gangs arose to protect property, and the *kalenda* bands started gang warfare at carnival. For some 40 years, bands of stick fighters stalked the streets, and when two met, their leaders would joust in song, in anticipation of the battle. This was an image that stigmatized calypso – an association with violence and the socially outcast.

Another important function of calypso, however, was that of a news transmitter. Like the town crier in Europe of old, news and cultural events were often passed along through song to an uneducated population, so that it has often been referred to as the nation's newspaper and has even served as a source for the study of cultural history. This role was under siege in the mid-19th century, as the British sought to anglicize the island. Trinidad had been a British colony for about half a century by that point, but its language was far from English. It was a French-African mix, as were its customs. The British tried to institutionalize their way of thinking as a means of ensuring political stability.

The first battleground was calypso and carnival. In 1884, drumming and *kalenda* bands were outlawed, which completely changed the sound of the music. *Tamboo bamboo*, tuned lengths of bamboo, produced rhythmic percussion like that of drums, but without the heaviness of the latter. Equally important, this rhythmic change brought in a whole new segment of society. With drummers gone, middle and upper classes more and more joined in calypso and carnival, increasing its acceptance but diluting the message. Years later the schism returned. Upper classes accompanied their singing with Venezuelan string bands. Poor blacks continued their performances with *tamboo bamboo* until the discovery in the 1930s that discarded oil drums could produce more notes. Despite this dissension, the British influence over Trinidad was proceeding at a fair clip. In 1899, the first calypso sung completely in English was performed. From then on, lyrics were increasingly sung in English rather than Creole, marking the beginning of the end of French culture in the country.

Above: Steel drums are not immune to being out of tune. Right: A quiet afternoon.

In the 20th century, this anglicizing trend continued, changing calypso, making it clearer and more oratorical. This would not last, though. By the 1920s, islanders were chafing under English rule and using the calypso songs to decry English rulers. Still, English was a permanent element to the mixture.

Between the 1920s and World War II, calypso enjoyed its golden age, flourishing with the support of local businessmen and, due to recordings and radio, spreading its message all over the world. In the U.S., Rudy Vallee and Bing Crosby were drawn to it and helped popularize it.

There was, however, a drawback to this newfound fame. Instruments popular with American bands began to infiltrate calypso and calypso musicians, tired of the bamboo bands, began to transform any castoff metal product into drums. By the 1930s percussion bands were popular at carnival, and oil drums came into play. Steel bands began their rise to fame. They figuratively exploded in the years after World War II when American soldiers took up residence in bases in the area. The number of calypso artists grew to entertain the soldiers, and singers changed to appeal to an international audience.

In 1951, the *Trinidad and Tobago All Steel Percussion Orchestra* represented Trinidad musically at the Festival of Britain. Audiences went wild. But the biggest international hit occurred in the late 1950s, when Harry Belafonte released a calypso album in the U.S., a fact that suddenly opened the door for their own musicians and bands, among them great Trinidadians like *The Mighty Sparrow*.

Steel bands continued in prominence through the 1960s but began to change. Women came to the forefront as singers and, in the 1970s, a new form, allied with soul music and called *soca*, emerged. This new style, with its hot horn sections and wild electrified tempos, is still popular and it worries some who see traditions disappearing. But to others it seems to be just one more ingredient in an amalgam of elements that is bound to change further as time goes on.

HURRICANES

Because of the devastation that hurricanes can cause, people fear these storms in the vulnerable Lesser Antilles during hurricane season, which is June through October. And there is ample evidence to justify such concern. In 1979, *hurricane Frederic*, for instance, caused $753 million worth of damage to the Bahamas, only two weeks after *hurricane David* had slammed into the Dominican Republic, killing about 1200 people. In 1988, *hurricane Gilbert* pounded Jamaica, damaging or destroying 80% of the island's homes and leaving some 500,000 people homeless. And it might have been worse if island residents had not taken precautions; 37 years earlier a hurricane had already leveled the island. In 1989, another murderous hurricane, *Hugo*, tore its way through the Lesser Antilles, smashing Puerto Rico, Montserrat, Nevis, Guadeloupe, Tortola, St. Kitts and the Virgin Islands, particularly St. Croix.

Officials usually downplay the hurricane threat, explaining that it seems to be so sinister because of the double punch of *Gilbert* and *Hugo* a year apart. The threat exists each year, they say, but the storms actually hit land more rarely than people think they do. Unfortunately, the storms develop in the Caribbean and gain their force from the water there. The fact that they often hit the U.S. the hardest is only of little consolation to islanders.

As the evidence suggests, most islands in the Caribbean are laboring with decreased resources to cope with a natural disaster – from inefficient communications to inadequate emergency services in, particularly, rural communities and crowded urban areas alike. Fear is no stranger to islanders faced with an oncoming storm. To this end, officials are for ever updating hurricane procedures, although the specifics usually seem a bit on the vague side.

Above and right: Hurricanes in the Caribbean take on biblical proportions in the lives and minds of the people.

HURRICANES

All of the islands say they are working at improving this situation, however. Early warning procedures have improved. They now have signals as long as three days ahead that a hurricane is on the way. But these storms can take unexpected turns and no one can really predict where one of them will hit until the very last moment.

No one who winds up in the middle of a storm like this can ever forget how it feels. The drenching rain and ripping winds provide a sense of powerlessness as nature tears apart buildings, trees and everything else in its path. But as the residents of one island learned, the aftermath of a hurricane can in its way be as treacherous as the winds themselves. After *hurricane Hugo* destroyed the buildings in St. Croix, looting on a grand scale erupted. The U.S. had to send troops to quell the disturbances. The reasons for the outbreak had little to do with hurricanes. Instead, what caused it was the poverty endured for generations by the people, and a lingering feeling of resentment about the fact that the smaller Virgin Island of St. Thomas was the capital. All it took was one external blast to blow the lid off the resentment. But, as captured on news video, the pictures of the island's citizens looting its stores and of store owners standing outside of their shops with shotguns probably did more damage to the island than the hurricane. As the 1990 season began, many wondered how many tourists, remembering those scenes, would choose to bypass a troubled place and go elsewhere. Lately it's been volcanoes that have been giving trouble, especially on Monserrat where the last erruption took place in August 1997. They are dangerous phenomena and should not be underestimated.

Of course, life goes on after a hurricane, and nature can recuperate with miraculous speed in the tropics. Buildings and homes are quickly repaired. But some of these storms leave disastrous effects that linger for years in the minds and memories of those who have had to bear the brunt of their destructiveness.

SHOPPING

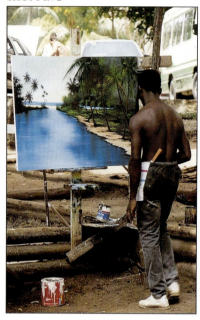

SHOPPING

Books do exist about shopping in the Caribbean. Travel is incomplete for some without the give and take of haggling with local artisans for their products and wares. This aspect of the Caribbean remains. On streets or in small shops the price is negotiable, though now the price may not drop to the irresistible lows of bygone days. Nor is duty-free shopping the great bargain that it was, but the prolific or casual shopper can still purchase a variety of imported goods including liquor, jewelry, watches, chinaware, perfumes, cameras and electronics. Mass-produced goods, and unique island crafts as well, or inexpensive souvenirs are all readily available almost everywhere, and there is always something for everyone, the choice being limited only by dictates of one's budget and tastes.

Above: Naive painting in the Caribbean was born in Haiti. Right: The island of Curaçao was named first, then the liqueur.

Unless money is no object, one should always compare prices in shops. Rates for the same goods may vary markedly. One should keep in mind that the first price quoted for a steel drum in Trinidad or a woven banana-leaf basket in Dominica may be many times more than the seller is really willing to accept. Haggling is part of the game, but some hungry street vendor may react brusquely if one negotiates all too hard and long. This is their livelihood, and sadly for most, not a highly remunerative one. Competition is fierce and the stakes high, so that a little empathy would not be out of place here.

Generally the best shopping for imports is always in stores on tourist strips, near cruise ports or resort hotels. Folk arts and crafts are found in local markets and small shops, or from roadside vendors selling batiks, cottons and silks, pottery, straw goods, and wooden carvings ranging from amateur to artful, or paintings, also of varying quality. Jewelry includes gold and precious stones, shells and corals. Rum is ubiquitous and French islands offer imported alcohol. Alcohol and tobacco are usually priced best at in-bound airport or cruise port stores. The following is only a brief description of what shoppers may expect to find in the Lesser Antilles.

Barbados: Barbados rum is probably the best-known island product, but the island offers reasonably good bargains oarticularly on British woolens and clothing, French perfumes, china, crystal, jewelry and watches. Best prices are in in-bond stores. Local crafts include shell work and coral jewelry, as well as wood carvings and straw goods.

Anguilla, **Antigua**, **Barbuda**, **Montserrat**, **Nevis**, **St. Kitts**: The British Leewards are not renowned as a shopper's paradise, but there are local brands of rum available at good prices, as well as local crafts, including batik fabrics and clothing in St. Kitts. The other islands offer imported British clothing.

Virgin Islands: Many imported goods are available here, from gold jewelry to sportswear, alongside local shell and coral jewelry, or ceramics, all well displayed in shops on Tortola. The place to shop for a good selection of quality wares that one does not mind paying more for.

Dominica, **Grenada**, **St. Lucia**, **St. Vincent** and **the Grenadines**: The British Windwards offer crafts produced by the last remaining Carib Indians in Dominica, who are known for their woven baskets. Grenada and St. Vincent offer handcrafted baskets, carvings and ceramics, as well as the many usual imported goods. Printed silk-screen fabrics are a remarkable specialty of St. Lucia.

Saba, **St. Eustatius**, **Sint Maarten**: Duty-free Dutch cheeses, jewelry and fine chinaware are sometimes a bargain in these Dutch Windward Islands. *Saba Spice* is that island's local rum, and linen and cotton goods, plus clothing, are made there. Only St. Eustatius is refreshingly free of shopping save for T-shirts, wood carvings, or else sea shells.

Guadeloupe, **Martinique**, **St. Martin**, **St. Barts**: The French West Indies presumably offer the best Caribbean prices on imported French perfumes, alcoholic beverages, jewelry, and silks. Also worthwhile looking out for are local fabrics, clothing and straw goods.

Aruba, **Bonaire** and **Curaçao**: The Netherlands Antilles are an import shoppers' haven, expanding especially upon extensive selections of French and British goods to include as well Oriental, Indian, South American and even African wares at bargain prices. And, of course, not to forget Curaçao liqueur.

Trinidad & Tobago: Although these islands mainly offer the usual British and French imports, the many indigenous local crafts are distinctive. They include namely items such as steel drums, various rhythm instruments, flutes, and other musical instruments. Local calypso recordings are also a very popular buy, as well as wood and straw handicrafts. The music-related products are not the bargains they once were.

PREPARATION

The more one knows ahead of time about potential bureaucratic, cultural or environmental problems, the better one's trip will be. The following points regarding climate, currency, entry/departure requirements, and health/emergency services will help to insure that one has fun instead of regrets in the Lesser Antilles.

Climate

Surrounded by warm tropical seas, the Caribbean has a predictable and stable climate: hottest in summer, but still quite warm in winter, combined with high humidity. Air temperatures generally stay within a range of 20 to 30°C (68 to 86°F). These temperatures are more or less guaranteed by limits set by the surface water and a location near enough to the equator to make not only temperature, but also sunlight variations between summer and winter slight, though elevated areas may see winter temperatures occasionally dip lower.

Sea temperatures also remain consistently high throughout the Lesser Antilles, averaging more than 20°Celsius (68°F) year-round, and topping 27°C (80°F) during summer months. Rainfall varies seasonally, with the greatest precipitation occurring between May and November, while the most popular tourist season from December through April is considerably drier.

Low lying islands or areas tend to be driest, while higher ones often trap clouds and force them to release their moisture. Even in the case of summer rains, which are far more likely throughout the Lesser Antilles, the rainy periods occur regularly each day, rather than in bursts of day- or week-long downpours. Except, of course, during hurricane season, which can combine drenching rains with cyclonic winds reaching upwards of 200 miles per hour, occurring with regularity in late summer through early fall.

Only Trinidad, remains safe due to a combination of factors, including its location near the equator and the gravitational forces at work as the earth rotates.

The strong Caribbean sun could cause problems for the careless. One should always use some sort of sunscreen, keep sunglasses handy and maybe even a hat. Sweaters can surely remain at home unless one is bothered by the chill of air-conditioning. Not even the summer rains dampen the sunshine, with little variance in hours of sunlight between winter and summer months. In Fort-de-France, for example, there is an average of 2790 hours of sunlight annually, varying from 8.5 hours daily in December to only 7.5 hours daily in August, the rainiest month. The following average temperatures and rainfall statistics (where available) may help one to decide on the most appropriate time to visit the Lesser Antilles.

Anguilla

January-February, temperatures average 21°C to 27°C (70°F to 80°F.). March-April, temperatures average 25°C to 28.5°C (83°F to 86.5°F). May-June, temperatures average 26°C to 31°C (77°F to 88°F). July-August, temperatures average 27.5 degrees to C 32°C (80°F to 90°F). September-October temperatures average 25.5°C to 31°C (76°F to 87°F). November-December, temperatures average 24.5°C to 30°C (83°F to 86°F).

Antigua, Barbuda

January-February, temperatures average 21.5°C to 26.5°C (70°F to 79°F). March-April, temperatures average 22°C to 28°C (71°F to 83°F). May-June, temperatures average 24°C to 28.5°C (75°F to 85°F). July-August, temperatures average 25°C to 30°C (77°F to 86°F). September-October, temperatures average 23.5°C to 30°C (75°F to 86°F). November-December, temperatures average 23°C to 29°C (74°F to 84°F).

Aruba, Bonaire & Curaçao

January, temperatures average 24°C to 28°C (76.5°F to 83°F); average rainfall 63 mm. February, temperatures average 24°C to 28°C (76.5°F to 83°F), average rainfall 30 mm. March, temperatures average 23.5°C to 29.5°C (75°F to 86°F), average rainfall 16 mm. April, temperatures average 25.5°C to 30.5°C (78°F to 87°F), average rainfall 15 mm. May, temperatures average 25.5°C to 30.5°C (78°F to 87°F), average rainfall 18 mm. June, temperatures average 24°Cto 31°C (76°F to 88°F), average rainfall 27 mm. July, temperatures average 24°C to 32°C (76°F to 90°F), average rainfall 29 mm. August, temperatures average 26°C to 31.5°C (79°F to 89°F), average rainfall 40 mm. September, temperatures average 26°C to 31.5°C (79°F to 89°F), average rainfall 33 mm. October, temperatures 25.5°C to 31°C (78°F to 87°F), rainfall 78 mm. November, temperatures average 24.5°C to 30.5°C (77°F to 87°F), average rainfall 128 mm. December, temperatures average 24°C to 30°C (76°F to 86.5°F), average rainfall 106 mm.

Barbados

January, temperatures average 22°C to 28°C (72°F to 83°F), average rainfall 68 mm. February, temperatures average 22°C to 28°C (72°F to 83°F), average rainfall 62 mm. March, temperatures average 23°C to 29°C (74°F to 85°F), average rainfall 37 mm. April, temperatures average 24°C to 30°C (76°F to 86°F), average rainfall 51 mm. May, temperatures average 25°C to 31°C (77°F to 88°F), average rainfall 70 mm. June, temperatures 25°C to 31°C (77°F to 88°F), rainfall 103 mm. July, temperatures average 25°C to 31°C (77°F to 88°F), average rainfall 141 mm. August, temperatures average 25.5°C to 31.5°C (78°F to 89°F), average rainfall 144 mm. September, temperatures 25.5°C to 31.5°C (78°F to 89°F), rainfall 168 mm. October, temperatures average 24°C to 30°C (76°F to 86.5°F), average rainfall 176 mm. November, temperatures average 21°C to 30°C (73°F to 86.5°F), average rainfall 160 mm. December, temperatures average 20.5°C to 30°C (69°F to 86.5°F), average rainfall 93 mm.

Dominica, Guadeloupe

January, temperatures average 20°C to 27°C (69°F to 81°F), average rainfall 91 mm. February, temperatures average 20°C to 27°C (69°F to 81°F), average rainfall 66 mm. March, temperatures average 21°C to 28°C (70°F to 83°F), average rainfall 66 mm. April, temperatures average 22°C to 29°C (72°F to 85°F), average rainfall 86 mm. May, temperatures average 23°C to 30°C (74°F to 86°F), average rainfall 135 mm. June, temperatures average 23.5°C to 30.5°C (75°F to 87°F), average rainfall 148 mm. July, temperatures average 23.5°C to 30.5°C (75°F to 87°F), average rainfall 179 mm. August, temperatures average 23.5°C to 30.5°C (75°F to 87°F), average rainfall 244 mm. September, temperatures average 23°C to 31°C (74°F to 88°F), average rainfall 196 mm. October, temperatures average 22°C to 30°C (72°F to 86°F), average rainfall 229 mm. November, temperatures average 21°C to 29°C (70°F to 85°F), average rainfall 231 mm. December, temperatures average 20°C to 28.5°C (68°F to 84°F), average rainfall 143 mm.

Grenada, St. Vincent, Grenadines

January-February, temperatures average 23°C to 29°C (74°F. to 85°F.). March-April, temperatures average 24°C to 29.5°C (76°F to 85.5°F). May-June, temperatures average 24°C to 30°C (76°F to 85°F). July-August, temperatures average 25 degrees C to 30.5°C (77°F to 87°F). September-October, temperatures average 24.5°C to 29.5°C (76.5°F to 85.5°F). November-December, temperatures average 24°C to 29.5°C (76°F to 85.5°F).

Martinique, St. Lucia

January-February, temperatures average 20°C to 28.5°C (68°F. to 84°F), average rainfall 82 mm. March-April, temperatures average 21°C to 29.5°C (70°F to 85.5°F), average rainfall 70 mm. May-June, temperatures average 22°C to 30.5°C (72°F to 87°F), average rainfall 143 mm. July-August, temperatures average 22°C to 31°C (72°F to 88°F), average rainfall 220 mm. September-October, temperatures average 22°C to 31°C (72°F to 88°F), average rainfall 226 mm. November-December, temperatures average 21.5°C to 29.5°C (71°F to 88.5°F), average rainfall 178 mm.

Montserrat, St.Kitts, Nevis

January-February, temperatures average 21.5°C to 28°C (68°F to 83°F). March-April temperatures average 21.5°C to 29.5°C (71°F to 85.5°F). May-June, temperatures average 23°C to 31°C (74°F to 88°F). July-August, temperatures average 24°C to 31°C (76°F to 88°F). September-October temperatures average 23°C to 31.5°C (74°F to 89°F). November-December temperatures average 22.5°C to 28.5°C (73°F to 84°F).

Saba, St. Barts, St. Eustatius

January-February, temperatures average 22°C to 29°C (72°F to 85°F). March-April, temperatures average 23°C to 30°C (74°F to 86°F). May-June, temperatures average 23.5°C to 31.5°C (75°F to 89°F). July-August, temperatures average 24°C to 32°C (76°F to 90°F). September-October, temperatures average 24°C to 32°C (76°F to 90°F). November-December, temperatures average 23°C to 30°C (74°F 86.5°F).

St. Martin / Sint Maarten

January-February, temperatures average 21°C to 27°C (70°F. to 81°F). March-April, temperatures average 22°C to 29°C (72°F to 85°F). May-June, temperatures average 23°C to 30°C (74°F to 86°F). July-August, temperatures average 24°C to 31°C (76°F to 88°F). September-October, temperatures average 24°C to 31°C (76°F to 88°F). November-December, temperatures average 21.5°C to 28°C (68°F to 83°F).

Trinidad and Tobago

January-February, temperatures average 20°C to 30°C (69°F. to 86°F.). March-April, temperatures average 21°C to 32°C (70°F to 88°F). May-June, temperatures average 22°C to 32°C (72°F to 90°F). July-August, temperatures average 22°C to 31°C (72°F to 88°F). September-October, temperatures average 21.5°C to 31°C (71°F to 88°F). November-December, temperatures average 21°C to 30.5°C (70°F to 87°F).

Virgin Islands

January-February, temperatures average 23°C to 29.5°C (74°F. to 85.5°F). March-April, temperatures average 22°C to 30°C (72°F to 86.5°F). May-June, temperatures average 23.5°C to 31°C (73°F to 88°F). July-August, temperatures average 25°C to 35°C (77°F to 95°F). September-October, temperatures average 24°C to 34°C (76°F to 93.5°). November-December, temperatures average 22°C to 29.5°C (72°F to 86°F).

Arriving in the Caribbean

All of the islands mentioned here will require some form of identification from visitors. The procedures will vary, depending upon the country of origin, and may be complicated in some cases. Visitors from North America are, for instance, not required to produce vaccination certificates, while people from other countries may be so required.

Each Caribbean country has a different bureaucracy, but all require, at the very least, some proof of citizenship. Acceptable documents are an original birth certificate, passport or voter's registration. Passports should be valid at least six

GUIDELINES

months after the end of the trip. Some will allow one to use a recently expired passport or a certified copy of a birth certificate. It is a good idea to carry a driver's license if one plans to rent a car or moped, but one may still be required to purchase a temporary local license in some islands.

Though not generally required of North Americans, certain countries require visas or tourist cards for tourists from other countries, and many immigration officials one encounters will ask for proof of onward passage in the form of an ongoing or return ticket. Some will ask for proof of sufficient funds for one's stay. It is a good idea to check with tourist authorities in each country and at home if one has any questions.

Departure

One should allow two hours for departure formalities such as ticketing, seat assignment and security checks, which can be elaborate in some Caribbean countries. Most countries charge a departure tax which is payable at the airport, in local currency.

There is usually an opportunity to spend the balance of any local funds at in-bond airport stores, or to re-convert funds at an airport exchange bureau, provided one has saved a purchase receipt from the original transaction. Flights should always be reconfirmed 24 to 72 hours prior to departure. It is also advisable to consult one's carrier for any additional departure requirements or fees that may be required.

Currency and Exchange

Currency and exchange facilities are different in each country, with details included in the guidepost section after each travel chapter. In general, it is best to carry travelers checks issued in U.S. currency, as opposed to cash or credit cards, in the Caribbean, and there is frequently a small benefit in the exchange rate granted by these checks over cash, depending, of course, on where the exchange is made. Banks typically provide slightly better rates than hotels, and using American dollars instead of local currency for smaller transactions, while widely acceptable, may exact a higher charge.

U.S. dollars are the official currency in some of the islands. On others the local currency is on a par with U.S. dollars. Official currencies and approximate rate of exchange for U.S. dollars are as follows: **Anguilla, Antigua, Dominica, Grenada, Montserrat, St. Kitts / Nevis, St. Lucia, St. Vincent** and **The Grenadines** all use the Eastern Caribbean dollar (EC), at a variable rate of exchange from island to island against the U.S. dollar. As of 1991 the rate was approximately EC 2.68 to 1 US$. **Barbados** uses the Barbadian dollar (BDS$) at a rate of exchange of approximately 1.85 BDS$ to 1 US$. **Guadeloupe, Martinique, St. Barts** and **St. Martin** use the French Franc, exchanged at approximately 5.5 FF to 1 US$. **Aruba, Bonaire, Curaçao, Saba, St. Eustatius** and **Sint Maarten**, all islands of the Netherlands Antilles, use the Dutch florin, also known as the guilder, currently exchanged at around 1.79 NAfl to 1 US$. **Trinidad & Tobago** use the Trinidad & Tobago dollar, currently exchanged at around 4 T$ to 1 US$. The U.S. dollar is the official currency of the U.S. Virgin Islands and is also universally acceptable within the British Virgin Islands.

Rates fluctuate and are posted at exchange facilities. Banking hours vary locally. Hotel and airport exchange facilities are generally available round-the-clock, or as needed, such as for arriving or departing flights, though in some out-of-the-way hotels that might not hold true. International credit cards, such as *Visa, American Express, Carte Blanche Mastercard,* and *Diner's Club,* may or may not be accepted in certain establishments, but can be used for cash advances.

239

GUIDELINES

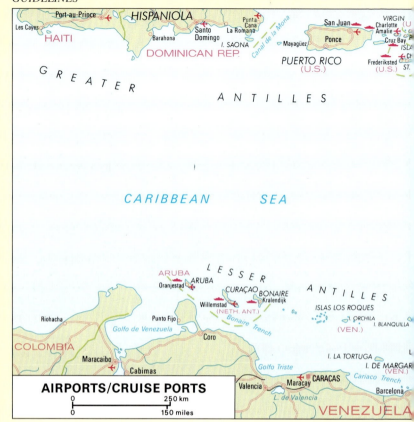

Customs

Duty-free allowances were recently increased for U.S. residents returning from certain Caribbean countries. For instance, it was increased from 400 US$ to 600 US$ for travelers returning from Antigua, Barbuda, Aruba, Barbados, Dominica, Grenada, Montserrat, the Netherlands Antilles, St. Kitts/Nevis, St. Lucia, St. Vincent and the Grenadines, Trinidad & Tobago, and the British Virgin Islands. The duty-free allowance was raised from 800 US$ to 1200 US$ for Americans returning from the U.S. Virgin Islands.

A number of restrictions apply as to what can and cannot become a souvenir, and these vary according to country of residence. In general, fresh fruit, meat, flowers, or anything alive, would be disqualified by customs, and there are limitations as to how much liquor and tobacco one may bring home duty-free. After reaching the duty-free allotments, a flat duty rate is imposed according to a local formula, although some craft items are duty-free regardless of their cost.

TRAVELING IN THE LESSER ANTILLES

Airlines

An increasing number of airlines are signing international agreements for Caribbean routes, while others drop out of this high stakes game. Many of the islands have national carriers, which tend

GUIDELINES

to dominate those markets in frequency of flights, if not service. And there are hundreds of charters and small airlines flying local routes. It is somewhat confusing, and made all the more bewildering by schedules clocked in on "Caribbean time", which can be flexible, to say the least.

And then there is the matter of air fares, which can show shocking variations from the last-minute full fare rate to the tempting low season bargains. Other variables affecting air fares are one's particular route, with extra savings often realized on heavily traveled routes, such as between the U.S. northeast and the U.S. Virgin Islands, special promotions sponsored by the airline or hotels,

or package deals that may include savings on airfare from certain cities. (E.g., ALM pass and ABC pass: Check in Curaçao, Tel: 461-3033/868-1322).

Depending on what is going on, such as "post-hurricane super savings," which may or may not be a bargain, there always seem to be fantastic Caribbean deals year-round. Check with a travel agent for current rates and offerings. Or if you prefer to work directly with airlines, consult the listings in the guideposts at the end of each chapter for airlines offering service to the various islands.

Cruise Directory

In 1990, the cruise industry had its biggest growth ever, with 16 new or refurbished ships sailing into service. Many of these ships will cruise the excellent harbors and year-round calm seas of the Lesser Antilles, making these islands the top cruise destination in the world.

The biggest cruising news of late has been the inauguration of the mega-ships offering service for 2500 or more passengers, including full-scale health spas, two-deck show-rooms, multi-story atriums, large cabins, numerous restaurants and so forth. The largest ship, for now, is Royal Caribbean Line's *Sovereign of the Seas*, although with several mega-ships currently under construction.

Other cruise news include: *Club Med I*, a sail-assisted ship offering seven-night Caribbean cruise itineraries; Princess Cruises' 1596-passenger *Crown Princess*, offering seven-day Caribbean itineraries out of Fort Lauderdale; Chandris Celebrity Cruises' *New Horizon* will carry 1354 passengers sailing out of San Juan on seven-day cruises in the Lesser Antilles; the *Crown Monarch*, Crown Cruise Line's latest entry into the Caribbean market is due to carry 550 passengers on seven-day itineraries out of Palm Beach, Florida; Royal Viking Line's refurbished *Royal Viking Star* is offering ten- and eleven-day cruises from

GUIDELINES

Fort Lauderdale to 17 Caribbean ports from November through March; Carnival Cruise Line's *Tropicale* sails out of San Juan for ports in the Lesser Antilles; Chandris Cruises' *Amerikanis* sails only in the Caribbean, out of San Juan.

The options available to cruise passengers only serve to point out one of the biggest changes in recent years, which is the number of cruise ship ports and departure points to choose from on the U.S. mainland (particularly Florida and New York), the Caribbean Islands and Europe.

Among cruise lines sailing the Lesser Antilles waters are the following (Note: all 800-numbers are toll-free in and from the U.S. and Canada!): **American Canadian Line**, 461 Water St., Warren, Rhode Island 02855, 1-401/247-0955, or 1-800/556-7450. **Canberra Cruise**, offers 22-day sailings on the *Canberra* from Southampton, England, to numerous Caribbean ports. **Carnival Cruise Lines**, 5225 NW 87th Ave., Miami, FL 33178, 1-305/599-2200, or 1-800/327-2058. **Chandris Celebrity Cruises/ Chandris Fantasy Cruises**, 4770 Biscayne Blvd., Miami, FL, 1-305/573-3140, fax 305/576-9520. **Clipper Cruise Line**, 7711 Bonhomme Ave., St. Louis, MO 63105, 1-314/727-2929, or 1-800/325-0010. **Club Mediteranée**, 40 West 57th St., New York, NY 10019, 1-212/977-2100. **Commodore Cruise Line**, 1007 N. America Way, Miami, FL 33132, 1-305/358-2622, or 1-800/327-5617, fax 305/371-9980. **Costa Cruises**, World Trade Center, 80 S.W. 8th St., Miami, FL 33130-3097, 1-305/358-7325, fax 305/375-0676. **Crown Cruise Line**, PO Box 3000, 2790 N. Federal Highway, Boca Raton, FL 33431, 1-407/394-7450. **Cunard Line**, 555 Fifth Ave., New York, NY 10017, 1-212/880-7500 or 1-800/221-4770. **Epirotiki Lines**, 551 Fifth Ave., New York, NY 10176, 1-212/599-1750, or 1-800/221-2470. **Holland America Line**, 300 Elliot Ave., Seattle, WA 98119, 1-206/281-3535, fax 206/281-7110. **Home Lines**, One World Trade Center, No 3969, New York, NY 10048, 1-212/432-1414, or 1-800/221-4041. **Norwegian Cruise Line**, 95 Merrick Way, Coral Gables, FL 33134, 1-305/445-0866. Ocean Cruise Lines, 1510 S.E. 17th St., Fort Lauderdale, FL 33316, 1-305/764-3500, departs from Aruba, Barbados and Curaçao. **Ocean Quest International**, 1-504/586-8686, or 1-800/338-3483, departs from St. Petersburg on Caribbean diving itineraries. **Pacquet French Lines**, 240 South Country Road, Palm Beach, FL 33480, 1-800-999-0555; *Paquet's Mermoz* sails from San Juan or Pointe-à-Pitre. **Premier Cruise Lines**, 400 Challenger Road, Cape Canaveral, FL 32920, 1-407/783-5061. **Princess Cruises**, 10100 Santa Monica Blvd., Los Angeles, CA 90067, 1-213/553-1666, fax 1-213/277-6175. **Regency Cruises**, 260 Madison Ave., New York, NY 10016, 1-800/457-5566, Fax: 1-212/687-2290; **Royal Caribbean Cruise Line**, 903 S. America Way, Miami, FL 33132, 1-305/379-2601. **Royal Cruise Line**, 1 Maritime Plaza, Suite 1400, San Francisco, CA 94111, 1-800/227-0925; *Royal's Golden Odyssey* sails from San Juan or Curaçao. **Royal Viking Line**, 95 Merrick Way, Coral Gables, FL 33134, 1-305/447-9660; **Seabourn Cruise Line**, 550 Francisco St., San Francisco, CA 94133, 1-415/391-7444. **Sun Line Cruises**, 1 Rockefeller Plaza, New York, NY 10020, 1-212/397-6400, or 1-800/223-5760. **Windjammer Barefoot Cruises**, Box 120, Miami Beach, FL 33119, 1/305-347-2090, classic sailing "tall" ships for 80 to 126 passengers. **Windstar Sail Cruises**, 7415 NW 19th St., Miami, FL 33126, 1-305/592-8008, ultra- modern sail assisted ships covering Lesser Antilles itineraries.

A further source of information on many cruise lines is the **Cruise Lines International Association**, 500 Fifth Ave., Suite 1407, New York, NY 10110, 1-212/921-0066.

GUIDELINES

PRACTICAL TIPS

Accommodation

Accommodations throughout the islands of the Lesser Antilles truly cover the entire range in cost and amenities. At the top end there are expensive private-staffed villas that come stocked with one's favorite food and drink, as well as cook, maid and chauffeur service. On the other hand, one could stay for a few dollars nightly, or no charge at all, in a sleeping bag on a Lesser Antilles beach, the surf quietly rolling, stars twinkling, and nearby mango trees swaying in a warm breeze. In between there are the state-of-the-art resort hotels, including some of the best-managed properties in the world, at least according to the likes and dislikes of royalty, rock stars and diplomats; or more democratic all-inclusives, a concept pioneered in Jamaica, but now spread throughout the Caribbean.

At an all-inclusive, guests who cannot afford to emulate royalty *à la carte* are granted the fantasy of access to everything the resort offers for a fixed price, including food, drinks and even cigarettes, as well as swimming, sailing, disco and so forth.

There are highrise hotels, with complete sports and entertainment facilities, as well as modest cottage hotels. Apartment, condo and villa rentals, ranging from the spartan to the fully-staffed, are another option. Small local hotels and guest houses are sometimes stronger on local color than upkeep or service. *Aficionados* of such subtly savored retreats appreciate the savings as well as the absence of the hordes of fellow tourists. And camping, although not allowed everywhere, is a growing alternative.

Accommodations listed in this book are meant to be among the best in each price range and category, although there are many, many more to choose from in most areas of the Caribbean. Tourism has become the number one industry in most of these islands. More private properties are being converted to guesthouses or seaside camping grounds all the time.

Of special note are the country inns or the small hotels that seem to proliferate throughout the Caribbean. Uniformly small in size, but large on charm and character, these properties offer the unique personalities of their diverse ownership, frequently the same person who greets you, drives and cooks your breakfast in this sort of multi-talented establishment. Under 50 rooms is indeed the only common element these lodgings share, and indeed they span a great range from the ultra-exclusive and expensive to more traditional bed & breakfasts, or clean and comfortable abodes, that will cost under $50 nightly, per double.

Despite the presence of more and more big chain mega-hotels, it actually comes as no surprise that more than 65 percent of the members of the Caribbean Hotel Association still qualify as small properties. They usually come from a strong tradition of family ownership and management. The people who run these places make it their business to know the islands and their people, and aim to provide personalized service.

In **Dominica** small hotels take advantage of the island's impressive geography. Roxy's Mountain Lodge is a six-room inn in Laudat, lying at the base of a volcano, near the entrance to a national park. The Papillotte Wilderness Retreat is set in a rain forest, beside a waterfall. Picard Beach Cottages Resorts is a cluster of 18 cottages at the foot of Mount Diablotin, the island's highest peak.

Bonaire, particularly known for diving, offers Captain Don's Habitat, featuring diving round-the-clock. The Sorobon Beach Resort is popular for its secluded location on Lac Bay, as well as for its clothes-optional policies.

Some of the small Caribbean properties, such as Point Pirouette, a villa on **Sint Maarten**, come complete with private pool and tennis court, maid service, VCR library and a satellite dish.

While some have their historic links to the past, having been converted from sugar mills, plantation houses or colonial government buildings, others are famous for having historic figures pass through them, including the likes of Mick Jagger and other members of the Rolling Stones, not to mention British Royalty, who favor retreats on the island of Mustique.

Some of the smaller hotels have formed associations, such as the Relais Hotels de la Guadeloupe, but for the most part a thorough travel agent is a valuable helper in sifting through the variety of choices in accommodations, as well as in planning all trip details for example with regard to airline flights or cruise bookings, rental cars or other local transport.

Most of the Caribbean accommodations have swimming pools, but then one is not likely to ever be far from a swimming beach, a river or a mountain waterfall. Amenities such as air-conditioning, although standard in some lodgings, are unnecessary in others thanks to congenial winds, or ceiling fans. But one should not be surprised to find a mosquito coil along with soap and shampoo in such places, or mosquito screens over bedding. Television is not yet all that very common in the Caribbean, although satellite dishes are becoming more so; and phones can be somewhat primitive in more out of the way locales. While large, modern resorts will likely offer all the conveniences, especially some of the Caribbean's historically better properties may not, although impeccable standards in service will probably more than compensate for any absence of modern equipment, at least in the higher-end properties.

Most rates are adjusted seasonally, with high season running from December 15 through April 15. Rates tend to be a little lower at other times of the year, with the lowest prices traditionally available during June, July and August, when the weather is a bit hotter and sometimes rainy, but the savings are substantial and the beaches far less crowded.

A lot of people prefer summers for this last reason. To enjoy the best of both worlds, one should skip the mid-summer, which can be incredibly hot and humid, and head for the Caribbean in May or November. Those months are almost exact duplicates of the high season weather-wise, but with fewer travelers and bigger savings that one would realize in the summer.

Very little changes in the Lesser Antilles on April 16 except prices. All sorts of package deals are available through tour wholesalers, hotels or airlines, as well as special-interest groups for divers, gamblers, shoppers and so forth. For these options a travel agent can be helpful, or consult with tourist offices for certified packages, as well as with airlines or individual properties.

Accommodating the Handicapped

Accommodations for handicapped travelers are happily becoming a consideration in the Caribbean, but due to the diversities of many countries, few common standards exist. The only way to be certain about facilities that can accommodate the needs of the disabled is to phone ahead and ask very specific questions, or to book through reliable agencies specializing in the requirements of the disabled.

Accommodation Information

Some Caribbean hotels and resorts are linked through marketing networks that can supply you with information and details at no cost through a toll-free phone number from the US or Canada. Increasingly, Caribbean properties are marketing to Europe as well, with a number of islands maintaining tourism offices in England or Germany, among others. Check local listings in your area, or consult the following hotel groups: **Ameri-**

cana Hotels, 405 Lexington Ave, New York, NY 10174, 1-800/ 228-3278. **Best Western**, Box 10203, Phoenix, AZ 85064, 1-800/334-7234. **Conrad International**, 301 Park Avenue, New York, NY 10022, 1-800/445-8667. **Club Mediterranée**, PO Box 4460, Scottsdale, AZ 85261, 1-800/528-3100. **Concorde Hotels**, 551 Fifth Avenue, Suite 2530, New York, NY, 1-800/228-9290. **Divi Hotels**, 54 Gunderman Road, Ithaca, NY 14850, 1-800/367-3484. **Hilton Reservation Service**, Waldorf Astoria Hotel, New York, NY 10021, 1-800/445-8667. **Holiday Inn Reservations,** 757 Lexington Ave., New York, NY 10022, 1-800/238-8000. **Hyatt Resorts Caribbean**, 341 Madison Ave., New York, NY 10017, 1-800/233-1234. **Jack Tar Resorts**, 1314 Wood St., Dallas, TX 75202, 1-800/527-9299. **Leading Hotels**, 747 Third Ave., New York, NY 10017, 1-800/223-6800. **Loews Reservation International**, One Park Ave., New York, NY 10016, 1-800/223-0888. **Marriott**, 420 Lexington Ave., New York, NY 10170, 1-800/228-9290. **Ramada Inns**, 7720 Crown Point Ave., Omaha, NE 68134, 1-800/272-6232. **Radisson Hotels**, 2223 North 91 Plaza, Omaha, NE 68134, 1-800/228-9822. **Sheraton Hotels**, 1700 Broadway, New York, NY, 1-800/ 334-8484. **Stouffer Hotels Reservations**, 29800 Bainbridge Rd., Solon, OH 44139, 1-800/468-3571. **Wyndham Hotels**, 5775 N.W. 11th St., Miami, FL 33126, 1-800/822-4200.

Business Hours

These vary widely throughout the Caribbean but stores roughly stay open from 8 a.m. to 6 p.m., Monday to Friday, and till noon, at least, on Saturday; banks generally open from 9 a.m. to noon, Monday to Friday, with afternoon hours on certain days only.

Museums and tourist attractions are generally open 9 a.m. to 5 p.m. Craft markets are open daily, while local produce markets are generally open Friday and Saturday. Roadside entrepreneurs and other small business people put in longer hours, often well into the night.

Clothing

Rarely does one need to be attired in more than a pair of shorts and a T-shirt. Of course, there are the clothes-conscious resorts where this will not always work, or the clothing-optional resorts where you are even heartily welcome to stay in your birthday suit, but mostly any casual clothing will suffice. In fact, in certain circles dressing ostentatiously tends to mark someone as fair game to be charged higher prices.

Just like on the cruise lines, which still have individual dress codes, some Caribbean resorts, hotels, restaurants and night spots require guests to be more formally attired particularly for evenings, which may mean a jacket without a tie for men, and pants or dress for women. Only the rarest number of establishments still require yet more formality.

Cool, loose-fitting clothing for the most part works best, in light-weight natural fibers, along with shorts, T-shirts, light sandals or sneakers. Swimwear, perhaps with a cover-up, is acceptable attire in most places during the day, less so away from the beach or at night. And at a great number of resorts and beach areas throughout the entire Caribbean, swimwear is not required on the beach. Inquire locally about nude beaches.

If one's visit is going to include any time in upland areas, a water-proof is recommended. Those who chill easily in air-conditioning may want to pack a sweater. Headgear is recommended. Sunscreen is always necessary outdoors. Insect repellant may come in handy. It is highly recommended when traveling by plane in the Caribbean to pack a day or so of clothing, toiletries and other necessities in a carry-on bag, in case there's a delay with the luggage.

Crime

The basic idea is the same that applies all over the world: Exercise common sense. Larger hotels and resorts do have room safes, or check valuables with the desk. Carry travelers checks, never cash. Keep your rental car locked, and remove all valuables.

Driving

Some driving is on the left, British-style, some on the right, Continental-style. Happily, there is consistency in this regard on each island, so one only has to remember where one is at any given moment. Some main roads are fairly good in some parts of the Caribbean, but most roads are not super-highways. They are rather narrow and winding. Frequently cars must share the middle of the road with people walking, cattle, stray pigs, dogs, goats and so forth. Driving in the Caribbean can therefore be a challenge, which you should consider whether or not you will relish ahead of time.

Most visitors are allowed to operate a motor vehicle in most Caribbean countries, provided they hold a valid license issued at home. Residents of certain countries may have to produce an international driver's permit.

And in certain Caribbean countries, drivers will have to buy a temporary local permit issued at the time they pick up their rental car. Tourism authorities should always be able to give you all the details for your specific situation, including listings of car rental agencies, which generally include particularly the major companies.

Electricity

Some countries covered in this book operate at the same electric current as the United States of America – 110 volts, 60 cycles, alternating current – although there could be local variations. On these islands, European appliances will require adapters. Other countries operate on European current – 220 volts, 50 cycles, direct current – requiring adapters for American appliances. It is best to inquire in advance regarding any special power requirements.

The following countries are off the U.S. standard: Antigua and Barbuda, 220 volts, 60 cycles AC Bonaire, 127 volts, 50 cycles AC Curaçao, 110 volts, 50 cycles AC French West Indies, Grenada, St. Lucia, 220 volts, 50 cycles AC Montserrat, 220 volts, 50 cycles AC St.Kitts / Nevis, 220 volts, 60 cycles AC Dominica, St. Vincent and the Grenadines, 220 volts 50 cycles AC

Emergencies

Some travelers experience health problems in the Caribbean due to changes in climate, drinking water or food, or from too much sun, insects or rum. Larger resorts and hotels will have a nurse or doctor on call. In the major towns, hospital or medical facilities may be surprisingly good or bad.

The farther out one goes, naturally, the less likely one is to be within easy reach of medical help. If you have an accident or medical emergency the following numbers will put you through to emergency services.

Anguilla, phone 911 for all emergency services, 497-2551 for ambulance services, 497-2333 for police.

Antigua, phone 462-0251 for ambulance service, 462-0125 for police.

Aruba, phone 411 for all emergency services, 24555 for police.

Barbados, phone 119 for all emergency services, 426-1113 for ambulance service, 426-1112 for police.

Bonaire, phone 8000 for all emergency services.

British Virgin Islands, phone 999 for all emergency services.

Curaçao, phone 599/962-5822 for ambulance service, 44444 for police.

Dominica, phone 999 for all emergency services.

GUIDELINES

Grenada, phone 434 for ambulance service, 911 for police.

Guadeloupe, phone 590/ 828933 for ambulance services, 590/17 for police.

Martinique, phone 596/ 703648 for ambulance services, 596/17 for police.

Montserrat, phone 491-2552 for ambulance service, 491-2555 for police.

St. Kitts/Nevis, phone 911 for all emergency services.

St. Lucia, phone 999 for all emergency services.

Sint Maarten, phone 599/5-22111 for ambulance service, 595/5-22222 for police.

St. Martin, phone 590/875414 for ambulance service, 590/855010 for police.

Saba, phone 63220 for all emergency services, or phone 599/46-3237 for police.

St. Barthelemy, phone 990 for ambulance service, 999 for police.

St. Eustatius, phone 82333 for all emergency services.

St. Vincent and the **Grenadines**, phone O for all emergency services, or 456-1185 for ambulance services, 457-1211 for police.

Trinidad & Tobago, phone 990 for ambulance services, 999 for police. for all emergency services.

U.S. Virgin Islands, phone 922 for ambulance services, 915 for police.

Etiquette

The variety of ethnic, social, religious and economic conditions existing here causes tensions you may not recognize, and others that you may see all too clearly.

Some local people may be helpful and favorable towards tourism, while others may consider tourism an unwanted extension of colonialism. At all times consider yourself a guest in a place where rules of behavior vary from Western standards. Punctuality, for example, is a general concept in the Caribbean. Things happen slowly, appointments are delayed and so forth. Hurried and harried visitors may be patronized with cynical humor, if not ignored. At the very least, those who are most rushed will inevitably face the longest delays.

The Caribbean operates at its own pace, and it is slow and worthy of respect. This, after all, is one of the reasons why tourists come here. Take time to be polite about taking photographs. Do not persist in taking photos if you are asked to stop. Common courtesy counts for almost everything in receiving friendly consideration from people. As in Rome, do like the Romans: Adapt to the slower pace of life, and make sure you have packed your sense of humor!

Festivals and Holidays

Festivals and holidays are an important part of the social fabric of Caribbean life, as well as a main attraction for more and more tourists. Many festivals and special events are listed in chapters of this book, or individual tourist offices can provide festival and holiday calendars. Write to the Caribbean Tourism Organization, 20 East 46th St., New York, NY 10017, 1-212/682-0435 that publishes a free Caribbean tourist calendar listing festivals and yearly events.

Guides

Multi-lingual guides are probably best set up through package tours. Most of the local guides, however, tend to be plentiful, usually youthful freelancers or else cab drivers who wait for flights at the airport or outside tourist sites. Many of these guides will be overly enthusiastic, although good connections can be made on the spot if one develops a quick rapport. Always negotiate a fee in advance. Local tourist offices can sometimes secure the services of a multi-lingual guide. For guided tours organized under a variety of special interests and itineraries, contact the tourist offices for a listing of approved operators.

Photography

Still photography and video recording are popular with Caribbean tourists. Although film, video tapes and batteries may be available in certain areas, they will be expensive. It is always advisable to bring everything you need from home. As mentioned before: It is advisable to ask before photographing people, and accept a no with grace.

Postal Services

Postal services and fees vary according to each country. Mail moves rather slowly in the Caribbean. Always use air mail, not surface. The latter is cheaper, but will presumably take a very long time.

Telephone Service

Telephone service is getting better throughout the Caribbean, although at times there are still problems. Service is by no means standardized, and you will need to check locally for idiosyncracies such as three- five- or seven-digit dialing, as well as for calls between islands. The Caribbean area code is 809 for all countries listed in this book except for the following: Aruba, French West Indies, Guadeloupe, Netherlands Antilles and St. Barts. For these islands you must dial 011 (the international access code), the individual country code, city code and the local number. Consult the operator for information on the codes.

Time

The islands of the Greater Antilles are all within the EST or Eastern Standard Time zone (i.e., 6 hours behind European standard time. The Lesser Antilles and Puerto Rico fall into the Atlantic time zone, 5 hours behind Euroipe and an hour ahead of EST. The Dutch Antilles are 5 1/2 hours behind Europe (1/2 hour ahead of EST). Daylight savings time can push the time on some islands foreward by an hour.

Tipping

Tipping is expected everywhere. Many times a service charge will be added to your hotel or restaurant bill. If it is not, count on tipping airport porters, bellhops and doormen $1 per bag; cab drivers some 15 percent – 20 percent of taxi fare; hotel maids $1-$2 daily; waiters, barbers or hairdressers 15 percent – 20 percent of total bill. Cruise lines usually offer their own guidelines for tipping.

Tourist Information

In addition to the numerous information sources listed throughout this book, the following additional sources can provide you with current information on rates, schedules, facilities and services.

In the United States, the **Caribbean Tourist Organization**, 20 East 46th St., New York, NY 10017, 1-212/682-0435 can provide detailed information, including further specific information sources, particularly on the following countries: Anguilla, Antigua, Barbuda, Aruba, Barbados, Bonaire, British Virgin Islands, Curaçao, Dominica, the French West Indies (Guadeloupe, Martinique, St. Barts, St. Martin), Grenada, Montserrat, Saba, St. Eustatius, St.Kitts / Nevis, St.Lucia, St. Vincent and the Grenadines, Trinidad and Tobago, U.S. Virgin Islands, Venezuela (Isla de Margarita).

For information on U.S. Customs call 1-212/466-5550. Information on U.S. State Department Travel Advisories are available by phoning 1-202/647-5225.

AUTHORS

Eva Ambros, who wrote the *Nelles Guide Egypt*, became an instant enthusiast of the Caribbean and its inhabitants at her first trip to the islands in 1979. She contributed to the editing of the second edition of the *Nelles Guide Lesser Antilles* and was co-author for the chapters on culture, Antigua, Guadeloupe, Dominica, Martinique, St. Lucia, Bar-

CREDITS

bados, St. Vincent, Trinidad, Grenada, Aruba and Curaçao.

Steve Cohen, project editor of this book, is a writer and photographer specializing in travel and world-wide adventure. His work appears regularly in major North American magazines and newspapers as well as more than 150 publications around the world. He is the author of the best-selling book *The Adventure Guide to Jamaica* and was project editor for the *Nelles Guides to Florida* and the *Greater Antilles*.

Janet Groene has traveled in the Caribbean by cruise ship and scheduled airlines, as well as her own boats and planes for 20 years. Her books, along with her husband, photographer Gordon Groene, include *How to Live Aboard a Boat and Dressing Ship*, published by Hearst/Morrow. Florida-based, she also contributed to the *Nelles Guides to Florida* and the *Greater Antilles*.

Laurie Werner is a New York-based writer and member of the Society of American Travel Writers. Her work appears in major North American newspapers and magazines including *Ladies Home Journal*, *Vis-a-Vis*, *USA Weekend*.

Ute Vladimir is a German-born writer who has lived in Florida for 30 years during which time she has sailed and traveled extensively in the Caribbean. She writes a travel column for Florida's *Palm Beach Post* along with her husband Andrew Vladimir.

Deborah Williams is a former newspaper reporter and editor (the same paper where Mark Twain served as editor many years earlier). She has traveled in the Caribbean for more than 20 years and her work has appeared in a wide variety of books, magazines and newspapers in the United States and Canada.

Claire Walter is an award-winning ski and travel writer. Her books include *The Best Ski Resorts in America*, and *The Berlitz Handbook to Skiing the Alps*. She is Western Editor of *Skiing Magazine*.

PHOTOGRAPHERS

Antigua & Barbuda Department of Tourism 123, 128
Barba, Dan (Viesti Ass.)S 54, 87
Batschari, Robert 31, 89, 170
Begsteiger, A. M. 1
Boisberranger (Viesti Ass.) 12/13, 24, 26, 27, 42, 46, 83, 88, 92/93, 94, 109, 113, 123, 130, 134, 140, 174, 175, 188, 189, 225
Bravo, J. (Viesti Ass.) 8/9, 72, 104/105, 112, 146, 157
Downey, Mark (Viesti Ass.) 48, 61, 71, 84, 197, 223
Dunn, Jeffrey (Viesti Ass.) 32, 233
Giersch, Werner 120
Hartl, Helene 69, 70, 75, 96, 213L, 214
Hoa Qui (Viesti Ass.) 142/143
Janicke, Volkmar 85, 164, 184, 186, 224
Kaestner, Reed (Viesti Ass.) 60, 62
Kanzler, Thomas 28, 29
Karl, Roland F. 10/11, 20, 78/79, 100, 151, 160/161, 162, 168, 173, 194, 212, 231, 235
Lovell, Craig (Viesti Ass.) 68
Morse, Randy (Viesti Ass.) 66, 218
Nikas, Greg (Viesti Ass.) 47, 57, 125
Purchia, Peter (Viesti Ass.) 14, 17, 44, 99, 101, 137
Renaudeau (Viesti Ass.) 124
Rosenstein, Carl (Viesti Ass.) 220
Ross, Ken (Viesti Ass.) 18, 25, 40, 202, 204, 205
Schaible, Herbert 167
Skupy, Hans-Horst 45, 63, 64, 65, 67, 73, 110, 199, 208/209, 213R, 215L, 215R, 221, 232, 234
Skupy, Jitka 126
Trox, Traudl 21, 30, 102, 108, 115, 135, 148, 150, 185, 219
Valentin (Viesti Ass.) 23, 41, 50/51, 97, 152, 154, 166, 211
Vandivier, Kevin (Viesti Ass.) 33
Viesti, Joe (Viesti Ass.) cover, 16, 22, 34, 35, 36, 37, 38, 39, 52/53, 56, 82, 86, 118/119, 147, 155, 156, 171, 172, 178/179, 180, 187, 192/193, 198, 217, 226, 227, 228, 229, 230.

INDEX

A

ABC Islands **195-207**, 198
Amerindian Museum 150
Andicouri Bay 197
Anegada 73, 74
Anguilla 17, **81-83**, 106
   Barnes Bay 82
   Cove Bay 82
   Maunday's Bay 82
   Rendezvous Bay 82
   Sandy Ground 82
   Sandy Hill 82
   Shoal Bay 82
   Shoal Bay West 82
   The Valley 82
   Wallblake House 82
Anse-à-l'Ane 147
Anse à Sable 156, 157
Anse Azerot 147
Anse Chastenat 157
Anse Diamant 147
Anse La Raye Point 157
Anse l'Ivrogne 157
Anse Mitan 147
Anse Turin 146
Anses d'Arlets 147
Antigua 15, 106, **121-127**
Antigua Sailing Week 124
Arawaks 19, 25, 37, 148, 151, 196, 198, 203, 222, 223, 224
Architecture **45-48**
Arima 186
Arikok 198
Aripo Range 186
Aruba 15, 18, 19, **195-198**, 205

B

Barbados 17, 145, **147-150**, 152
Barbados Bay 189
Barbuda 15, 26, 106, 121, **127-128**
Barrouallie 166
Bashiribana 197
Basseterre 109
   Church of St. George 109
   Clock Tower 109
   Independence Square 109
   St. Kitts Sugar Factory 109
   The Circus 109
Basse-Terre 133, 135
   Jardin Botanique 133
Bath House 111
Bathsheba 150
Bath Village 111
Batik 49, 155, 234
Beef Island 73, 75
   Trellis Bay 73
Belafonte, Harry 231
Bequia 163, 172, 216
Birdwatching 155, 166, 190
Black Caribs 163
Blanchisseuse 187
Bligh, Captain 164, 171, 224
Bloody Point 19
Blue Basin Falls 185
Bocas 185, 217
Boca-Mahos Bay 197
Boca Slagbaai National Park 202
Boiling Lake 138
Bolivar, Simon 203, 205
Bonaire 195, **198-203**
Bonaire Marine Park 200
Bridgetown 148, 150
   Barbados Museum 148
   Bay Street 148
   Careenage-harbor 148
   Constitution River 148
   Garrison Savannah 148
   St. Michael's Cathedral 148
   Synagogue 148
   Trafalgar Square 147
Brimstone Hill 45, 106, 110
Brion, Pedro Luis 204
British Leeward Islands 106, 121
British Virgin Islands 72-75
Buccament Valley 166
Buccoo Reef 190, 217

C

Cabrits National Park 138
Caiquetios 19, 203
Calibishie 138
Calypso 36, 39, 168, 188, 228, 229, 230, 231
Camerhonge 168
Camping 216, 219
Canefield 138
Canouan 163, 173
Capesterre-Belle-Eau 134, 136
Caravelle Peninsula 146
Carbet 146
Careenage, harbor 150
Carib Reserve 140
Caribs 19, 106, 137, 138, 145, 146, 148, 151, 163, 168, 181, 198, 222
Carib's Leap 19
Carnival 36, 168, 181, 188, 230, 231
Caroni Bird Sanctuary 186
Carriacou 168, 173
Carriacou Regatta 174
Case Pilote, Baroque church 146
Castle Bruce 138
Castries 48, 155
   Harbor 155
   Market 155
   Morne Fortune Fortress 155
   Museum 154
   Pointe Séraphine 152
Casuarina 175
Caurita Plantation 185
Caves 205
Cayman Brac 32
Central Forest Reserve 155, 157
Chaguanas 186
Chaguaramas Bay 186
Chances Peak 115
Charlestown 111
   Alexander Hamilton Museum 111
   Jewish Cemetery 111
   St. Paul's Church 111
   St. Thomas Church 111
Charter companies 210, 211
Charter yachts 210
Chateaubelair 166
Christiansted 63
Cibrahacha Dancers 40
Clay Ghaunt Estate 112
Clifton Harbor 175
Coco Point Lodge 128
Codrington, Christopher 127, 128
Columbus, Christopher 16, 17, 20, 55, 72, 81, 84, 95, 99, 106, 110, 113, 121, 131, 137, 145, 146, 148, 151, 163, 167, 181, 224
Compas 41
Concepción 168
Conch 222, 224
Cooper Island 74
Cortez, Hernando 17
Cotton House 174
Cousteau, Jacques 56
Creole 41
Crooks Castle Beach 102
Cruises 211
Cuevos Beach 186
Cuisine 222-223
Culture 35-49
Curaçao 19, 195, **203-205**
Curaçao Undersea Park 205

D

Dance 37
Dead Chest Island 74
Deep-sea fishing 56
Dennery 154
Desolation Valley 138
Devil's Bridge 127
Diamond Falls 154
Dickenson Bay 127
Diego Martin River Valley 185
Dieppe Bay 110
Diorite boulders 198
Distillerie Poisson 135

INDEX

Divali 36
Dividing Wall 128
Divi-divi tree 197
Diving 75, 216
Dockyard Day 124
Doctor Doolittle 156
Domaine de la Grivelière 134
Dominica 19, 22, 131, **137-138**
Dominica Undersea National Park 138
Dougaldston Estate 170
Douglas Bay 138
Drake, Sir Francis 24, 55, 72
Dulcina 127
Dutch West India Company 198

E

East End 124, 127
   Archeological excavation 127
   Devil's Bridge 124
   Indian Town 127
Eden Brown Estate 113
El Dorado 181
Emerald Island 166
English Harbour 121, 123, 125
   Admiral's House 126
   Admiral's Inn 126
   Clarence House 126
   Copper & Lumber Store Hotel 126
   Nelson's Dockyard 125

F

Fairley Hill House 150
Falls of Baleine 166
Fat Hog Bay 44
Fête Annuelle 36
Fig Tree Drive 124
Fig Tree Village 111
Flamingo colony 202
Fontein Cave 198
Forest Reserve 189
Fort-de-France 145, 146
   Baie des Flamands 147
   Bibliothèque Schoelcher 145
   Cathédrale St. Louis 145
   Fish Market 145
   Fort Louis 145
   Fruit and Vegetable Market 145
   La Savanne 145, 146
   Musée Départemental 145
   Rivière Madame 145
Fort Fleur D'Épée 135
Fort George 185
Fountain Estate 109
Frederiksted 63
Freshwater Lake 138
Frigate Bay 110
Frigate Bird Sanctuary 128

G

Galway's Soufrière, volcano 115
Gambling 225
Gauguin, Paul 48
Ginger Island 75
Gold Mines 197
Gosier 135, 136, 137
Gouyave 170
Grafton Beach 190
Grande Anse 147, 155, 170
Grande Anse de Salines 147
   Anse Trabaud 147
   Baham 147
   Dunkerque 147
Grand Étang 170
Grand Étang Forest Lake 170
   Crater Lake 170
   Qua Qua Mt. 170
Grande-Terre 133, 134, 135
Grand Piton 156
Great Alps Waterfall 115
Great Courland Bay 189
   Fort James 189
   Grafton Estate 189
Grenada 19, 163, **167-172**
Grenadines 32, 163, 167, **173-175**
Grenville 171
Gros Islet 157
Guadeloupe 131-137, 131, 138
Gulf of Paria 183
Gun Hill 150
Gustavia 95, 217

H

Haiti 28, 29
Half Moon Bay 124
Hampstead 138
Handicrafts 48
Harvey Vale 174
Hiking 138, 216, 218
Hillsborough 174
   Carriacou Historical Society 174
Hilton, Anthony 111
Hispaniola 16, 17
History 15-33
HMS Boreas 122
Hodge, Arthur William 27
Hooiberg (Haystack Mountain) 198
Horseshoe Bay 171
Hosein festival 36
Hurricanes 32, 232

I

Îles-des-Saintes 135
   Fort Napoléon 135
   Terre-de-Haut 135
Indian Town 127
Inkle, Thomas 27
Irish settlers 113
Isla de Margarita 190
   La Asunción 190
   Pampatar 190
   Porlamar 190
   Santa Ana 190

J

Jackson, Henry 24
Jamanota 198
Jardin de Balata 146
Joséphine, Empress 145
Jost Van Dyke, island 73, 74
   Little Dix Bay 74
   Little Harbour 73

K

Karukera (Guadeloupe) 131
Kingstown 164
   Bay Street 164
   Botanical Gardens 164
   Bounty Café 164
   Fort Charlotte 164
   National Museum 164
   St. George's Cathedral 164
   St. Mary's Church 164
Klein Bonaire 199, 200
Kralendijk 199, 200
   Island Museum 199, 200

L

Labrelotte Bay 156
La Créole Beach 136
Lady of Laventille, church 185
Lamentin 133
Language 41
La Rivière Salée 133, 134
La Rosette 135
   Musée d'Archéologie 135
La Sagesse Nature Center 170
La Traversée 133
Laudat 138
Layou 166
Leeward Islands 127, 211
Le Moule 135, 136
Les Gorges de la Falaise 146
Levera Beach 170, 171
Liberta 127
   St. Barnabas Church 127
Lignumvitae Bay 127
Limbo 39, 188
Little England (Barbados) 148
Little Tobago 189

M

Madinina (Martinique) 146

INDEX

Mahault 133
Manchioneel Bay 74
Man O'War Beach 190
Maracas Bay 185
Maraval 189
  Moka 188
Mardi Gras 36
Maria Galanda 131
Maria Island 157
Marie-Galante 131, 135
  Anse Canot 136
  Capesterre 136
  Château Murat 135
  Distillerie Poisson 135
  Gueule du Gouffre 135
  La Grande Barre 135
  Trou au Diable 135
  Vieux Fort 136
Marigot 138
Marigot Bay 156
Marine life 200
Marley, Bob 227
Marquis 168
Martello Tower 128
Martinica (Martinique) 145
Martinique 20, 131, **145-147**
Massacre 138
Matura Bay 187
Mayaro Bay 187
Mayreau 174
Mayreu 164
Mero 138
Mesopotamia Valley 167
Middleham Trails 138
Middle Island Village 109
  St. Thomas Church 109
Miramar Pass 198
Molinère Reef 172
Monkey Hill 110
Montagne Pelée 33, 145, 146, 147
Montpelier Estate 111, 112
Montserrat 15, 21, 32, 106, 113-115
Morel 135
  Arawak Village 135
Morne Diablotin, mountain 138
Morne Gimie 155
Morne Trois Pitons Natn.Park 140
Morning Star Plantation 112
Morris 115
Moruga 181
José de Oruna (St. Joseph) 181
Moule-à-Chique Peninsula 152
Mount Christoffel 205
Mount Liamuiga 108
Mount Misery 108
Mount Parnassus 175
Mount St. Benedict Monastery 185
Musée de Rhum 133

Musquetta Beach 171
Mustique 163, 174

N

Naipaul, V.S. 186
Nariva Swamp 187
Nelson, Horatio 21, 110, 112, 122, 147
Nelson Museum 112
Netherlands Antilles 195, 196
Nevis 84, 106, **110-113**
Nisbet, Frances 111, 112, 122
Nonsuch Bay 127
Norman Island 74
  Treasure Point 74
Northern Forest Reserve 138
Northern Range 185

O

Oil 183, 195, 196
O'Keefe, Georgia 121
Old Road Town 109
Oranjestad (Sint Eustatius) 101, 102
  Dutch Reformed Church 102
  Fort Oranje 101, 102
  Fortstraat 102
  Lower Town 101, 102
  St. Eustatius Historical Museum 102
  Synagogue 102
  Three Widows Corner 102
  Upper Town 101
Oranjestad (Aruba) 197
  Nassaustraat 197
  Schooner Market 197
Ovando, Nicolás de 16

P

Palm Island 164, 175
Papiamento 41, 195
Parang 36
Parc Naturel 134, 219
  Cascade aux Ecrevisses 134
  Chutes du Carbet 134
  Soufrière, volcano 134
Parham
  St. Peter Church 127
Paria Bay 186
Paria Falls 186
Patois 140
Peter Island 74, 75
Petit-Canal 136
Petit Martinique 168, 175
Petit Piton 156
Petit St. Vincent 164, 175
Petroglyphs 19, 166, 205
Pigeon Island 136, 155, 216

  National Park 155
  Open-air Museum 155
  Rodney Fortress 155
Pigeon Point (Tobago) 190
Pinney's Beach 113
Pirates 23
Pirate's Castle 197
Pitch Lake 181, 186
Pitch pits 15
Plena 39
Plymouth 114, 115
  Government House 114
  Market Day 115
  National Trust Museum 115
  Richmond Hill 115
  St. Anthony's Church 115
Pointe-à-Pierre 183
Pointe-à-Pitre 133, 135
  Basilique de St. Pierre et St. Paul 135
  Librairie Général 136
  Musée Saint-John Perse 135
  Musée Schoelcher 135
  Place de la Victoire 134
Pointe Baptiste 138
Pointe de Bout 147
Pointe du Cap 152
Point Fortin 183
Point Salines Intl. Airport 168
Pont de la Gabare 133
Pont Cassé 138
Port Elizabeth 173
  Admiralty Bay 173
  Whaling & Sailing Museum 173
Port Louis 136
Port of Spain 181, 184
  Botanic Gardens 185
  Cathedral of the Immaculate Conception 184
  Cathedral of the Holy Trinity 184
  Emperor Zoo 185
  Fort George 185
  Frederick Street 184
  Independence Square 184
  Jama Masjid Mosque 184
  Lady Chancellor Rd. 185
  National Museum 184
  Our Lady of Laventille
  Queen's Park Savannah 184
  Queen Street 184
  Red Hause 184
  San Andres Fort 183
  South Quay 184
  Woodford Square 184
Portsmouth 138
Pottery 49
Potwork's Dam 127
Powell, John 148
Prince of Wales Bastion 110
Prince Rupert Bay 138

INDEX

Pte. Tarare 136
Puerto Rico 29

Q

Quakers 43
Queen's Drive 166
Questelles 166
Quill volcano 101

R

Rabacca Falls 164
Radio Antilles 115
Raleigh, Walter 181
Rastafari 227-231
Redonda 121
Réduit Bay 157
Refineries 30
Reggae 39, 157, 227
Religion 43-45
Rendezvous Bay 127
Rendezvous Beach 115
Richmond Great House 189
Rijstafel 203
Rivière du Galion 133
Road Town 72
Rodney Bay 156
Rogers, Woodes 25
Romney Manor 109
Rosalie 138
Roseau 138, 140
  Bay Street 138
  Botanical Gardens 138
  Old Market Plaza 138
  Saturday Market 138
Roseau River 138
Route de la Trace 146
Rum 171, 172, 187, 223, 224, 234, 235
Rumba 39

S

Saba 15, **98-101**
  Crispeen 99
  Flat Point 99
  Fort Bay 99, 100
  Hell's Gate 99
  H.L.Johnson Memorial Museum 100
  Ladder Bay 100
  Mount Scenery 99
  St. John's 100
  The Bottom 99, 100
  Windwardside 100
Sacré-Coeur de Balata 46, 146
Sailing 210 -211
Saint Martin 83
  Baie Longue 86
  Baie Orientale 86
  Baie Rouge 86
  Fort St. Louis 89
  French Cul-de-Sac 86
  Grand Case 86
  Guana Bay Point 87
  Marigot 86
  Orléans 86
  Oyster Pond 87
  Paradise Peak 89
  Pointe du Bluff 86
Salsa 39
Salt Island 75
  Wreck of the Rhone 75
Salybria 140
Sandy Bay 163
San Fernando 186, 188
Santa Maria 16
Sauteurs 170
  Caribs Leap 170
Scarborough 189, 190
  Botanical Gardens 189
  King George Fort 189
  House of Assembly 189
Schoelcher-Library 46
Scotland District
  St. John's Church 150
Scott's Head 138
Scuba diving 87, 147
Sea moss milk 172
Shirley Heights 123
Shopping 234-235
Simadan 37
Sint Christoffelberg National Park 205
Sint Maarten 203
  Fort Amsterdam 86
  Fort William 88
  Great Bay 88
  Juliana Airport 86
  Little Bay 88
  Maho Bay 86
  Mullet Bay 86
  Philipsburg 85
  Point Blanche 88
  see Saint Martin 83
Slagbaai National Park 202
Slavery 26, 28, 73, 145, 168, 183, 195, 199
Smith, John 111
Smoke Alley Beach 102
Snorkeling 216
Soca 41
Solar saltworks 202
Soufrière 33, 138, 151
  Historical Architectural Walk 154
  Soufrière Heritage Center 154
Soufrière Estate Waterfalls 154
Soufrière, volcano 155, 164, 166, 167
Souvenirs 48

Speyside 189
Spice Island
  see Grenada 172
Spring Hills Estate 186
  Asa Wright Nature Center 186
  Dunston Cave 186
Spyglass Reef 75
Standfast Point 127
St. Barts 21, 84, **95-98**
  Anse des Flamands 97
  Anse du Gouverneur 97
  Corossol 96
  Forst Gustave 97
  Grande Saline 97
  Gustavia 96
  Inter-Oceans Museum 97
  Lorient 97
  Marigot 97
  St. Jean 97
  Swedish Town Hall 96
  Toiny Coast 97
St. Croix 62
  Apothecary Hall 69
  Buck Island 69
  Cane Bay 72
  Christiansted 69
  Cramer Park 72
  Cruzan Rum Distillery 71
  Davis Bay 72
  Fisher Street 70
  Fort Christansvaern 69
  Fort Frederik 70
  Frederiksted 70
  Government House 69
  Grapetree Bay 72
  Old Scale House 69
  Protestant Bay 72
  Sandy Point 72
  Sprat Beach 72
  Sprat Hall 71
  Steeple Building 69
  St. George Village 71
  St. Patrick's Church 70
  The Reef 72
  Visitor's Bureau 69
  Whim Plantation 70
Ste. Anne 147
Steel Bands 39, 170, 227, 231
St. Eustatius 22, **101-102**
Stewart, Don 200
St. François 135
St. George's 168, 170
  Carenage-Pier 167, 168
  Fort George 168
  Markets 168, 171
  National Institute of Handicrafts 168
  National Museum 168
  Queen's Park 168
St. John, island 28, 62, 67, 68, 150

253

INDEX

Annaberg Plantation 68
Cinnamon Bay 68
Cruz Bay 67
Maho Bay 68
Villa Nova 150
St. John's 123, 124
  Antigua Rum Distillery 126
  Archeology Museum 126
  Deepwater Harbor 123
  Fort James 126
  Heritage Quay 123
  Police Headquarters Newgate 126
  Redcliff Quay 123
  St. John's Cathedral 123
  St. John the Divine Cathedral 125
St. Joseph 185
  Jinnah Mosque 185
St. Kitts 19, **106-110**
St. Lucia 15, 145, **151-157**
St. Lucia Artists Association 49
St. Lucy 148
  Animal Flower Cave 148
St. Peter 150
  St. Nicholas Abbey 150
St. Philip 150
  Barbados Park Zoo 150
  Sunbury Plantation 150
St. Pierre 33, 146
St. Thomas 63-67
  99 Steps 64
  Baby Shark Pond 65
  Blackbeard's Castle 64
  Bluebeard's Castle 66
  Bluebeard's Castle 64
  Bordeaux 63
  Brewer's Beach 65
  Buck Island 67
  Charlotte Amalie 63
  Coki Beach 65
  Coral World 65
  Crown House 64
  Crystal Gade 64
  Drake's Seat 65
  Emancipation Square 63
  Fort Christian 63
  Frenchcap Cay 67
  Harrison Cave 148
  Hotel 1829 64
  Hull Bay 65
  Limetree Beach 65
  Lindbergh Beach 66
  Little Buck Island 67
  Lutheran Church 63
  Magens Bay 65, 66
  Main Street 64
  Morningstar Beach 66
  Mountain Top 65
  Packet Rock 67
  Raadets Gade 64
  Red Hook 63
  Salt River 67
  Sapphire Beach 66
  Sea Turtle Pool 65
  Sprat Point 67
  Thatch Cay 67
  Touch Pond 65
  Visitors' Center 63
  Wreck of the Rhone 67
Stuyvesant, Peter 21, 47, 196, 203
St. Vincent 19, 28, **163-167**
St. Vincent Craftsmen Centre 164
Sta. Cruz (Aruba) 198

T

The Pinnacles 157
Ti Trou Gorge 138
Tobago 28, **189-190**
Tobago Bays 164
Tobago Cays 174
Tortola 17, 29, **73-74**
  Botanic Garden 74
  Brewer's Bay 73
  Cane Garden Bay 74
  Dungeon Fort 74
  Mount Sage National Park 74
  Road Town 73, 74
  Skyworld 74
  West End 73
Tourism 220-221
Trafalgar Falls 138
Transinsular Road 140
Trinidad 22, 30, **183-188**
Trois-Ilets 146, 147
Trois-Rivières 134
  Roches Gravées 134
Tuma 39
Turtles 155
Tyrell Bay 174
Tyrico Bay 186

U

Union Island 164, 175
U.S. Virgin Islands 61-72

V

Vaval 36
Vernou 134
Vespucci, Amerigo 17
Vieux Fort 151
Vigie Bay 157
Vigie Beach 157
Virgin Gorda 15, 75
  Old mines 75
  The Baths 75
Virgin Islands 55-77, 210
Volcanic eruptions 33
Voodoo 44, 220

W

Warner, Thomas 106, 109
Washington, George 21, 148
Welshman Hall Gully 150
West Indian English 42
Westpunt Baai 205
White River Falls 115
White River Valley 115
Wild Fowl Trust 186
Willemstad 195, 203
  Bredestraat 205
  Columbusstraat 205
  Curaçao Museum 204
  Floating market 204
  Jewish Museum 204
  Konigin Emmabrug 204
  Konigin Julianabrug 204
  Mikve Israel-Emanuel Synagogue 205
  Otrabanda 204
  Punda 204, 205
  Schottegat (Harbor) 204, 205
  St. Anna Baai 204
Windjammer Cruises 211
Windward 174
Windward Islands 148, 151, 163, 211
Wingfield Estate 109
World Wildlife Fund 200
Wreck of the Antilla 198
Wreck of the Hilma Hooker 202
Wright Nature Center 185

Y

Yachting 57, 97
Yellow Poui Art Gallery 168
Young Island 163

Z

Zevallos mansion 135
Zoo 146

Explore the World

AVAILABLE TITLES

Australia
Bali / Lombok
Berlin and Potsdam
Brittany
California
  Las Vegas, Reno, Baja California
Cambodia / Laos
Canada
  Ontario, Québec, Atlantic Provinces
Caribbean
  The Greater Antilles, Bermuda, Bahamas
Caribbean
  The Lesser Antilles
China – Hong Kong
Corsica
Crete
Cyprus
Egypt
Florida
Greece – *The Mainland*
Hawai'i
Hungary
India
  Northern, Northeastern and Central India
India – *Southern India*

Indonesia
  Sumatra, Java, Bali, Lombok, Sulawesi
Ireland
Israel - *with Excursions to Jordan*
Kenya
London, England and Wales
Malaysia
Mexico
Morocco
Moscow / St Petersburg
Munich
  Excursions to Castels, Lakes & Mountains
Nepal
New York – *City and State*
New Zealand
Paris
Philippines
Portugal
Prague / Czech Republic
Provence
Rome
Scotland
South Africa
Spain – *Pyrenees, Atlantic Coast, Central Spain*

Spain
  Mediterranean Coast, Southern Spain, Balearic Islands
Sri Lanka
Thailand
Turkey
Tuscany
U.S.A.
  The East, Midwest and South
U.S.A.
  The West, Rockies and Texas
Vietnam

FORTHCOMING

Brazil
Croatia – *Adriatic Coast*
Canada
  The Rockies, Pacific, Prairie, and the Territories
Myanmar (Burma)
Norway
South Pacific Islands
Syria – Lebanon
Tanzania

Nelles Guides – authorative, informed and informative.
Always up-to-date, extensivley illustrated, and with first-rate relief maps.
256 pages, appr. 150 color photos, appr. 25 maps

Explore the World
NELLES MAPS

AVAIBLABE TITLES

Afghanistan 1 : 1 500 000
Australia 1 : 4 000 000
Bangkok - *Greater Bangkok, Bangkok City* 1 : 75 000 / 1 : 15 000
Burma → *Myanmar*
Caribbean Islands 1 *Bermuda, Bahamas, Greater Antilles* 1 : 2 500 000
Caribbean Islands 2 *Lesser Antilles* 1 : 2 500 000
Central America 1 : 1 750 000
Colombia - Ecuador 1 : 2 500 000
Crete - *Kreta* 1 : 200 000
China 1 - *Northeastern* 1 : 1 500 000
China 2 - *Northern* 1 : 1 500 000
China 3 - *Central* 1 : 1 500 000
China 4 - *Southern* 1 : 1 500 000
Egypt 1 : 2 500 000 / 1 : 750 000
Hawaiian Islands 1 : 330 000 / 1 : 125 000
Hawaiian Islands 1 *Kauai* 1 : 125 000
Hawaiian Islands 2 *Honolulu - Oahu* 1 : 125 000
Hawaiian Islands 3 *Maui - Molokai - Lanai* 1 : 125 000
Hawaiian Islands 4 *Hawaii, The Big Island* 1 : 330 000 / 1 : 125 000

Himalaya 1 : 1 500 000
Hong Kong 1 : 22 500
Indian Subcontinent 1 : 4 000 000
India 1 - *Northern* 1 : 1 500 000
India 2 - *Western* 1 : 1 500 000
India 3 - *Eastern* 1 : 1 500 000
India 4 - *Southern* 1 : 1 500 000
India 5 - *Northeastern - Bangladesh* 1 : 1 500 000
Indonesia 1 : 4 000 000
Indonesia 1 *Sumatra* 1 : 1 500 000
Indonesia 2 *Java + Nusa Tenggara* 1 : 1 500 000
Indonesia 3 *Bali* 1 : 180 000
Indonesia 4 *Kalimantan* 1 : 1 500 000
Indonesia 5 *Java + Bali* 1 : 650 000
Indonesia 6 *Sulawesi* 1 : 1 500 000
Indonesia 7 *Irian Jaya + Maluku* 1 : 1 500 000
Jakarta 1 : 22 500
Japan 1 : 1 500 000
Kenya 1 : 1 100 000
Korea 1 : 1 500 000
Malaysia 1 : 1 500 000
West Malaysia 1 : 650 000
Manila 1 : 17 500
Mexico 1 : 2 500 000
Myanmar (Burma) 1 : 1 500 000

Nepal 1 : 500 000 / 1 : 1 500 000
Trekking Map *Khumbu Himal / Solu Khumbu* 1 : 75 000
New Zealand 1 : 1 250 000
Pakistan 1 : 1 500 000
Peru - Ecuador 1 : 2 500 000
Philippines 1 : 1 500 000
Singapore 1 : 22 500
Southeast Asia 1 : 4 000 000
Sri Lanka 1 : 450 000
Tanzania - *Rwanda, Burundi* 1 : 1 500 000
Thailand 1 : 1 500 000
Taiwan 1 : 400 000
Uganda 1 : 700 000
Venezuela - *Guyana, Suriname, French Guiana* 1 : 2 500 000
Vietnam, Laos, Cambodia 1 : 1 500 000

FORTHCOMING

Dominican Republic - Haiti 1 : 600 000
South Pacific Islands
Trekking Map *Kathmandu Valley / Helambu, Langtang* 1 : 75 000

Nelles Maps in european top quality!
Relief mapping, kilometer charts and tourist attractions.
Always up-to-date!